MICHIGAN LEGAL STUDIES

UNREPORTED OPINIONS

OF THE

SUPREME COURT OF MICHIGAN

1836 - 1843

PUBLISHED UNDER THE AUSPICES OF THE UNIVERSITY OF MICHIGAN LAW SCHOOL (WHICH, HOWEVER, ASSUMES NO RESPONSIBILITY FOR THE VIEWS EXPRESSED) WITH THE AID OF FUNDS DERIVED FROM GIFTS TO THE UNIVERSITY OF MICHIGAN BY WILLIAM W. COOK.

MICHIGAN LEGAL STUDIES

Hessel E. Yntema, Editor

Discovery Before Trial
George Ragland, Jr.

Torts in the Conflict of Laws
Moffatt Hancock

The Amending of the Federal Constitution
Lester B. Orfield

Review of Administrative Acts
Armin Uhler

The Prevention of Repeated Crime
John Barker Waite

The Conflict of Laws: A Comparative Study
Ernst Rabel

Unreported Opinions of the Supreme Court of
Michigan 1836-1843
William Wirt Blume, *Editor*

UNREPORTED OPINIONS

OF THE

SUPREME COURT OF MICHIGAN
1836-1843

Edited

by

WILLIAM WIRT BLUME
PROFESSOR OF LAW, UNIVERSITY OF MICHIGAN

Foreword

by

WALTER H. NORTH
JUSTICE, SUPREME COURT OF MICHIGAN

Historical Introduction

by

CLARK F. NORTON
INSTRUCTOR IN POLITICAL SCIENCE, UNIVERSITY OF MICHIGAN

Ann Arbor

THE UNIVERSITY OF MICHIGAN PRESS

1945

Paperback ISBN: 978-0-472-75031-3

Foreword

IN July 1836 final jurisdiction of non-federal litigation passed from the Michigan Territorial Supreme Court to the Supreme Court of the State of Michigan. Then, substantially as now, the Constitution provided: "The judicial power shall be vested in one supreme court, and such other courts as the legislature may from time to time establish." Mich. Const. 1835, Art. VI, §1. Those who are interested in the judicial history of Michigan prior to 1836 are fortunate in having access to much of such history contained in the six volumes entitled "Transactions of the Supreme Court of Michigan," edited by Professor William Wirt Blume of the Michigan Law School faculty. Along with other interesting material, he has included therein and thus made available some seventy of the opinions of the Michigan Territorial Supreme Court. His present volume of "Unreported Opinions of the Supreme Court of Michigan, 1836-1843" brings to light and for the first time makes accessible the Michigan Supreme Court decisions therein contained which were rendered during the indicated period of seven years.

Contrary to the prevailing assumption among laymen and some members of the legal profession, the Michigan Supreme Court Reports do not (with a few exceptions) contain the Supreme Court opinions which were rendered during this seven year period from 1836 to 1843. This failure to perpetuate opinions of the Supreme Court from 1836 to 1843 may in part be attributed to the fact there had been no printed reports of the Michigan Territorial Court during the immediately preceding period. Seemingly there was no orderly procedure adopted for permanent preservation of the Michigan Supreme Court's opinions during the first years following its creation. Thus quite naturally such of the Court's opinions as were reduced to writing found lodgment in diversified repositories and often in obscure places. The fact that during the noted period the Supreme Court held its sessions in various localities doubtless was a contributing circumstance to the disappearance of many of its records. But since the informative introduction to this volume by Doctor Clark F. Norton of the University of Michigan so amply narrates the circumstances which produced this hiatus in Michigan's judicial history, there is no need of amplification in this foreword; but the circumstance is worthy of note as indicative of the value of Professor Blume's present contribution to Michigan's judicial history.

The authenticity of this volume's contents is vouchsafed by the detailed references painstakingly provided by the editor to many manuscripts, public records, etc. Readers of this volume will find therein the earlier and probably the first utterances of the Supreme Court of Michigan relative to many interesting phases of our law. Suffice to note among them the following:

Lack of legislative power to revive abated suits. Calhoun v. Cable, et al. Jurors in justice court are judges of both law and facts, hence it was error for justice to direct a jury in matters affecting verdict. Burhans v. Reynolds. General appearance in a civil case waives objections to process; and decision by lower court on issues of fact will be affirmed though not entirely free from doubt. Dorr, et al. v. Dreyer. A witnessed memorandum purporting to dispose of his property approved orally by one in his last sickness, though not written or signed by him, constitutes a nuncupative will. Brewster, et al. v. Hastings, et al. Receipt of security by an endorser of a promissory note to indemnify him against his contingent liability, does not waive his right of demand and notice. Brewster v. Drew. Validity of a will requires that a subscribing witness saw testator sign. McCall, et al. v. Hough, et al.

In addition to the subject matter hereinbefore noted, Professor Blume has preserved for us in this volume the early rule making activities of Michigan State Courts. He notes that at the outset (1837) the State Supreme Court adopted the rules of the Michigan Territorial Court. And by reproduction to some extent of the early promulgated court rules, we are given the genesis of the exercise of the rule making power by the judicial branch of our State government, thereby seeming to exemplify the fact that this is an inherent power of Michigan's judiciary.

The compiler of this volume has, as it were, saved from complete loss much of the subject matter presented. By its perusal the reader can gain a closer touch with the manner in which cases were presented in the State Supreme Court by early and noted practitioners, among them such outstanding members of the legal profession as Henry M. Walker, Alpheus Felch, E. Burke Harrington, G. E. Hand, B. F. H. Witherell, E. Farnsworth, and Samuel T. Douglass.

In this volume and the preceding volumes of "Transactions of the Supreme Court of Michigan" we seemingly have as complete an assemblage of the record from 1805 to 1843 of both the Michigan Territorial Court and the Michigan State Supreme Court as could well be accomplished. These volumes are a merited tribute to the patience, industry and ingenuity of Professor Blume, and likewise a credit to the Michigan Law School which has made their publication possible. For this work the bench and bar of the State, historians, and others interested owe a debt of gratitude to those who have made it accessible.

WALTER H. NORTH
Justice, Michigan Supreme Court

Table of Contents

Historical Introduction*

I T IS a commonly known fact that, although Michigan was admitted to the Union in 1837 (many of her citizens had claimed statehood for more than a year prior to her formal admission), few opinions of the state supreme court written before 1843 have ever been published. Why a period of almost ten years should have elapsed before the first volume of state reports was issued in 1846 (with the exception of two volumes of chancery reports), or why the early reporters seem, from a casual examination, to have neglected decisions of the court before 1843, or what happened to the opinions, if any, that were rendered by supreme court justices during the first seven years of the state's existence, are questions which have never been answered adequately.

The historical setting of this subject may be summarized for present purposes in a few sentences. During the summer of 1835 a constitutional convention, which had been elected by the people of the Territory of Michigan, drew up and submitted to the electorate for ratification the first constitution of the state. This document was approved by a large majority of the people voting at a surprisingly small election in October of that year.[1] At the same time a governor, lieutenant-governor, and members of the state legislature were chosen, all of whom shortly thereafter assumed office and, without Congres-

---

* This introduction is a shortened and revised version of the sixth chapter of the writer's unpublished doctoral dissertation, A HISTORY OF THE SUPREME COURT OF THE STATE OF MICHIGAN, 1836-1857, pp. 220-273 (1940) (Legal Research Library, University of Michigan). It appeared in slightly different form in 42 MICHIGAN LAW REVIEW, 87 (August, 1943).

[1] The total vote was: Yes—6,299; No—1,359. In only one county (Branch) were there more ballots cast against than for the constitution, and that was by the narrow margin of 29 to 32. JOURNAL OF THE SENATE OF THE STATE OF MICHIGAN (hereafter cited as SENATE JOUR.), 1835-1836, Doc. No. 1.

sional sanction, attempted to establish a state government and
to cast off the territorial government.[2] Of the various measures undertaken in the interim preceding final entrance into
the Union, it is necessary to note here only that the new legislature early in the next year adopted laws which provided for
the cessation on July 4, 1836, of the terms and functions of
the territorial officers,[3] for the establishment of a peripatetic
supreme court whose members were to act singly as presiding
judges in the circuit courts of the various counties and jointly
as the highest court of review, and for the selection of the new
state judges.[4] Subsequently, the governor in July nominated
for the positions of chief justice and associate justices of the
state supreme court three men who were approved almost
unanimously by the senate.[5] Within a week after their appointment these men began to assume control of Michigan's judicial business.[6]

[2] For a detailed account of the actions taken by the governor and legislature
of Michigan, counter measures carried out by President Jackson and his aides,
and the arguments presented on both sides in regard to the right of Michigan
to proceed as a state previous to approval by Congress of her constitution, see
NORTON, A HISTORY OF THE SUPREME COURT OF THE STATE OF MICHIGAN,
1836-1857, pp. 68-111 (1940). Also see the treatment of the same subject in
1 TRANSACTIONS OF THE SUPREME COURT OF THE TERRITORY OF MICHIGAN,
1825-1836, pp. xlv-liii (1940) (edited by W. W. Blume).
[3] Mich. Pub. Acts (1836), pp. 14-23, 30-35.
[4] Id. 30-35.
[5] The three were William A. Fletcher, George Morell, and Epaphroditus
Ransom, all nominated and approved on July 18, 1836. EXECUTIVE JOURNAL
OF THE SENATE OF THE STATE OF MICHIGAN, 1835-1836, pp. 17-18.
[6] Although no session of the state supreme court as a whole was held until
January 1837, the individual justices, as required by law, presided in the state
circuit courts which were held in several counties during the latter part of 1836.
See the STATE JOURNAL (Ann Arbor), Oct. 20, 1836, and the Journal of the
Washtenaw County Circuit Court for the session of circuit court held in Wash-
tenaw County; for reports on circuit court terms in Kalamazoo and St. Clair
Counties, see Ransom, "Kalamazoo County," 7 MICHIGAN PIONEER COLLEC-
TIONS 469 at 473 (1886), (Michigan Historical Commission) and 1 W. L.
JENKS, ST. CLAIR COUNTY, MICHIGAN: ITS HISTORY AND ITS PEOPLE 196
(1912). In addition there were at least three writs issued before August 1, 1836,
which bore the heading "State Supreme Court": a writ of certiorari, dated July
25, in Batty v. Fraser, Sup. Ct., 1st circ., file No. 23; a writ of certiorari, dated
July 30, in Lee v. Force, Sup. Ct., 2d circ., file No. 18; and a writ of error,
dated July 30, in Mathews v. Howell, Sup. Ct., 1st circ., file No. 8.

Little emphasis had been placed upon the reporting and publishing of judicial opinions during the thirty-one years Michigan had territorial status. As far as is known, the Supreme Court of Michigan Territory never appointed an official reporter of its decisions, although for two years (1819-1821) a court rule was in force which provided that reports of the judges' opinions should be kept by some person appointed by the court, and James Duane Doty, clerk of the supreme court at that time, appears to have made an attempt to report several cases.[7] In 1825 another private venture at reporting the supreme court decisions at least was projected,[8] apparently without success. The legislative council adopted a resolution in 1828 instructing the committee on the judiciary to inquire whether it would be advisable to require the judges when sitting in bank to file written opinions on the cases disposed.[9] While there were no immediate tangible results of this resolution, in 1831 a law was passed by the legislative council which required the judges of the Territorial Supreme Court and of the Wayne County Circuit Court to write decisions "in such cases and matters as are usually reported in the several States of the United States, where there are reporters provided by law," and such opinions to be filed and preserved by the clerks of the courts.[10] However, no collection of decisions by the Territorial Supreme Court was published until recently,[11] and the few opinions which were printed

[7] Doty's reportorial activities, as well as his manuscript volume of reports, have been recorded in 1 TRANSACTIONS OF THE SUPREME COURT OF THE TERRITORY OF MICHIGAN, 1814-1824, pp. 365-427 (1938).

[8] Notice was given in 1825 that A. G. Whitney, United States District Attorney, was engaged in taking notes on the arguments of counsel and on the decisions by the supreme court with the intention of collecting materials for a report of cases in that court. MICHIGAN HERALD (Detroit), Dec. 13, 1825 (photostatic copy in the Legal Research Library, University of Michigan).

[9] JOURNAL OF THE LEGISLATIVE COUNCIL OF THE TERRITORY OF MICHIGAN, 1828, pp. 18, 27.

[10] Act of March 3, 1831, 3 Mich. Terr. Laws (1874 ed.), p. 886.

[11] All available opinions which could be located have been printed in the

contemporaneously appeared mainly in newspapers.

In view of these precedents, as well as the examples of similar practices followed by many other states during their early history, it is not surprising that neither the constitution of 1835, nor the acts which established the state supreme court in 1836, provided that the justices should write their opinions or that a reporter should edit and publish them. Some evidence exists that at least Chief Justice William A. Fletcher intended to write some opinions during 1837, which was the first year sessions of the court were held,[12] but no extant opinions have been found which date prior to 1838.[13]

The latter year marked the earliest statutory provision for a court reporter. According to the revision of the laws made in 1838, this official was to report the decisions of both the supreme court and the court of chancery, and was required to attend all terms of those courts, to make "true reports of their decisions upon all such causes and matters as are usually reported," and to publish every year the decisions of each court separately. His appointment and tenure of office were subject to the action of a majority of the justices and the chancellor, but in the selection of cases to be reported he was given a certain amount of discretion on the basis of their importance. In turn it was made the duty of the courts to give their opinions to the reporter in writing as soon as convenient. Although the compensation of the reporter was fixed at six

six volumes of TRANSACTIONS OF THE SUPREME COURT OF THE TERRITORY OF MICHIGAN (1935-1940).

[12] In 1842 newly appointed Chief Justice George Morell wrote a notation on the wrapper of a case file that Fletcher had taken the papers in that particular file at the June term, 1837, "to draw up the opinion of the court." Fletcher did not return the papers until March 31, 1842. United States v. Cornell, Sup. Ct., 1st circ., file No. 62.

[13] There are thirty-seven cases decided before 1843 in which opinions, manuscript and printed, are known to be in existence. By year, these are 1838, six; 1839, four; 1840, two; 1841, eight, and 1842, seventeen. Eight of the thirty-seven have been published in full and one in part. The remainder are published for the first time in the present volume.

hundred dollars annually, payable quarterly, he was to receive in addition any profits which might result from the sale of the reports. Under this law the reporter, while nominally a state official, was forced to assume personally the risk and expense of publishing the reports, although, as will be seen, state assistance was sometimes extended.[14]

Available information indicates that the only two active candidates for the new position were Charles H. Stewart[15] and Ebenezer Burke Harrington. The latter, a young lawyer, was selected by the court. Much of Harrington's early life is obscure. He apparently left the home of his parents in Michigan while still a youth, learned the trade of a cabinetmaker at Jamestown, New York, then later studied law at Whitestown in the same state.[16] Before he returned to Michigan in 1836 he had been one of the compilers of Barbour's and Harrington's *Equity Digest* for the state of New York.[17]

[14] Mich. Rev. Stat. (1838), p. 414. For a brief sketch of the office of reporter by Justice James V. Campbell, who was a contemporary and had business connections with at least two of the reporters (Walker and Douglass), see his opinion in People ex rel. Ayres v. State Auditors, 42 Mich. 422 at 431-435, 4 N. W. 274 (1880).

[15] In soliciting the support of William Woodbridge for the office, Stewart claimed that he had received favorable expressions from most of the Detroit bar, including A. D. Fraser. An inclosure from Fraser stated the opinion that Stewart would make an excellent reporter. Dec. 4, 1838, WOODBRIDGE PAPERS (Burton Historical Collection, Detroit Public Library).

[16] "Daniel B. Harrington," 5 MICHIGAN PIONEER COLLECTIONS 138 at 141-142 (1884). Authorities differ on whether Harrington's first name was "Ebenezer" or "Edmund." The above article, along with 1 MICHIGAN BIOGRAPHIES 374 (1924) (Michigan Historical Commission) and 1 JENKS, ST. CLAIR COUNTY, MICHIGAN: ITS HISTORY AND ITS PEOPLE 196 (1912), use the former name, but the supreme court journal calls him by the latter. SUP. CT. JOURN., 1st circ., vol. 1, pp. 299, 350. In 1836 he signed his name as "Ebenezer" (Fisk v. Leroy, Sup. Ct., 1st circ., file No. 5), which should be conclusive unless he had it legally changed. A short biographical sketch of Harrington can be found in R. B. Ross, THE EARLY BENCH AND BAR OF DETROIT 85 (1907).

[17] An article had appeared in the Detroit ADVERTISER, Sept. 21, 1838, purporting to be an extract from the American Jurist, which charged that Harrington had acted as no more than a clerk in the compilation of the Equity Digest. Harrington replied in a letter to the editor of the Free Press that the charge was false, that a contract had been made by Barbour and by himself, providing that both their names should appear on the title page, and that he had actually done

He was reputed to have been admitted on October 20, 1836, to the bar in the circuit court of St. Clair county, and then to have opened a law office in the village of Desmond, Michigan.[18] During the next few months he edited and published the *Lake Huron Observer* at Port Huron, made a venture in real estate speculation which was a complete failure, and then moved in 1838 to Detroit, where he practiced law as a partner of James A. Van Dyke.[19] Governor Stevens T. Mason appointed him and E. J. Roberts to edit and superintend the publication of the revision of Michigan laws made in 1838.[20] A practical politician, he was a delegate from St. Clair county to the Democratic state convention at Ann Arbor, July 20, 1837, and was nominated and elected state senator from the fourth district in 1838.[21] He continued to hold his senatorship through the 1839 session and was called "as useful a legislator, as any man in the senate."[22] Moreover, he was in 1840, while still state reporter, the prosecuting attorney for Michilimackinac county.[23] These activities, in addition to his continuous services as an attorney and counselor at law, would seem to indicate that the duties of reporting were not then very onerous.

The exact date of Harrington's appointment as reporter has not been determined, but it was probably about February

more work on it than had Barbour because the latter was at the same time the chancellor's clerk. See the FREE PRESS (Detroit), Dec. 25, 1838.

[18] 1 JENKS, ST. CLAIR COUNTY, MICHIGAN: ITS HISTORY AND ITS PEOPLE 196-197 (1912).

[19] Id.; 1 MICHIGAN BIOGRAPHIES 374 (1924); "A Good Chancery Lawyer but Unlucky in Real Estate," newspaper clipping, undated, in 2 C. M. BURTON, SCRAPBOOK 106 (Burton Coll.). Harrington laid out a "paper town" on Lake Huron north of Port Huron in 1837 but failed to sell any lots.

[20] Mich. Rev. Stat. (1838), p. 3.

[21] FREE PRESS, July 24, 1837; Sept. 19, 1838; Nov. 24, 1838. In the Senate he was a member of the committee on the judiciary. SENATE JOURN., 1839, p. 7.

[22] MACOMB DEMOCRAT, quoted in the FREE PRESS, March 28, 1839.

[23] See the notice (July 10, 1840) and the subpoena (July 20, 1840) in the examination of A. R. Davenport, ". . . Inspector of Fish for Michilimackinac County." WOODBRIDGE PAPERS, folder July 11-20, 1840 (Burton Coll.).

20, 1839.[24] "To handsome talents and much legal learning and experience, Mr. Harrington unites habits of industry which well qualify him for the proper discharge of the duties of the office," was the comment of the *Detroit Free Press*.[25] In view of the fact that the only volume of reports which he edited was that of the court of chancery, and that no opinions of the supreme court were published while he was in office, the question whether Harrington adequately fulfilled his duties as reporter may well be raised. Existing manuscript opinions prove without doubt that he did edit several opinions, complete with headnotes, statement of facts, arguments of counsel, and revisions of the original drafts of opinions written by the justices of the supreme court. Included in the files of the court are six opinions in cases decided at the January terms of 1838, held at Detroit and Ann Arbor, all of which are in the handwriting of Associate Justice Epaphroditus Ransom. They are accompanied by other drafts of the same opinions written by Harrington in the form of reports.[26] Some of these contain a penciled annotation, "not to be reported," written by an unidentified person, probably a later reporter; there are also short memoranda penned by Harrington for both the majority and dissenting opinions delivered in a case decided in 1839.[27] However, the

[24] There is no entry in any of the extant Journals of the Supreme Court indicating the date of appointment, but H. N. Walker, Harrington's successor as reporter, stated that it was in February 1839. See the preface to MICHIGAN CHANCERY REPORTS (Harrington). The leading Democratic newspaper of the state did not announce the appointment until May 22. FREE PRESS, May 22, 1839. However, there is documentary proof that his salary must have begun sometime in February, because on April 23 he was paid $162, more than a quarter of a year's salary. DOCUMENTS OF THE SENATE OF THE STATE OF MICHIGAN (hereafter cited as SENATE DOCS.), 1840, I, 518.

[25] May 22, 1839.

[26] Burhans v. Reynolds, Sup. Ct., 2d circ., file No. 1160 (Index of 1902); Calhoun v. Cable, Sup. Ct., Mich. Terr., file No. 1491; Hubble v. Burch, Sup. Ct., 1st circ., file No. 70; Mundy v. Sargent, Sup. Ct., 2d circ., file No. 1158 (Index of 1902); Norris v. Hawks, Sup. Ct., 2d circ., file No. 66; Whitcomb v. Porter, Sup. Ct. 1st circ., file No. 88.

[27] Henretty v. City of Detroit, Sup. Ct., 1st circ., file No. 159.

remaining manuscript opinions, most of which were written by Chief Justice Fletcher, show no marks of editing by the reporter.

This paucity of existing opinions reported by Harrington does not by itself constitute sufficient evidence to censure him for neglecting his duties; because of the incomplete status of the files, and the probability that many of his reported opinions were never in the official files, it would be unjust, without more positive evidence, to make such a charge. Moreover, there are strong grounds to believe that he intended as early as 1840 to publish a volume of chancery court and supreme court reports.[28]

Formal notice of the delay in publishing the reports was taken by the state senate in 1841, which adopted a resolution directing Harrington to inform the senate in the near future "the number of cases decided by the supreme court, designating the title of the cause, what judges have furnished him with a written opinion, and the time when furnished, and in what circuit the cause has been decided, and also the same, as near as may be, in the court of chancery, and at what time a volume of reports of the decisions of the supreme court, or of the court of chancery will be published."[29]

Harrington's reply to this legislative request is most instructive. He claimed that since the date of his appointment as reporter he had attended nearly all the terms of both the supreme court and the chancery courts, that he had kept an accurate list of cases with notes on their principal points, and

---

[28] A notice appeared in the newspapers requesting the clerks of the several counties to send to Harrington at Detroit the names of attorneys in their counties, because he is "now preparing the first number of reports of the cases decided in the court of chancery and supreme court of this state, which will be published during the ensuing winter, and is desirous of ascertaining the number of Attorneys in the State, that he may the better judge how large an edition will be necessary." FREE PRESS, Nov. 28, 1839; MICHIGAN STATE JOURNAL (Ann Arbor), Jan. 1, 1840.

[29] SENATE JOUR., 1841, p. 74. Adopted on Jan. 15.

that he had examined the papers in over seven hundred causes. However, it was his contention that the justices of the supreme court had directed him to report only seventy-three decisions. According to Harrington, up to 1841 only one member of the court, Justice Ransom, had sent in his opinions; these, the reporter asserted, he had prepared for the press, but he had been informed by the chief justice that opinions had been written in most of the cases in "schedule B" and were then ready for the reporter. Furthermore, Harrington stated that in September, 1840, he had contracted with Dawson and Bates for the printing of one volume of reports for each court, that this printing had begun in October, and that about three hundred pages of the chancery volume were finished and about one hundred more pages ready to be printed. "The cases in the supreme court will be printed and ready for delivery by the fifteenth of June next [1841]."[30]

The following year, when the advisability of maintaining the office of reporter was questioned by the new economy-minded governor, John S. Barry,[31] the legislature proceeded

[30] SENATE DOCS., 1841, No. 38, pp. 147-148. On the last day of the legislative session in 1841, a resolution was offered that Dawson and Bates should be paid the sum of $912 for printing the first volume of chancery reports, provided that the reporter should relinquish all his right and title to any profits from the sale of the reports, but it was not adopted. SENATE JOUR., 1841, pp. 489-490. However, it appears that Harrington proceeded with his plans and published a pamphlet volume of chancery reports which extended through 1840 and was ready for sale in the summer of 1841. See the DAILY ADVERTISER (Detroit), July 7, 1841.

[31] In his annual address (1842) Governor Barry repeated most of the information which Harrington had conveyed to the senate in 1841, but said that enough opinions had been received from Justice Ransom to make about 100 pages and none from the other justices. "These facts naturally suggest the inquiry whether, under the present legislation upon the subject, the public are likely to receive an adequate benefit for the expense incurred in providing a reporter." He said that the subject required the attention of the legislature, and that either the reporter should be abolished or more effectual means should be provided to publish supreme court decisions. JOURNAL OF THE HOUSE OF REPRESENTATIVES OF THE STATE OF MICHIGAN (hereafter cited as HOUSE JOUR.), 1842, p. 48.

to investigate the whole subject. A petition by Harrington
asking for relief in return for the printing of three hundred
and seventy-two pages of chancery reports was rejected on
the recommendation of the house committee on claims, which
held that the law giving the reporter a salary and allowing
him profits from sale of reports rendered such relief unnecessary.[32] In reply to inquiries sent by the house committee
on the judiciary to the members of the supreme court to
ascertain their views upon the subject and to learn the "true
reasons" why the reports had not been published, letters
were received from each of the four justices.[33]

Chief Justice William A. Fletcher's answer was a conditional one: "If the present judicial system is to continue, I
think some other means of publishing the reports, as they can
be prepared, might be adopted which would be attended with
less expense."[34] Justice Ransom stated that the creation of a
reporter was entirely premature, that in 1838 there had been
few cases pending which, when decided, would settle the law,
and that the benefits derived from reporting them would not
equal the expense to the treasury. He suggested that instead
of abolishing the office, it would be necessary only to repeal
the law providing for the reporter's salary, as the incumbent
would thereupon resign; by this procedure the office would
be left in existence so that when a reporter was needed one
could be provided by merely restoring the salary. He also
suggested that until a new reporter should be appointed, the
opinions of the supreme and chancery courts ought to be filed

---

[32] Id., pp. 127, 327.

[33] DOCUMENTS OF THE HOUSE OF REPRESENTATIVES OF THE STATE OF
MICHIGAN (hereafter cited as HOUSE DOCS.), 1842, No. 21, pp. 85-94. The
judiciary committee included the letters of the justices in full in their report
because of the complete information they contained and because "they so
perfectly exculpate those functionaries from what a cursory reader of the
governor's message might suppose a censure upon them," but asserted that
the only desire of the governor was "to discharge his whole duty to the people
of this state." Id., 87.

[34] Id.

with the secretary of state, who should publish a synopsis of each case in the newspapers at no cost to the state.[35] Justice Charles W. Whipple wrote that

> ". . . under existing circumstances, the office of reporter is of but little practical importance, and might well be dispensed with. In expressing this opinion, I am not insensible of the great importance of perfecting the judgments and opinions of the highest judicial tribunal in the state; but under the present system, this cannot be done."[36]

Of the four justices, the only one who believed that it was proper for the position of reporter as constituted to be continued was George W. Morell, who stated that the business of the supreme court had accumulated and in the near future would be increasing sufficiently to justify retention of the office.[37]

Although a majority of the court seemed to have been inclined to doubt the necessity for an official reporter, the fundamental reason for their stand clearly arose from the belief that they did not have enough opportunity (because of their burdensome task of presiding in the circuit courts) to perform the research and to spend the time necessary for the writing of adequate opinions. Each one of them stressed this point emphatically in his letter to the house judiciary committee. For example, Chief Justice Fletcher wrote that

> ". . . we have not time, under the present system, to do that which we think the interest of the public requires, to draw up with care, opinions in the great variety of cases which are presented, many of them involving new and important principles, and which opinions are to become written law."[38]

[35] Id., p. 89.
[36] Id., p. 91.
[37] Id., p. 94.
[38] Id., p. 88.

Associate Justices Ransom, Whipple, and Morell expressed similar views, all of them blaming the requirement of circuit duty as the chief obstacle to thoughtful consideration and preparation of opinions in the majority of decisions.[39] With the exception of Ransom, none of them intimated the belief that the quality of causes which had been adjudicated by the supreme court since the appointment of a reporter in 1838 was of so minor a character that written and published opinions were not justified or desirable, at least in many cases. Even the statement of Ransom on this point (referred to above) appears to be rather singular in the light of the fact that he himself had written at least six opinions for the year 1838.[40] Moreover, Justice Whipple very pointedly called attention in a later decision to the handicap that resulted from a lack of published opinions before 1843,[41] and neither Fletcher nor Morell was opposed to the principle of printing reports of the supreme court's decisions. Nevertheless, the judiciary committee of the house recommended, as Ransom had advised, the repeal of the law which had provided for the salary of the reporter,[42] and a joint resolution to that effect was adopted by the legislature and approved by the governor on February 16, 1842.[43]

[39] Id., pp. 90, 91-92, 93-94. Whipple suggested another justice be added to the supreme court, which would help both the supreme and the circuit courts and allow the members more time to write opinions.

[40] See note 26 above.

[41] In the case of Robinson v. Steam Boat Red Jacket, 1 Mich. 171 at 173 (1849), Whipple wrote: "The learned counsel for the plaintiff was not advised, until the argument of the case, that a construction had been given to the statute in question by this court—the opinion never having been published [referring to Moses v. Steam Boat Missouri, decided Jan. 1842]. Had the fact of its promulgation been known, it must have narrowed a discussion which assumed a wider range in consequence of the prominence given to a question which it was supposed had not been judicially determined."

[42] HOUSE DOCS., 1842, No. 21, p. 94.

[43] Mich. Pub. Acts (1842), J. Res. 28, p. 168. For legislative proceedings on this Joint Resolution, see HOUSE JOUR., 1842, pp. 313, 361, and SENATE JOUR., 1842, p. 254.

Perhaps more important than the fate of either Harrington or the office of reporter is the question how many opinions were written by the justices of the supreme court prior to 1843 and what happened to them. To summarize briefly, opinions from thirty-seven cases which date from that period are known to be in existence.[44] All these cases are listed in a table of cases, *infra* p. lii. The opinions in twenty-eight cases are published for the first time in the present volume, two others for which the manuscripts are still in the court files have been printed, and the remaining seven can be found only in later published reports. The assertions by Harrington noted above concerning his intentions to publish a volume of supreme court reports during 1840-1841 were of a prospective nature and can be relied upon only as an indication that he expected to have collected enough opinions by those dates to constitute a volume, but the significance of his statement that the supreme court had directed him, by 1841, to report seventy-three cases cannot be waived lightly. If true, it would mean that nearly two years before 1843 the supreme court had selected twice as many cases to be reported as now exist for the whole period, and had, presumably, assigned them to the various members to be written. Even more striking is the fact that of the thirty-seven opinions now extant which were delivered before 1843, seventeen bear the date 1842, so that for the years in which the Supreme Court intended at least seventy-three cases to be reported we have opinions in only twenty cases.

It is certain that as late as 1842 many of the opinions were still in the hands of the justices who wrote them and not in the possession of the reporter. For instance, Whipple stated

[44] Of these, one case is represented only by a dissenting opinion (*Infra*, p. 36) and another only by a long quotation in a later case (*Infra*, p. 69). In one case (*Infra*, p. 85) there is both a majority and a dissenting opinion.

that all of the opinions which he had delivered were in written form and were ready to be given to the reporter, who had been advised of their availability but had neglected to collect them.[45] Truly mysterious are the circumstances involving the Morell opinions. Justice Morell's own words testify that he wrote them, as well as to the fact that they were mainly dissenting ones,[46] but most of them have completely disappeared. Morell's wife, daughter, and son, after the justice's death in 1845, accused Justice Ransom of having called at their home and taken away the supreme court opinions of their husband and father, but Ransom vigorously denied the charge and countered with the statement that no such opinions ever existed.[47] However, another authority who cannot be entirely disregarded maintained directly the opposite view. He said:

> ". . . Judge Morell always wrote out in full his important opinions, and a full series of his manuscripts was found, but they could not well be published with-

[45] HOUSE DOCS., 1842, No. 21, p. 92.

[46] According to Morell, Chief Justice Fletcher was to have prepared his opinions in the cases he thought proper to report and give a list of them to the reporter, who was to submit it to Morell for his examination. If Morell approved the list he was to give the reporter his own decisions in cases they thought advisable to report, but he claimed that no such list had been furnished him. "The reporter was informed long ago, that my decisions, (which are most all *dissenting* ones,) would be furnished at a moment's notice, whenever he got the opinions of a majority of the court, for I supposed it would hardly be admissable [sic] to publish a minority decision before publishing that of the majority. The fact is, that I have had so many legal opinions to give and write out, in cases arising alone in the county of Wayne, that I have had but very little time to draw up opinions for publication in the Supreme Court, and as my brethren are willing to spread their opinions upon the record, I was perfectly willing to accommodate them." HOUSE DOCS., 1842, No. 21, p. 93.

[47] Epaphroditus Ransom to S. T. Douglass, Kalamazoo, Dec. 1, 1845, HERBERT BOWEN PAPERS (Burton Coll.). Ransom said in this letter that he had at one time examined some opinions delivered by Morell in Wayne Circuit Court, but that he had returned them immediately, and that the only time he had visited the Morell home since 1843 was at attend Morell's funeral in 1845. He claimed that Morell had not drawn up or delivered a written opinion in a single case during the year prior to the expiration of his term, except at Kalamazoo in 1843, when he delivered two or three opinions.

out the rest [of the court's opinions]. The Reporter [Douglass] therefore, although his friend and admirer, was reluctantly compelled to begin his work at a time when the materials were more complete; and our series, for this reason, contains but a few of his opinions, and these all belong to the later years of his judicial career."[48]

The full significance of these words can be understood better if it is remembered that their author, Justice James V. Campbell, had been from 1845 to 1850 a law partner of Samuel T. Douglass, who was without doubt the "Reporter" to whom Campbell referred, and that a few years later Douglass, by his marriage to Campbell's sister, became his brother-in-law. These circumstances would make for an intimate acquaintance both in business and personal affairs between the two men and add credence and authenticity to Campbell's words. Certainly Douglass had made efforts to locate Morell's opinions, for he wrote to Chief Justice Ransom in 1845 asking for them,[49] and, if we are to believe what Justice Campbell said, Douglass found but did not print them. Only two opinions written by Justice Morell are known to exist today, both delivered in 1843, and both have been published.[50]

In addition to the above-mentioned six manuscript opinions of 1838 by Ransom, we have but one other of his previous to 1843.[51] Nine of Justice Whipple's opinions before 1843 are extant, five of which have been printed.[52] Chief Justice

---

[48] Justice James V. Campbell's address delivered at the acceptance of Judge Morell's portrait by the Supreme Court in 1880, printed in 43 Mich. xviii (1880).

[49] See note 47 above.

[50] Beach v. Botsford, 1 Doug. 199 (1843); Taylor v. Kneeland, 1 Doug. 67 (1843).

[51] Owen v. Farmers' Bank of Sandstone, 2 Doug. 134, note (1841).

[52] Davis v. Ingersoll, 2 Doug. 372 (1840); Godfrey v. Beach, Sup. Ct., 1st circ., file No. 188; Caswell v. Ward, 2 Doug. 374 (1842); Slaughter v. People, 2 Doug. 334, note (1842), and also with the BY-LAWS AND ORDINANCES OF THE CITY OF DETROIT, 1842 in the Burton Historical Collection,

Fletcher before his retirement in 1842 wrote nineteen opinions, or nearly two-thirds of all those prior to 1843 which are still available, but only two of his have been included in later reports.[53] Moreover, it should be noted that of Fletcher's nineteen opinions, only eight were written before the year (1842) he resigned from the bench: two in 1839, one in 1840, and five in 1841.[54] The very fact that Chief Justice Fletcher, in the few months of 1842 during which he was a member of the supreme court, wrote nearly as many opinions as did any one justice during any full year of the whole period between 1836 and 1857 permits the inference that he probably drew up more opinions than eight during the five years he served on the bench prior to 1842. We know that as early as the June term, 1837, he had taken the papers from a certain file with the intention of writing an opinion in that particular case.[55] Although it has been stated that some of Fletcher's opinions were printed in contemporary newspapers,[56] the present writer has found none in any of the newspaper files which he has searched.[57]

Detroit; Royce v. Bradburn, 2 Doug. 377 (1842). In Campbell, Appellant, 2 Doug. 144 (1845), Justice Ransom quoted a long paragraph that supposedly was an excerpt from an opinion written by Justice Whipple in the case of Godfroy v. Brooks. He undoubtedly meant Godfrey v. Beach, above. See *infra*, p. 69.

[53] Bomier v. Caldwell, 8 Mich. 463 (1841); Chamberlin v. Brown, 2 Doug. 120, note (1842). A manuscript copy of the latter opinion in the handwriting of Harrington is also extant, but it is not identical with the printed report. See Sup. Ct., 1st circ., file No. 195.

[54] See opinions, *infra*.

[55] See note 12 above.

[56] Both R. B. ROSS and G. B. CATLIN, LANDMARKS OF DETROIT, Burton rev. ed., 394 (1898), and R. B. ROSS, EARLY BENCH AND BAR OF DETROIT 64 (1907), make such statements. The latter quotes Alpheus Felch as having supposedly said the following: "Some of his [Fletcher's] opinions, however, found their way into the newspapers of the day; and many are treasured up in the memory of early members of the bar. The latter were often cited by them in Court, and even at this late day they are sometimes quoted, and always regarded as high authority."

[57] Their nonexistence in the newspapers is corroborated by another worker

In spite of the fact that his salary as reporter was suspended by the legislature on February 16, 1842, Harrington did not stop his attempts to report the cases of both the supreme and the chancery courts. His interest in the decisions and in their publication was so genuine that he continued his work, providing the public press with abstracts of many chancery court opinions and presumably of some supreme court opinions. In a letter to the editor of the *Detroit Free Press* he explained his position admirably:

> "The Legislature of this state have made no provision for the preservation or publication of the judicial decisions of our Supreme Court or Court of Chancery. Although these decisions form an important part of the law they are only known to the judges themselves, and those who are in constant attendance upon the courts. Many of these opinions have been written out with care and placed in my hands as Reporter for publication, and I have prepared them for the press, but I am unable to publish them without compensation. I will hereafter furnish you with the headnotes for publication from time to time as my leisure will permit."[58]

The headnotes of at least nineteen chancery court cases were printed in the *Free Press* between December 15, 1842 and July 25, 1843;[59] unfortunately none has been found for supreme court cases.

Early in 1843 Governor Barry formally recognized Harrington's continued services as well as the need for publication of the supreme court and chancery court opinions.[60]

---

who has searched for them. POTTER, ADDRESS AT THE UNVEILING OF A MARKER ERECTED TO THE MEMORY OF WILLIAM ASA FLETCHER 9-10 (1935).

[58] FREE PRESS, Dec. 15, 1842.

[59] Dec. 15, 1842, four cases; Dec. 29, 1842, five cases; July 25, 1843, ten cases.

[60] Barry noted that the salary of the reporter had been suspended but said that the incumbent had continued to discharge the duties of the office. "It

Apparently the governor's attitude had changed considerably since his first annual message; nevertheless he still expressed hope that "if such reports were judiciously prepared under well digested regulations of law, the proceeds from their sale would nearly, if not altogether, reimburse the expense of their publication."[61] The legislature, however, was not willing to carry out completely the governor's recommendations and adopted a compromise scheme. According to the new law it was provided that in any matter adjudicated by the supreme court, the justices thereof must pronounce an opinion and prepare an abstract of it in writing. These abstracts were to be filed by the first Monday in January of each year with the secretary of state, who was to have them published in one newspaper of each judicial circuit with the printing costs borne by the state. When enough abstracts of opinions had been accumulated to compose a volume of about three hundred and fifty pages, the secretary of state was directed to have them edited and to have one thousand copies printed at state expense and offered for sale, any profits derived therefrom to go to the state.[62] As a consequence of this statute, the task of reporting what condensed opinions the justices might

seems to me that the best interest of [the] state requires the decisions of its courts to be published, and that much other printing is now required which is of less importance and less beneficial. Indeed I consider the reports of decisions which give construction to the statutes, as important as the statutes themselves, and as necessary to be distributed among the citizens of the state for their information and guidance." HOUSE JOUR., 1843, p. 16.

[61] Id.

[62] Mich. Pub. Acts (1843), pp. 169-170. This act was approved by the governor March 9, 1843, and given immediate effect. On Feb. 3, 1843, a statement made by Harrington had been presented to the house of representatives by Justus Goodwin of Calhoun County, and as a result the question what would be the best method and means of procuring reports of the decisions of the supreme court and the court of chancery was referred to the judiciary committee. HOUSE JOUR., 1843, p. 225. Further action on the bill can be found in id., 1843, pp. 534, 535, 537, and in SENATE JOUR., 1843, pp. 268, 281, 422, 429, 430, 431. A second bill which provided for the publication of the reports was adopted by the senate but not by the house. See id. 1843, pp. 363, 374-375; HOUSE JOUR., 1843, pp. 495, 499.

furnish was added to the regular duties of a state officer who had little connection with the courts and who might not possess any interest in their decisions. It is not surprising that, as far as can be learned, there were never any tangible results from this act;[63] certainly it was not an adequate solution of the problem.

Great influence must have been exercised upon the legislators by the very able report made in the house of representatives early in 1844 by H. N. Walker, a member of the house from Detroit who, after a few months, succeeded Harrington as reporter. Petitions by Harrington concerning publication of the opinions had been presented in both the senate and the house, and the latter body referred the matter to a select committee of which Mr. Walker was the chairman.[64] As a result of their deliberations, the representatives composing this committee concluded that the decisions of the highest state courts were too important a part of the law for their publication to be neglected. They believed that the establishment of legal principles, the interpretation of constitutional provisions, and the construction of important laws, all of which in their reasoning were essential to the administration of justice, could not be understood by the people without printed opinions. Other points the committee emphasized were that requiring written opinions would insure careful attention and examination by the courts to the questions before them, and that their publication would create a guide for future courts which would make for uniformity in practice and procedure.

[63] Not one such abstract has ever been found in any of the newspapers searched by this writer. Moreover, it was stated in the house of representatives in 1844 that this act had never been complied with and that it never could be "with any benefit or advantage to the state." HOUSE JOUR., 1844, p. 118.

[64] S. M. Green, later a justice of the supreme court, presented the petition in the senate and Mr. Walker presented it in the house, both on Jan. 15, 1844. See SENATE JOUR., 1844, p. 50, and HOUSE JOUR., 1844, p. 52.

Rather strangely, the committee adopted the view that published court decisions would be a means of preserving the separation of powers guaranteed by the state constitution, and would thus constitute a "guard against encroachments by the judiciary upon other departments, and the assumption of powers which do not belong to them. . . ." The statute of 1843 which required justices of the supreme court to prepare abstracts of their opinions and which provided for the publication of these abstracts in various newspapers at the expense of the state was scoffed at in the committee report. It was pointed out that the cost of such an undertaking would equal that of the regular form of reports, and that "the publication of an abstract of an opinion of the court without the statement of the case, and without the care and attention of a proper and competent person to correct the proof, would be of no more authority in legal proceedings than any other article found inserted in a newspaper would be evidence of the facts therein contained. . . ."[65] Consequently, the committee introduced a bill to provide for publication of the decisions of the supreme court and of the court of chancery; after much discussion and several amendments,[66] the bill was passed by both houses and approved by the governor on February 29, 1844.[67]

With one exception this new law established the reports and the office of reporter on a basis similar to that set forth in 1838 by the *Revised Statutes.* By virtue of its provisions the justices of the supreme court and the chancellor, or any

[65] The entire report of the select committee is in the HOUSE JOUR., 1844, pp. 116-119.

[66] The greatest amount of controversy over the bill occurred in the house, where the question of salary to be paid the reporter was much disputed, but the senate made several amendments and set the salary at $600 per year. See HOUSE JOUR., 1844, pp. 119, 195, 209, 279-280, 297, 314-315, 319, 324, 353, 359, 364, 389; SENATE JOUR., 1844, pp. 230, 245, 246, 251.

[67] Mich. Pub. Acts (1844), pp. 19-21.

three of them, were authorized to select the reporter, who would hold office entirely at their pleasure. For those cases which were considered to be of enough importance, they were directed to send full notes of the decisions to the reporter, who was to prepare them for publication, along with condensed arguments of counsel, in volumes of approximately six hundred pages. Of the one thousand copies ordered to be printed, nine hundred were to be sold at a price not over three and one-half dollars each in Michigan or five dollars each out of the state; the remaining one hundred copies were to be sent to the secretary of state, whose duty it was to distribute two of them to the Library of Congress, one to each of the state libraries of the United States, one to each county clerk in Michigan, and the remaining ones to the Michigan State Library. A very fundamental change, however, was made by the fourth section of the law, which relieved the reporter of the risk of publishing the works at his own expense. This desirable removal of responsibility was to some degree neutralized, however, by the requirement that payment to him for cost of publication was to be made only after completion of a volume. In addition the reporter's compensation was reduced to five hundred dollars annually; however, he was still entitled to any profits from the sale of reports.[68]

Although this act was given immediate effect, the justices and the chancellor, apparently anticipating by one day their powers thus conferred, reappointed Harrington as reporter on February 28, 1844.[69] This action constituted definite endorsement of his services as reporter since 1839, but it was not

[68] Id. The act specifically repealed those provisions of the Revised Statutes of 1838 and of the law of 1843 which concerned the reports and the reporter.
[69] SUP. CT. JOUR., 1st circ., vol. 1, p. 299. The appointment was dated Feb. 28, 1844, but the entry does not appear to have been made in the Journal until May 3, 1844. It is possible but not certain that the appointment was not made until the later date, but was effective retroactively to the former. Justices Ransom, Whipple, Felch, and Goodwin and Chancellor Manning signed the appointment.

destined that Harrington should live to vindicate himself of the last vestige of suspicion concerning the adequate performance of his duties; he died in early August, 1844, a little over five months after his second appointment and before a single volume of reports, either of the supreme court or of the court of chancery, had been issued to the public.[70]

In addition to the evidence already presented to indicate that the justices of the supreme court before 1843 wrote more opinions than are known to be extant, there is good proof that Harrington himself possessed many more opinions of that period than we now have. For instance, it was said as early as January 2, 1843, that "All the present justices of the supreme court, have furnished to the reporter their written opinions in cases decided by them previous to the January term of 1842, which, together with the opinions now in the hands of the late chief justice for revision, will make a volume of reports of that court."[71]

Again in 1844 it was stated that the reporter had sufficient manuscript opinions delivered by the supreme court justices to make a volume of about six hundred pages, which, along with the volume of chancery court reports (the publication of which had already been commenced), would "embrace all the decisions of the supreme court and court of chancery, of

---

[70] The Proceedings and Resolutions on the death of Harrington, adopted by the Bar of Detroit on Aug. 5, 1844, may be found in SUP. CT. JOUR., 1st circ., vol. 1, 350 (1845), and in the FREE PRESS, Aug. 6, 1844. J. A. Van Dyke, Harrington's law partner, expressed his great respect for the deceased, and H. N. Walker and G. C. Bates were appointed members of a committee to write the resolutions of the bar. It was resolved in part that "we cherish the highest respect for the professional learning of the deceased, for the purity and uprightness of his public and private character, for his uniformly honorable and correct deportment in every relation of life, and for the many excellent qualities which belonged to him as a man." Id.

[71] Annual Address of Governor Barry, HOUSE JOUR., 1843, p. 16. The "late chief justice" referred to was W. A. Fletcher, who, it would seem, still had in his possession several opinions to revise. Possibly some or all of them were the eleven Fletcher opinions delivered in 1842 which are now in the files or in later reports.

sufficient importance to report from the organization of the state government down to the present time."[72] Some time previous to June 22, 1844, Harrington had made overtures and had received a proposition for the publishing of a volume of supreme court reports,[73] but there is no proof that any had been printed before his death. The wide discrepancy between the number of opinions which would have been necessary to constitute a volume of supreme court reports of approximately six hundred pages[74] and the number of opinions which are known to exist—many of which are, indeed, quite brief—makes it appear that, even if the decisions which never came into the possession of the reporter are disregarded and not counted, the justices of the state supreme court wrote opinions in more cases during the first seven or eight years of their incumbency than the thirty-seven which are now in the files or included in later volumes of reports.

In September, 1844, Henry N. Walker was appointed by the supreme court justices and by the chancellor to be the second state reporter.[75] Mr. Walker, a graduate of the Academy at Fredonia, New York, came to Michigan in 1835, entered the office of Elon Farnsworth and A. D. Bates as a law student, and was admitted to the bar, becoming Bates' partner after Farnsworth was appointed chancellor.[76] Walker

[72] Report of H. N. Walker from the select committee to consider the petition of E. B. Harrington, HOUSE JOUR., 1844, p. 118.

[73] A memorandum written by Harrington on June 22, 1844, assured the firm of Wilcox and Harsha that they could depend upon publishing the second volume of his chancery reports "according to the proposition to publish the Supreme Court Reports. . . ." E. W. MORGAN PAPERS (Burton Coll.).

[74] There were nearly sixty opinions, delivered between 1843 and 1845, printed in the first volume of Douglass' Michigan Supreme Court Reports, and several of them were of great length.

[75] FREE PRESS, Sept. 10, 1844.

[76] See the obituary of Walker in 9 MICHIGAN PIONEER COLLECTIONS 88-89 (1886). This law partnership of Bates and Walker was changed during the late thirties and early forties first to Bates, Walker, and Douglass, then to Douglass and Walker, and finally to Walker, Douglass and Campbell, the two new members being S. T. Douglass and J. V. Campbell, both of whom later became justices of the supreme court.

had been elected to serve in the 1844 session of the legislature, where, it will be recalled, he introduced and supported in the house the bill, which later became law, providing for restoration of the reporter's salary and for publishing the reports of the supreme court and court of chancery.[77] Quite likely his legislative work on this bill had some influence on his selection by the justices and the chancellor. Walker's efforts to obtain the position indicate that he desired it and that it was neither unwanted nor thrust upon him without notice.[78] His appointment was approved by the Democratic press of the state and probably by the bar in general.[79]

Undertaking his duties immediately, the new reporter soon brought out the first large volume of reports of the decisions of any court in Michigan's history, those of the court of chancery under Chancellor Elon Farnsworth, 1836-1842. It was fittingly termed *Harrington's Chancery Reports*, inasmuch as practically all of the work on it had been done by the first reporter and not by Walker. In fact, as early as 1841 nearly three hundred pages of chancery opinions had been printed by Harrington at his own expense.[80] Although the

---

[77] See notes 64 and 65 above.

[78] On Aug. 24, 1844, he wrote to Lucius Lyon that the supreme court was about to appoint a reporter, that his (Walker's) name had been presented as a candidate, and that he wished Lyon to write to Chief Justice Ransom in his favor because of Lyon's "strong influence" with the Chief Justice. LYON LETTERS (William L. Clements Library, University of Michigan).

[79] "The high legal attainments and untiring industry of Mr. Walker render him peculiarly well qualified for the proper discharge of the duties of the office in question." FREE PRESS, Sept. 10, 1844.

[80] Harrington's bill for printing ($831.43) was not allowed by the legislature because the reporter had been required to publish the volumes at his own expense, although the statute had not been very clear on the question. See HOUSE JOUR., 1843, p. 16, and id., 1844, pp. 117-118. A committee of the house recommended in 1844 that Harrington should be reimbursed for the reports already printed and should be paid reasonable compensation for his services (id., 1844, p. 119), and an act of the same year authorized the state treasurer, auditor general, and secretary of state to settle his claim. Mich. Pub. Acts (1844), pp. 20-21. In the "Annual Report of the Auditor General" dated Nov. 30, 1844, an item shows that the sum of $2,323.66 had been paid for the supreme and chancery courts' reports, including the salary of reporter, but

burning of the printing office destroyed a portion of the rest
of the manuscript, the volume was prepared almost entirely
by Harrington and the last half of it was partly in press
when Walker assumed office.[81] A contemporary newspaper
notice stated that "A portion of the volume is composed of
the pamphlet volume of reports published sometime prior to
Mr. Harrington's decease, and the remainder has since been
made up from his manuscripts and notes,"[82] which would indicate that some of the sets of pages printed by Harrington in
1841 and 1842 were perhaps bound into pamphlet form
before the full volume was issued. However, no copy has
been found, nor even any confirmation that one ever existed.

Although Walker was appointed attorney-general of
Michigan by the governor and the senate on March 24,
1845,[83] this date does not mark the end of his activities as
reporter; at least, the preface he wrote to the second volume
of chancery reports, published under his auspices, bears the
date April 10, 1845,[84] and his successor was not named until
the following July. However, in the preparation of this
second volume Walker was aided by Chancellor Manning,

there is no indication of how much of this went to Harrington or his estate,
to the printer, or to Walker. JOINT DOCUMENTS OF THE SENATE AND HOUSE
OF REPRESENTATIVES OF THE STATE OF MICHIGAN (hereafter cited as JOINT
DOCS.), 1845, No. 2, p. 10.

[81] See the preface by H. N. Walker to HARRINGTON, MICHIGAN CHANCERY
REPORTS.

[82] FREE PRESS, March 13, 1845. There is evidence that in the summer of
1841 the first portion of the volume, containing decisions through 1840, was
bound up in some fashion and offered for sale at three dollars per copy. See
the advertisement in DAILY ADVERTISER (Detroit), July 7, 1841. No copy of
this volume has been seen or located by this writer.

[83] FREE PRESS, March 25, 1845.

[84] Governor Barry claimed too optimistically on Jan. 6, 1845, that the
second volume of chancery reports was already in press and would be published
the ensuing month. "Annual Message of the Governor," JOINT DOCS., 1845, p.
6. Walker authorized J. V. Campbell to act as his agent in the sale of the
volumes. See the power of attorney and the agreements for sale made by
Campbell, March 5 and 6, 1845, in H. N. WALKER PAPERS (Burton Coll.).

whose decisions between April, 1842 and March, 1845 were recorded therein, and who personally inspected the work, offered suggestions, and even wrote some of the headnotes.[85] In addition, it is probable that Harrington before his death had labored to some extent upon the manuscript which later constituted this volume,[86] but the major credit must be given to Walker. Both volumes of chancery reports were well executed for their time, but they have been superseded for most practical purposes by later annotated editions.[87] It is not to be supposed that Walker confined himself in his capacity as reporter solely to the decisions of the court of chancery; on the other hand, no reports of supreme court cases were published while he was in that office, and the only discovered contemporary reference located from which could be inferred any intention on his part to publish such reports lacks authoritative support and appears to be erroneous.[88]

Upon Walker's tranfer to the office of attorney-general, several candidates for the position of reporter appeared and an active campaign was carried on for at least two months before an appointment was made. The three men most prominently mentioned as worthy of holding the post were Samuel T. Douglass, Andrew Harvie, and G. V. N. Lothrop, with

[85] MICHIGAN CHANCERY REPORTS (Walker), Preface (1845).

[86] Harrington wrote that a part of the manuscript for his *second* volume of chancery reports would be ready by the first of August 1844. E. B. Harrington to Wilcox and Harsha, June 22, 1844, in E. W. MORGAN PAPERS (Burton Coll.).

[87] In 1872 and 1878 second editions, edited by T. M. Cooley and J. V. Campbell respectively, were published.

[88] It was stated by Governor Barry on Jan. 6, 1845, that the first volume of reports of supreme court decisions was in the hands of the printer and that there was hope that it would be completed before the session of the legislature ended. "Annual Message of the Governor," JOINT DOCS., 1845, p. 6. Actually, the first volume was not printed until 1846. It is interesting to note that the governor anticipated "most salutary results" from the publication of the reports, because "A judicial construction will thus be given to the statutes, and a uniformity secured in the administration of justice in the various circuits, and in courts of inferior jurisdiction throughout the state, which could not otherwise be obtained." Id. 7.

Douglass apparently having the greatest number of advocates. Among the prominent supporters of Douglass were George Miles, who soon became a justice of the supreme court, Jefferson G. Thurber, who later was speaker of the house of representatives, and James B. Hunt, a representative in Congress from Michigan (1843-1847); however, Douglass was opposed quite bitterly by the former attorney-general, Peter Morey.[89] Douglass himself was not above soliciting support; following the example of Walker (his law partner) he requested Lucius Lyon, an influential personage in Michigan politics at that time, to recommend him to the justices and to the chancellor for the position.[90] His comments in his letter to Lyon are illuminating:

"The office will necessarily be filled by someone residing here. It is not worth at the most as far as I can judge over $700 & will occupy nearly all of a persons [sic] time for the next two years at least and always a great part of it. My acceptance of it will be a pecuniary sacrifice but a sacrifice which I feel willing to make for the sake of the more active life it would enable me to lead, requiring as it would my attendance upon the terms of the Sup: & Ch: cour[t]'s in the several circuits.—It is my intention in case I receive the appointment to retire from my present business connexion. My health suffers too severely from my present confinement."[91]

<hr>

[89] In letters to Justice Alpheus Felch, Miles wrote on April 28, 1845, that Douglass had the two very important requisites of accuracy and great industry; Thurber wrote on May 31, 1845, that Douglass was a gentleman of integrity, ability, good legal acquirements, and an irreproachable character; and Hunt on Sept. 23 [?], 1845, wrote that Douglass was a sound lawyer, a good Democrat, and would give general satisfaction. On the other hand, Morey wrote Felch on May 1, 1845, that he believed Harvie was the best fitted for the position; he also protested against "the principle of permitting Mr. Walker to transfer the office of Reporter to his partner [Douglass]" and stated that "Douglass is a Whig every inch of him." These letters may be found under the appropriate dates in the ALPHEUS FELCH PAPERS (Burton Coll.).

[90] S. T. Douglass to L. Lyon, Detroit, June 13, 1845, LYON LETTERS (William L. Clements Library, University of Michigan).

[91] Id.

Why the reporter would have to reside in Detroit is not clear, unless Douglass meant that the largest share of the business of the supreme and chancery courts was done in the first circuit, but the argument was proved unsound by the fact that both of the next two reporters were not residents of Detroit.[92] Presumably Douglass believed that only two hundred dollars in profits could be made annually from the sale of the reports, because the salary of the reporter was still five hundred dollars per year, and, as he stated, anyone who gave up a lucrative business to accept the office of reporter would entail a "pecuniary sacrifice." However, it should be noted that, contrary to his expressed intentions, Douglass did not retire from his law partnership when he received the appointment, but continued in active practice of his profession throughout the period of his incumbency as reporter.[93] His appointment, announced in Detroit on July 7, 1845,[94] was probably made at the July term of the second circuit of the supreme court held at Ann Arbor.[95]

Although Samuel T. Douglass was born in Vermont in 1814, his parents moved to New York state when he was still a young child. There he was educated at Fredonia Academy, and later studied law in the offices of James Mullet and of Esek Cowen, both noted attorneys. He came to Michigan in 1837, was admitted to the bar in 1838, and, after a few months spent in Ann Arbor, settled in Detroit, where he

[92] Randolph Manning of Pontiac and George C. Gibbs of Marshall.

[93] See 8 DOUGLASS, WALKER, and CAMPBELL, LETTERPRESS BOOK, 1847-1850, in the Michigan Historical Collections, University of Michigan.

[94] The FREE PRESS, July 7, 1845, commended the appointment highly: "The selection is an excellent one. Mr. Douglass is a sound, well read and industrious lawyer; and both in professional and private life has, in an unusual measure, secured the confidence and respect of his fellow citizens." Justice Ransom called Douglass his "own much esteemed friend . . . to whom I am strongly attached, & whom I regard as one of the most valuable & promising men of his age, in our profession—." E. Ransom to H. N. Walker, Aug. 22, 1846, H. N. WALKER LETTERS (Burton Coll.).

[95] Inasmuch as the JOURNAL for the second circuit of the supreme court, 1836-1851, is missing, we have no official record of the appointment.

entered the law firm of Asher B. Bates and Henry N. Walker. When Bates retired in 1840 a partnership was formed with Walker under the name of Douglass and Walker, and in 1845 James V. Campbell was added as a partner. Douglass held the offices of city attorney of Detroit and of president of the Detroit Young Men's Society in 1843. Somewhat interested in science and geology in addition to the law, he accompanied his cousin, Douglass Houghton, the first state geologist of Michigan, on at least two of his journeys to the Lake Superior regions. A Democrat in politics, but not strongly partisan, he was highly regarded both legally and personally, and, until he was elected to the bench in 1851, his law firm ranked among the best and most prominent in Detroit.[96]

Soon after his appointment Douglass exhibited vigor in the prosecution of his duties as reporter, taking steps to secure and edit the opinions delivered by the justices of the supreme court.[97] By October 7, 1845, he wrote that he was so hard at

[96] These facts have been gathered from the following biographical sketches of Douglass: Buel, "The Bench and Bar of Detroit," 3 MAG. WEST HIST. 669 at 700-704 (1886); Chaney, "The Supreme Court of Michigan," 2 GREEN BAG 377 at 385-386 (1890); CYCLOPEDIA OF MICHIGAN 170-171 (1890); FARMER, THE HISTORY OF DETROIT AND MICHIGAN, biog. ed., 1115-1116 (1889); 1 MICHIGAN BIOGRAPHIES 249 (1924); 2 W. W. POTTER, COURTS AND LAWYERS OF MICHIGAN 1166-1167 (unpublished MS., 1936); G. I. REED, BENCH AND BAR OF MICHIGAN 244 (1897); R. B. ROSS, THE EARLY BENCH AND BAR OF DETROIT 48-53 (1907); Walker, "The Detroit Bar," 2 MICH. L. J. 1 at 12-13 (1893); MICHIGAN, NISI PRIUS CASES (Howell) 342-343 (1884); O. Kirchner, 121 Mich. xxxv-xliv (1899). Some discrepancy exists in the dates cited by these as to the year when Douglass was admitted to practice, Farmer, Potter and Reed stating that it was 1837, but the Cyclopedia of Michigan and a "Roll of Michigan Lawyers" in the Appendix of Reed's Bench and Bar, both cite 1838. The last named source seems to be the best since it supposedly was copied from the original roll of attorneys kept in the office of the clerk of the supreme court.

[97] Felch sent his earlier opinions to Douglass on Sept. 29, 1845, but reserved the remainder for use and reference in the circuit courts. A. Felch to S. T. Douglass, Sept. 29, 1845, FELCH PAPERS (Burton Coll.). C. W. Whipple to S. T. Douglass, Pontiac, Dec. 1, 1845, HERBERT BOWEN PAPERS (Burton Coll.). Whipple said that he wrote an opinion in the case of Ketchum v. Pierce, (Sup. Ct. Calendar, 3d circ., No. 72 [1844]) which he was unable to find at

work that he could not find even an hour's leisure time.[98] Douglass seems to have entertained some thought of publishing the opinions of the supreme court which had been written before 1843, but Ransom, chief justice since 1843, counseled against such a move, stating that "a report of them would be neither useful to the publik or the Profession, nor very creditable to the Court. The truth is, that while Judge Fletcher was on the Bench, most of the decisions were announced *orally*, by him, & the opinions written out—I speak of those held by myself—were but hasty & imperfect sketches of the decision."[99] It is quite probable that Douglass, through his predecessor and law partner, Walker, fell heir to the papers, notes, and opinions gathered by the first reporter, Harrington. At least we know that Walker employed Harrington's manuscript for nearly all of the first, and part of the second, volume of chancery reports, and there is little reason to suppose that Walker did not turn over to Douglass all of the materials pertaining to the office of reporter.

No opinions before 1843 were included in the first volume (1846) of reports published by Douglass, but in his second volume (1849) there are six, one of which had been delivered in 1840, one in 1841, and four in 1842.[100] He himself explained as follows the failure to print more of them:

"No complete series of the decisions of the court prior to 1843 can now be obtained, and the recent re-

a later date. C. W. Whipple to S. T. Douglass, Pontiac, Aug. 21, 1846, HERBERT BOWEN PAPERS. It has never been published or located.

[98] S. T. Douglass to Silas H. Douglass, Detroit, Oct. 7, 1845, S. H. DOUGLASS LETTERS (University of Michigan Library).

[99] E. Ransom to S. T. Douglass, Kalamazoo, Dec. 1, 1845, HERBERT BOWEN PAPERS (Burton Coll.).

[100] All six were printed as footnotes to later cases in which similar questions were involved. They were: Davis v. Ingersoll, 2 Doug. 372 (1840); Owen v. Farmers' Bank of Sandstone, 2 Doug. 134 (1841); Caswell v. Ward, 2 Doug. 374 (1842); Chamberlin v. Brown, 2 Doug. 120 (1842); Royce v. Bradburn, 2 Doug. 377 (1842); and Slaughter v. People, 2 Doug. 334 (1842).

vision of the statutes has rendered many of those which have been preserved, of comparatively little value. Some of them, however, are of permanent interest, and these, together with the decisions made subsequently to the time when the above mentioned volume closes, will be published in another volume now in the course of preparation, and which it is hoped will be issued from the press during the next summer."[101]

Of the six earlier opinions printed in volume two, a manuscript copy of only one of them is known to exist;[102] this fact suggests the possibility that Douglass might have possessed many more manuscript opinions which never were filed with the clerk of the supreme court. As late as 1848 Douglass wrote that a manuscript opinion in a certain case decided in 1842 "is now before me."[103]

Governor Alpheus Felch, who had been a justice of the supreme court from 1842 to 1845, in January 1846 estimated that probably three volumes would be required to report the supreme court cases already decided; in actuality, however, less than a volume and a half were filled by the decisions which, by a strict interpretation, should have been comprehended in the period mentioned by Felch.[104] Although the

---

[101] FREE PRESS, Jan. 20, 1847.

[102] Chamberlin v. Brown, Sup. Ct., 1st circ., file No. 195.

[103] S. T. Douglass to H. C. Wright, Detroit, Feb. 22, 1848, in 8 WALKER, DOUGLASS, and CAMPBELL, LETTERPRESS BOOK 263 (Mich. Hist. Coll., University of Michigan). The case was that of Moses v. Steamboat Missouri, which was printed in 1852 in 1 Mich. (Manning) 507 Appendix (1842).

[104] "Annual Message of the Governor," JOINT DOCS., 1846, p. 6. Governor Felch also called attention to the great importance of publishing the decisions, and said that Douglass intended to present during the year 1846 the reports of all important cases in both the supreme court and the chancery court. Id. No opinions of the court of chancery between March 1845 and March 1847, when the separate chancery court ceased to exist, have ever been printed. Manning remained chancellor until the Revised Statutes of 1846 (which provided for the abolition of the court in 1847) were adopted, when he resigned; former chancellor Elon Farnsworth was reappointed to the post in June 1846, and served for the remaining months of the court's existence. Nothing has been found except the reference by Felch that Douglass intended to publish a volume of chancery reports.

governor may have been mistaken or misinformed, his reputation for accuracy and truthfulness permits one to conjecture upon the possibility of the existence of many other opinions that were not printed. It is certain that when Douglass in 1850 delivered the manuscript opinions to his successor in the office of reporter, Randolph Manning, only those after 1845 and none prior to 1843 were included.[105] Nevertheless, a search of the available Douglass papers has failed to disclose any supreme court opinions.[106]

Douglass had planned to issue a third volume in August or September of 1850, but he retired from the office before that time.[107] It appears that he was instrumental in the selection of Randolph Manning, former chancellor,[108] as the new

[105] Douglass drew up an inventory which listed, according to the year and to the justice who delivered them, all of the manuscript opinions which he was turning over to his successor. When Manning received them on July 11, 1850, he had to acknowledge by his signature that the opinions were in his possession. Although it is not important in the present study, this list is significant because it proves that many supreme court opinions were written after 1843 that were never included in the printed reports. Nearly forty opinions, composed between 1846-1850, that have not been published and are not known to exist in manuscript, were cited by Douglass. 8 WALKER, DOUGLASS, and CAMPBELL, LETTER-PRESS BOOK 847-852 (Mich. Hist. Coll., University of Michigan). Douglass himself wrote that he had an opinion for the case of Stowell v. Walker (Sup. Ct., 1st circ., file No. 318) decided in 1844, but that he was not publishing it. See 1 Doug. 524, note (1845).

[106] While searching through a part of Douglass' papers in his old homestead on Grosse Ile, the writer and Mr. Henry Brown of the Michigan Historical Collections located five of the eight volumes of letterpress books kept between 1837 and 1850 by the law firm of which Mr. Douglass was a member. Volume 8 has proved most helpful.

[107] GRAND RAPIDS ENQUIRER, Jan. 16, 1850, quoting the DETROIT FREE PRESS. There must have been some public interest in the reports, because Douglass wrote the editor that he had received many inquiries as to when the third volume would be published. Douglass offered his resignation at the May 1850 term of court and it was accepted by the supreme court in July. FREE PRESS, July 6, 1850.

[108] Biographical sketches of Manning may be found in the following: AMERICAN BIOGRAPHICAL HISTORY OF EMINENT AND SELF-MADE MEN: REPRESENTATIVE MEN OF MICHIGAN, part VI, p. 49 (1878); Baldwin, "Judge Randolph Manning," 14 MICHIGAN PIONEER AND HISTORICAL COLLECTIONS 418-421 (1890) (Michigan Historical Commission); Felch, "Michigan's Court of Chancery," 21 id. 325 at 329 (1894); 2 MICHIGAN BIOGRAPHIES 73-74 (1924); G. I. REED, BENCH AND BAR OF MICHIGAN 12 (1897);

reporter.[109] Manning's appointment was conferred the first week in July, when the supreme court was in session at Jackson.[110] His first and only volume of reports was not published until 1852. It is important here to note only that in the appendix he included one opinion which had been written and delivered before 1843.[111] Since this opinion had been in the possession of Douglass in 1848[112] but was not cited in the list of those which Douglass had turned over to Manning in 1850, one might be tempted to draw the hasty conclusion that Douglass had transferred all of the decisions of the supreme court which he possessed, while making a record of only those dating after 1845. However, because inquiries had been made about this particular opinion, it seems more logical to suppose that Douglass himself had determined to publish it in the third volume of reports which he had contemplated issuing in 1850, in consequence of which Manning had acquired it along with any other work Douglass might have done on volume three. The entire matter is highly conjectural and with present sources cannot be determined with finality.

It is not known definitely whether Manning resigned or was removed from the office of reporter; at any rate George C. Gibbs of Marshall[113] was appointed to the position on

R. B. Ross, THE EARLY BENCH AND BAR OF DETROIT 131-133 (1907); MICHIGAN, NISI PRIUS CASES (Howell) 343 (1884); remarks by A. C. Baldwin, A. B. Maynard, Chief Justice Sherwood, and Justice Campbell in 65 Mich. li-lix (1889).

[109] Manning wrote to Douglass that he knew of nothing "to prevent my accepting the appointment mentioned by you, should the Judges of the Supreme Court think proper to confer it on me." Pontiac, May 15, 1850, HERBERT BOWEN PAPERS (Burton Coll.).

[110] FREE PRESS, July 6, 1850. As the Journal for the second circuit, 1836-1851, is missing, no official record of the appointment has been found.

[111] Moses v. Steamboat Missouri, 1 Mich. 507 (1842).

[112] 8 WALKER, DOUGLASS, and CAMPBELL, LETTERPRESS BOOK 263 (Mich. Hist. Coll. University of Michigan).

[113] For a sketch of Gibbs' life, see 1 MICHIGAN BIOGRAPHIES 323 (1924). A contemporary said of Gibbs that "A discriminating mind, accurate education, habits of thought and industry, and above all a courteous bearing, fully qualify

January 6, 1853.[114] During the four years in which he held
the office, Gibbs published as many volumes (three) of supreme court reports as had his four predecessors in twelve
years or as had his two immediate predecessors in seven years,
but in none of them did he print any opinions that had been
written before 1843. There is no evidence that he possessed
such material, or that any manuscripts had been transferred
to him by Manning. However, the next state reporter,
Thomas M. Cooley, obtained and printed in 1860 an opinion
in a case that had been decided in 1841![115] It would seem that
until a law of 1855 made it the duty of the reporter to have
accurate copies of the supreme court opinions made and the
originals returned to the proper offices for filing,[116] the reporters had been in the habit of retaining the original manuscripts in their personal possession, at least until the end of
their term.

In view of the fact that the early supreme court records
are incomplete[117] and that the available opinions are not
numerous, it is to be regretted that the newspapers of the day
did not devote more space to the business of the court and to
its decisions. Prior to 1847 the discussion in the press of supreme court cases was very spasmodic, limited mainly to decisions which were of great public moment or in which the
editors themselves might have had a personal or political
interest.[118] Only one instance has been found before that date

him for the discharge of the responsible duties of the station." FREE PRESS,
Jan. 8, 1853. Just why a "courteous bearing" should be important for the
office of reporter is not clear. See also the MICHIGAN ARGUS (Ann Arbor),
Jan. 12, 1853.

[114] 2 SUP. CT. JOUR., 1st circ., 260 (1853).
[115] Bomier v. Caldwell, 8 Mich. 463 (1841).
[116] Mich. Pub. Acts (1855), pp. 46-47.
[117] For a description of the supreme court calendars, journals, and files
known to be extant, see Norton, "Missing Supreme Court Documents," 26
MICH. HISTORY MAG. 518 (1942).
[118] For example, discussion of individual cases appeared in the MICHIGAN

in which an attempt was made to list even so much as the names and judgments of all cases decided at a particular term. However, that one article proved most helpful because the journal is not extant for that session of the court.[119] Not until 1845 did any Michigan newspaper, as far as is known, print a copy of a full opinion delivered by a justice of the state supreme court.[120]

If we discount the headnotes of chancery opinions published through the efforts of Harrington in 1842 and 1843,[121] no systematic account of superior court decisions appeared in the newspapers until Samuel T. Douglass, as reporter, undertook the task of providing one in 1847;[122] during his remaining years in office he supplied the *Free Press*, the main organ of the Democratic Party, with abstracts of many of the supreme court opinions, lists of judgments, and names of justices who delivered opinions in the cases not abstracted.[123] This practice was followed by later reporters, while in addition the same newspaper often published synopses of decisions and proceedings in court written by some attorney or staff member who was present at the session.[124]

ARGUS (Ann Arbor), May 10 and May 31, 1843, and May 27, 1846; in the MICHIGAN STATE JOURNAL (Ann Arbor), Feb. 28, 1844 and Oct. 1, 1845; in the FREE PRESS, Oct. 7, 1837, March 3, 1843, and Feb. 12, 16, and 23, 1844; in the PONTIAC COURIER, May 18, 1838.

[119] The MICHIGAN ARGUS (Ann Arbor), Jan. 24, 1839, listed eight decisions given by the supreme court at its Jan. term, 1839, in Ann Arbor. No other record is known to exist for three of the cases—Culver v. Raney, Carter v. Clark alias Turrill, and Davidson v. Smith—and the exact judgment of the court was not known for three of the others.

[120] FREE PRESS, April 2, 1845, published Felch's opinion in Cahill v. Kalamazoo Mutual Ins. Co., 2 Doug. 124 (1845).

[121] See note 59 above.

[122] FREE PRESS, Jan. 20, 1847.

[123] Abstracts of opinions or lists of the justices who delivered opinions will be found in the FREE PRESS for the following dates: Jan. 20, March 24 and 26, April 2, 3, 6, 24, 27, and 30, May 1, June 2, July 22, 23, and 27, Aug. 7, Dec. 7, 1847; Jan. 24, Feb. 14, March 2, 6, and 18, May 3, 4, and 5, 1848; March 23 and 29, 1849; March 7, 19, and 21, May 11, 1850.

[124] See the FREE PRESS for Jan. 20, 24, 28, 30, and 31, Feb. 11, April 1,

Some of the weeklies throughout the state occasionally copied the information given in the Detriot papers about the January terms, but rarely did they take the initiative to print such news originally, even when the supreme court was holding its term in their particular localities.[125] It is exasperating to note how, year after year, the journals of Ann Arbor, Jackson, Pontiac, Kalamazoo, and Adrian, all towns in which the supreme court met annually at different times, rarely did more in their pages than to call attention to the fact that the court would soon begin its session, or had just closed its term, or had admitted certain persons to the bar;[126] seldom before 1847 did they print so much as a list of cases on the docket or of the decisions rendered at any particular term.

Conclusion

It should not be supposed that the Supreme Court of Michigan between 1838 and 1843, or between 1843 and 1857, delivered written opinions in the majority, or even one-half, of the causes which they decided during those years. As a matter of fact, opinions are available for but a little more than one-tenth of the total number of cases disposed before 1843, and for about one-fourth of those disposed before

---

1851; March 13, 1852; March 12 and 14, 1853; Jan. 11, 14, 15, 27, 28, and 31, Feb. 1, 2, 3, 5, 7, 8, and 10, March 5, and 10, 1854; Jan. 3, 9, 13, 16, 18, 19, 20, and 31, Feb. 2, March 8, 9, 14, 16, 17, and 20, July 11, 1855; Jan. 12, 26, 27, Feb. 6, 7, 8, 23, 27, March 14, 15, 1856; Jan. 4, 6, 7, 8, 9, 11, 13, 15, and 31, March 10, 1857.

[125] See the OAKLAND GAZETTE (Pontiac), Jan. 27, 1847; PONTIAC JACKSONIAN, Dec. 25, 1850; PONTIAC GAZETTE, March 24, 1855, and Feb. 7, 1857; LANSING REPUBLICAN, March 18 and 26, April 1, 1850; MICHIGAN EXPOSITOR (Adrian), July 11, 1857. However, the ADRIAN WATCHTOWER on July 12, 1853, carried a rather full and very useful account of the court's session held there earlier in that same month.

[126] See the STATE JOURNAL (Ann Arbor), Jan. 12, 1837; PONTIAC JACKSONIAN, Jan. 21, 1842; KALAMAZOO GAZETTE, Sept. 9, 1842; MICHIGAN STATE JOURNAL, Jan. 25, 1843; PONTIAC JACKSONIAN, Jan. 20, 1843; OAKLAND GAZETTE (Pontiac) Jan. 20, 1847.

1858.[127] In the early years it was quite common for many decisions to be given orally or for no formal opinion in addition to the judgment of the court to be rendered.[128] There is proof that as late as 1849, if a case was of no great importance, the court might not direct an opinion to be written for it.[129] Notwithstanding, the evidence seems incontrovertible that many more decisions were written by the justices of the supreme court before 1843 than those which were published or which still remain in the files. Although it is not pertinent to the present inquiry, it might be mentioned that a total of fifty-six other opinions for which no copies are available have been cited in various contemporary sources as having been delivered between 1843 and 1858.[130]

The fate or present whereabouts of these and other opinions which probably were written cannot be answered satisfactorily. Thomas M. Cooley intended in 1858 to publish at least some of them.[131] Although he was forced to relinquish that plan,[132] he did include in one of his later volumes two

[127] See NORTON, A HISTORY OF THE SUPREME COURT OF THE STATE OF MICHIGAN, 1836-1857, Table XXII, Appendix, p. 31 (1940).

[128] E. Ransom to S. T. Douglass, Kalamazoo, Dec. 1, 1845, HERBERT BOWEN PAPERS (Burton Coll.).

[129] The reporter stated in 1849 that he had been informed by Judge Wing "that no written opinion was delivered by the Supreme Court in the license case, at Jackson, the case having been decided upon a point not deemed of any practical importance. . . ." S. T. Douglass to [?] Smith [?], Detroit, Sept. 14, 1849, 8 WALKER, DOUGLASS, and CAMPBELL, LETTERPRESS BOOK 671 (Mich. Hist. Coll., University of Michigan).

[130] See NORTON, A HISTORY OF THE SUPREME COURT OF THE STATE OF MICHIGAN, 1836-1857, Table XXIII, Appendix, p. 32 (1940).

[131] A note in the front of Cooley's first volume of reports (5 Mich.), dated at Adrian, December, 1858, stated: "The unreported decisions of the late Supreme Court, it is hoped, may be collected and included in the next volume. There are, among them, some cases of importance which the profession would doubtless be glad to have preserved in an accessible form."

[132] A note in the front of his second volume (6 Mich.) explained why he failed to report them as he had contemplated: "The hope was expressed . . . that the unreported decisions of the former bench could be collected, and included in this volume. It has, however, been found impracticable to obtain the most important of those decisions, and the intention to publish any is therefore abandoned." This statement would seem to indicate that Cooley

opinions, dated 1841 and 1857 respectively, giving as his reason for doing so the fact that many inquiries had been made about them.[133] The certainty that Cooley had access in 1860 to an opinion which had been written as early as 1841 may or may not be of great significance. If he obtained it from the official files, there is little cause for worry; but, if it was only one of many more which he might possibly have inherited by virtue of his office as reporter, that fact would be most disheartening and disconcerting to anyone searching for more decisions of the supreme court, because many of Cooley's earlier papers were destroyed about 1894.[134] There is no doubt that the justices of the supreme court frequently borrowed from the reporter, previous to their publication, various opinions that had been written either by themselves or by their brethren on the bench;[135] likewise, it is certain that the reporter in turn withdrew the opinions from the files of the court for the purpose of reporting.[136] With such a system of record-keeping it is conceivable that many original manuscript opinions might have found their way into the private papers of any one of twenty-five or more contemporary dignitaries and have been lost, destroyed, or interred in some unknown depository.

knew about the existence and the location of at least several opinions which, for some reason, he could not obtain for publication.

[133] Bomier v. Caldwell, 8 Mich. 463 (1841); Jackson v. Evans, 8 Mich. 477 (1857).

[134] "Most of my letters prior to 1882 were destroyed Jan. 2, 1894." Index to Scrapbook, p. A, COOLEY PAPERS (Mich. Hist. Coll., University of Michigan).

[135] For example, see a series of letters by Justice George Miles to the reporter, S. T. Douglass, requesting the loan of several different opinions. Aug. 11 and 17, Sept. 12, 1847, and Aug. 6, 1849, HERBERT BOWEN PAPERS (Burton Coll.).

[136] Gibbs in 1856 wrote to E. Hawley, clerk of the court at Detroit, asking Hawley to send him three opinions field by Justice Copeland "subsequent to the time I [Gibbs] called for the opinions of last Jan. term, I presume. If filed will you have the kindness to forward to me by express." Marshall, Feb. 7, 1856, Sup. Ct., Miscellaneous files.

In respect to the publication of its highest court decisions, the state of Michigan was unfortunate during the first years of its existence. The first volume of reports did not come from the press until 1846, and, during the whole twenty-one year period from the appointment of the first justices to the establishment in 1858 of the so-called "independent" supreme court, there were but six volumes of supreme court cases and two volumes of chancery court cases issued. Only a few supreme court opinions delivered before 1843 have previously been printed, while many of those which were rendered both before and after that date are not available at present. The men who were selected as reporters, all of whom were able, industrious, and well qualified for the position, were not solely at fault for the delay and omissions; the legislature, and even a few of the justices of the supreme court, exhibited at times much lethargy in their support of the reports and the reporter. Furthermore, it must not be forgotten that the history of reporting in many other states had been quite similar to that in Michigan, that often private individuals rather than public officials had undertaken the publication of opinions, and that Michigan is not unique in the lack of full, complete reports. But to any student who is interested in judicial history and the development of law, this deficiency, while possibly excusable, is extremely regrettable.

The long-existing incompleteness in early Michigan court reports has not in the past presented a mere academic question of no practical importance. Ignorance of these formerly unavailable opinions of the supreme court has not been confined to the layman, or even to the attorney; on occasion no less a figure than a member of the highest state bench could have profited if it had been possible for him to examine the unpublished opinions of former justices. For instance, Justice

Warner Wing, in a decision rendered in 1849,[137] while
referring to a case which had been decided more than ten
years previously,[138] wrote that "The opinion of the supreme
court was not reduced to writing, and, therefore, we can only
state the fact handed down to us by tradition."[139] As a matter
of fact, the opinion in the earlier case had been written by
Justice Ransom, is still extant in the files of the court, and is
printed in this volume for the first time.[140] The present publication of all the known supreme court opinions before 1843
will partially fill a heretofore unfortunate gap in Michigan
legal records.

September, 1944.   CLARK F. NORTON

[137] Scott v. Smart's Executors, 1 Mich. 295 (1849).
[138] Calhoun v. Cable, Sup. Ct., 1st circ., Chancery Calendar (1838), case
13, p. 25.
[139] 1 Mich. at 298 (1849).
[140] Mich. Terr. Sup. Ct., file No. 1491; see *infra*, p. 4.

JUSTICES OF THE SUPREME COURT

William A. Fletcher, July 1836—April 1842

George Morell, July 1836—July 1843

Epaphroditus Ransom, July 1836—December 1847

Charles W. Whipple, April 1839—October 1855

Alpheus Felch, April 1842—November 1845

Fletcher was chief justice. Upon his retirement
Morell became chief justice.

Table of Cases

Opinions

EDITOR's NOTE: The original manuscripts of the following opinions, together with other records of the Michigan Supreme Court prior to 1857, are now in the Legal Research Building at the University of Michigan. The notes following the opinions have been prepared from data gathered by Dr. Norton, author of the Introduction, in the course of his study of the early history of the court.

EDWARD MUNDY *versus* JOHN SARGENT
January 9, 1838

1. *A person may not be sued in a justice's court in a county other than that of his residence except when the action is commenced by warrant and it appears that the defendant is about to* REMOVE *from the county or the plaintiff is in danger of losing his debt. (Terr. Laws of 1833, pp. 195, 209.)*

2. *Where the only basis for issuing a warrant against a non-resident was the fact that he was about to* LEAVE *the county, the justice erred in not sustaining a plea in abatement.*

Supreme Court, Second Circuit. Certiorari to a justice of the peace, Jackson County. Opinion by Ransom, J. Judgment reversed.

Edward Mundy, in propria persona.

...... Morgan, attorney for defendant in certiorari.

[INDORSEMENT]

Edward Mundy

vs.

John Sargeant

In Error

[OPINION]

Edward Mundy
vs.   } Sup. Ct. Second Cir. Jan. Tr.
John Sargeant   1838.

Certio. to Justice of the Peace.

By return of Justice it appears—

That original action was commenced by warrant Feb. 1834 before Justice Thompson, Co. of Jackson, on application of Justice Goodwin—

Both parties resided out of Co. of Jackson—

Plf. & Deft. resided in Co. of Washtenaw—

The Deft. plead in Abatement "that he was a resident of Washtenaw Co. Mich. that he was sued out of the Co. in which he resided without proof to the Justice, that the Plf. was in danger of losing his debt or that Deft. was about to remove from the Co. of Jackson.

The plea overruled—Justice decided on the ground that Deft. residing out of Co. in which action was brought, was a *non resident*, within meaning of the Statute—

A question was also made, touching authority of Goodwin, to appear for Plf. Not necessary to decide that question here— First point perfectly clear—

By our Statute, no person may be proceeded against, except by warrant, out of the Co. in which he resides—

By 41. Sec. Justice Act. it is provided that no person who is a resident of Michigan shall be sued out of the Co. in which he resides, unless it be by warrant obtained on the *same* proof as warrants are obtained where both parties are residents of same Co.—

By 6th Sec. same Act it is provided that any person his Att^y &° applying for warrant, shall prove to the satisfaction of the Justice—*One* of two things, that the Deft. is about to *remove* from the Co. *or* that the Plf. will be in danger of losing his debt &ᶜ unless the process agsᵗ Deft. be by warrant—

The Stat. evidently, requires the same proof in cases where warrants are applied for agsᵗ Deft. *out* of Co. in which he resides, as would be, where he proceeded agsᵗ in Co. in which he resides—

The reason is apparent—were otherwise might be continually embarrassed by arrests, when going out of their Coˢ on business—

The same reasons apply to both cases—

The reason, for which a warrant is granted is in our case, when Deft. is about to remove—is that Plf. may not be put to inconvenience of going into another County or out of the State perhaps, to collect his debt of Deft. The Plf. need not lie by & see Deft. remove his person & effects, out of Co.

So, if Deft. be making such disposition of his property, as would endanger Plf's debt unless he proceed forthwith, he is enabled by the Stat., to take warrant, & arrest the Deft. at once—

Was there proof in this case of *either* fact which authorizes Justice to issue warrant?

Goodwin as agᵗ of Plf. applied for warrant, & on oath testified to Justice, that he was not afraid of Defts. responsibility but that he was about to *leave* the Co. not *remove*.

The Justice decided on the ground, that the Deft. not living in Co. of Jackson where action was brought, was a [""]*non resident"* he so returns expressly—

This was clearly erroneous—the judgᵗ of the Justice must therefore be reversed & the Plf. in Error recover his costs—

EDITOR'S NOTE: The above opinion, in the handwriting of Justice Ransom, was found in file No. 1158 (as renumbered in 1902) Supreme Court, Second Circuit. A draft of a report by Harrington is also in the file. The case was transferred to the Supreme Court from the territorial Superior Circuit Court, Washtenaw County. The Judgment Record of the Supreme Court, Second Circuit, contains: p. 127 (March 5, 1834) affidavit of Mundy; p. 129 (April 4, 1834) writ of certiorari; p. 129 (July 8, 1834) return of J. P.; p. 131 (Jan. 9, 1838) judgment of reversal.

A. B. CALHOUN *versus* DAVID CABLE, A. H. STOWELL, and CALEB CROSS
January 13, 1838

1. *The schedule of the Constitution of 1835, declaring that all writs, actions, etc., pending in the territorial courts shall continue, preserves these matters until the legislature acts. After the legislature has acted, any matter not provided for abates.*

2. *The act of March 26, 1836 (Pub. Acts, 1835-36, p. 30), which provided that civil suits* AT LAW *and criminal prosecutions be transferred to the state supreme court or to a circuit court of the state, did not authorize the transfer of suits in equity.*

3. *The act of March 26, 1836 (Pub. Acts, 1835-36, p. 38), which provided that suits in equity be transferred to the state court of chancery, excluded cases in which the chancellor had served as counsel.*

4. *This suit, being one in which the chancellor served as counsel, and no provision having been made for its transfer, has abated.*

5. *As the legislature has no power to revive suits which have abated, the act of February 11, 1837 (Pub. Acts, 1837, p. 11) directing that suits in which the chancellor is interested be transferred from the territorial supreme court to the state supreme court is invalid.*

Supreme Court, First Circuit. In chancery. Motion to strike from docket. Opinion by Ransom, J. Stricken from docket.

H. N. Walker, for the motion.

A. S. Porter, contra.

[INDORSEMENT]

[None]

[OPINION]

<table>
<tr><td>A. B. Calhoun
vs.
David Cable et als.
In Chancery</td><td>Supreme Court—First Circuit
Jan. Tr. 1838</td></tr>
</table>

On motion to strike the cause from the docket.

This action was originally commenced in the Sup. Court of the late territory of Michigan & was there pending when that Court was abolished by the Act of the State legislature, approved March 1836.

When the territorial Courts ceased to exist, all matters therein pending, also expired, unless continued in life by some legislative enactment.

That causes pending in any court are abated by the expiring of that court, seems not to be questioned.

Does the Act of March, 1836, wrest this cause from the operation of the common law principle just attended to?

I think, most clearly it does not. By the 8th Sec. of that Act, all civil suits *at law* & criminal prosecutions, appeals indictments & all cases where there might be a trial by jury, *then* pending in any of the courts of record—All writs warrants & process whatever relating to any civil suit *at law*, or criminal prosecution, which had issued & then existed, or which should be issued before the 4th day of July then next— were transferred & made returnable to the Supreme or Circuit Court of the State, as they severally might have juridiction thereof.

And by the same section all the dockets records documents writings & proceedings of causes, civil & criminal, are in like manner transferred to the Supreme or Circuit Courts. And those courts are empowered to hear, try & determine all such causes & matters so transferred &c. Stat. of 1836 P. 31-32.

What class of cases did the legislature intend to transfer from the territorial courts to the State Courts, by that Act?

Evidently, all suits *at law*, civil & criminal & no others.

It is said in argument, that inasmuch as *all the dockets, records, documents,* & proceedings of causes, *civil* & criminal, making no *express* reservation of the dockets &c. &c. pertaining to the cases in chancery, are, by the Act, transferred to the Supreme & Circuit courts, that this court *may* assume jurisdiction of this cause.

If that be the legitimate construction of the Act of 1836, *all* the causes, as well, *in chancery* as *at law*, pending in the territorial Courts, at the time of their extinction, were, by that act transferred to the Supreme and Circuit Courts of the State.

A construction so broad in its application, it seems to me, can hardly be contended for, indeed such a construction is entirely precluded by the provisions of the Act to establish a court of chancery, enacted cotemporaneously with the act creating the Supreme & Circuit Courts.

By the second Section of the Act establishing the Court of Chancery, exclusive original jurisdiction, in all matters properly cognisable by courts of chancery, is conferred on the Chancellor, by the 3ᵈ Section, all the powers & jurisdiction conferred on the Supreme Court of the late territory of Michigan by a certain Act, are conferred on the Court of Chancery, and by the 9th Sec. all suits & matters in Chancery pending in any of the territorial courts—all writs or process whatsoever, which then had issued &c. concerning matters in chancery, and all the dockets, records, documents, writings & proceedings in said suits & matters, are in like manner, transferred to the court of chancery.

The legislature obviously intended to confer jurisdiction of all matters *at law* & such only, on the Sup. & Circuit Courts, and of matters in chancery on the Court of Chancery. —But in the same 9th Sec. of the Act last alluded to, it is expressly provided, that no suit or matter, in which the Chancellor may have been interested, as Counsel or otherwise, shall be transferred to the Court of Chancery, but that such suits & matters shall be proceeded in by the Courts in which the same originated—

If then, by the Act, creating the Supreme Court, no suits or matters in chancery be transferred to that tribunal, and if also, by the Act establishing the Court of Chancery, all causes in which the Chancellor was interested, be excluded from his jurisdiction, it necessarily follows, that when the Supreme Court of the territory was abolished by the Act of March 1836, this cause, being one in which the Chancellor was interested as counsel, was abated.

Now the question arises whether the legislature by a subsequent Act could revive, and confer on this or any other Court, the power to rehear & try, a cause, which by operation of law was abated and consequently determined?

Suppose a suit was abated for any ordinary cause, would it be competent for the legislature by subsequent enactment to declare that such suit should be revived, and the parties compelled, in violation of the settled rules of law to proceed to a trial of the merits? That will not be pretended—

Does this case differ from the one supposed? I confess, I am unable to discover any distinction.

But it is insisted again in argument, that the Act of the legislature in this case only affects the remedy, not the rights of the parties.

The argument is correct in principle, but as it strikes me, wrong in application.

If this cause were abated & determined by the abolition of the Court in which it was pending the rights of the parties were thereby fixed, and in any view could not be disturbed by any subsequent legislation.

The constitutional provision, relied upon, does not affect this case—By the first Section of the Schedule of the Constitution it is declared that all *writs, actions* &c shall continue as if no change had taken place in the government—Suppose no change had taken place in the government, and the territorial legislature had abolished the then existing courts & substituted others, making the same provisions the state legislature has done, would not this cause have been abated? Unquestionably it would—

The constitution preserves the matters pending in the territorial courts, for the future action of the state legislature, —that action has been had, and the purpose of the constitution fully accomplished.

EDITOR'S NOTE: The above opinion, in the handwriting of Justice Ransom, was found in file No. 1491 (as re-numbered for *Transactions of the Supreme Court of the Territory of Michigan,* Blume, ed.). A draft of a report by Harrington is also in the file. Volume I of the Journal of the Supreme Court, First Circuit, contains the following entries: p. 28 (Jan. 2, 1838) defendants move to strike from docket; p. 31 (Jan. 5, 1838) motion argued and submitted; p. 40 (Jan. 13, 1838) stricken from docket. For later proceedings in this case see p. 70, *infra.* In 1849 the act of February 11, 1837, was held valid. *Scott* v. *Smart's Exrs.,* 1 Mich. 295.

NATHAN HUBBLE *versus* ETHEL BURCH
January 13, 1838.

1. *The justice did not err in permitting an attorney at law to appear for the plaintiff on the trial, without express authority, the attorney having appeared many times without objection.*

2. *Where the defendant has pleaded the general issue and a special plea and the return of the justice states that issue was joined, the appellate court will presume that plaintiff added a similiter to the general issue and traversed the special plea. The omission of a similiter is a mere matter of form which is aided by verdict.*

3. *In an action for the escape of a person taken in execution it is not necessary that the jury find specially that the officer consented or was negligent. A general verdict is sufficient.*

4. *In an action against a sheriff for an escape, the sheriff's deputy who released the prisoner on an insufficient bond was interested in the event of the action, and, therefore, properly rejected as a witness.*

5. *In an action for an escape, it is error to reject as a witness the escaped prisoner when called by the defendant. If interested, his interest is against the party calling him.*

Supreme Court, First Circuit. Certiorari to a justice of the peace, Monroe County. Opinion by Ransom, J. Judgment reversed.

P. R. Adams and R. McCleland, attorneys for plaintiff in certiorari.

A. Felch, attorney for defendant in certiorari.

[INDORSEMENT]

Ethel Burch Deft.
in Error
vs—
Nathan Hubble
Plf. in Error.

[OPINION]

Ethel Burch Deft.
in Error.

v—

Nathan Hubble Plf.
in Error

Sup. Court, First Circuit Jany Tr.
1838.

Certiorari to a Justice of the Peace.

This cause is brought into this court upon a writ of
certiorari to a Justice of the Peace.

By the return of the justice it appears that the Deft. in
Error, on the 6th day of Oct. 1832, before P. P. Ferry a
justice of the peace, recovered a judgment against one
Couture for about $74 which judg^t he afterwards assigned
to H. B. Hopkins—that on the first day of March 1834 an
execution was prayed out on the judg^t and delivered to John
Mulholland, (a deputy of the Plf. in Error Hubble, who was
then sheriff of the County of Munroe), to levy serve &
return—That on the 21st day of April then next, Mulholland
arrested Couture, and proceeded with him to the common
jail of the County—that Couture with a view to obtain the
benefit of the prison limits, gave a bond, to *H. B. Hopkins,*
conditioned that P. P. Ferry should not depart without the
prison limits &c. and that upon the delivery of that bond to
the keeper of the prison, Mulholland permitted Couture to
go at large—

That afterwards on the 28th day of June 1834 a suit was
instituted by Burch against Hubble, before Justice Curtis—
that on the return day of the writ, the Plf. declared against
Hubble in debt, upon the escape of Couture, in one count for
a voluntary escape & in another for a negligent escape, suffered by Mulholland—that to this declaration the Plf. in
Error, plead the general issue, and specially also that Couture
had been committed to prison on the Plf's execution & having

given a limit bond pursuant to the Statute, was admitted to the benefit of the prison limits—that issue was joined and the cause continued from time to time till the 4th day of Aug. 1834 when it was tried by a jury, a verdict for $69.21 Dam[s] returned for the Plf. and judgment rendered on the verdict.

It further appears that this suit was commenced in the name of the Plf. Burch, by A. Felch Esq. an Attorney duly admitted to practice law, in the courts of this state—that said Felch had appeared & answered to the suit, without objection being made by the Deft. until the day of the final trial, when the Deft. objected to Felch's being permitted to prosecute the suit farther without proof of authority from the Plf.—the objection was overruled by the justice—on the trial of the cause the Deft. Hubble, to prove the issue on his part, offered as witnesses, the said Couture & Mulholland, they were objected to by the Plf. on the ground of interest & rejected by the Justice.

To these proceedings the Plf. in Error, takes exceptions— he contends—First—that the justice committed error in permitting Felch to appear & prosecute the suit without express authority from the Plf. Burch. But without deciding that question, it is sufficient to say that this case is relieved from all difficulty upon that point, by the fact, that Felch had been permitted to appear for the Plf. many times, without objection, and we think the magistrate correctly decided that the objection, if tenable under any circumstances, came too late in this case.

Another objection is that no issue was made, which the jury could properly try—

Technical nicety or legal precision is not required in Justice's Courts, when this court can reasonably intend that the merits have been fairly tried, we will not test by technical rules, the formality of the pleadings.

It would seem, however, in this case, the pleadings were sufficiently formal. Whenever one of the parties concludes to the country, he refers the trial to the jury & the issue is joined & ready for trial, by the adverse party's adding the *similiter*, and the similiter being no part of the pleadings, but a mere matter of form, it would seem that its omission should be aided by verdict.

The Justice's return here shews that the general issue was plead & also a special plea in bar, and upon those pleadings issue was joined—we feel bound to presume from this return that to the general issue tendered the Plf. added the similiter & traversed the special plea in bar, making a material & proper issue for the jury.

The third exception taken, is, that, agreeably to the declaratory act concerning the escape of prisoners in certain cases, no judg^t could be rendered against the Deft. in this case—that it should appear from the record that the jury *expressly* found that the debtor escaped with the consent, or through the negligence of the Deft. or that he might have been retaken & that the Deft. neglected to make immediate pursuit. Had the debtor been in custody upon mesne process, the objection would be well founded—but the statute obviously creates a distinction, between escapes of debtors arrested upon mesne process & those taken in execution.

By a proviso to the act just referred to, any sheriff or other officer, who shall have taken the body of any debtor in *execution*, & shall wilfully or negligently suffer such debtor to escape, is made liable to the execution creditor, in an action of debt, for the amount of the execution—this case is clearly within the contemplation of the proviso—and a general verdict of the jury sufficient.

Again it is said the Justice erred in rejecting the witnesses, Mulholland & Couture, offered by the Deft.—We think

Mulholland was properly rejected, being directly responsible to his principal, Hubble, for the amount of any judg^t that might be recovered against him for the escape of Couture— Since it is apparent from the return that Mulholland failed to comply with the requisitions of the Statute in the service of the execution—he neither committed the ex^n debtor to the keeper of the prison nor did he take a proper limit bond, before discharging him from custody—But the rejection of the debtor, Couture was manifest error, if interested at all in the event of this suit, his interest was against the party calling him   he was therefore a competent witness and should have been permitted to testify—

The judg^t of the justice must be reversed therefore, and the Deft. Hubble recover his costs.

EDITOR'S NOTE: The above opinion, in the handwriting of Justice Ransom, was found in file No. 70, Supreme Court, First Circuit— Law. A draft of a report by Harrington is also in the file. The case was transferred to the Supreme Court from the territorial Superior Circuit Court, Monroe County. Volume I of the Journal of the Supreme Court, First Circuit, contains the following entries: p. 30 (Jan. 4, 1838) argued and submitted; p. 40 (Jan. 13, 1838) judgment reversed. Also see Calendar, First Circuit, Vol. I, case No. 70.

HIRAM WHITCOMB *versus* IRA PORTER
January 13, 1838.

1. *In a summary proceeding against an officer for failing to levy or return a writ of execution (Terr. Laws of 1833, p. 200) a justice of the peace does not exceed his jurisdiction by rendering a judgment for more than $100.*
2. *A renewal of an execution at the instance of the officer without the request or consent of the plaintiff will not defeat a claim against the officer for failing to levy or return the writ in time.*

Supreme Court, First Circuit. Certiorari to a justice of the peace, St. Clair County. Opinion by Ransom, J. Judgment affirmed.

E. B. Harrington, attorney for plaintiff in certiorari.

A. D. Fraser, attorney for defendant in certiorari.

[INDORSEMENT]

Ira Porter Deft. in Error

vs—

Hiram Whitcomb Plf. in Error

[OPINION]

Ira Porter Deft. in Error
vs—
Hiram Whitcomb Plf. in Error
}
Sup. Ct. first Circuit Jany Tr. 1838

Certiorari to a Justice of the Peace.

By the record certified to this Court by the justice, it appears that on the 29th Decr 1835, the Deft. in Error, Porter recovered a judg^t before Justice Baker against one Chamberlin, for $88.20—execution was stayed pursuant to the Statute, on the 20th day of Jany 1837 Porter prayed out an execution upon the judg^t which was renewed by a proper endorsement, by the Justice on the 21st May 1837, and on the same day placed in the hands of Whitcomb, then a constable of the town of   to levy serve and return—On the 29th day of the same May, Whitcomb, having made no levy or return of the execution, and the time having elapsed in which it could be levied, the creditor moved the Justice that judg^t be entered in his favor against the constable, Whitcomb, for the Am^t of the execution, with damages, interest & cost—On the same day the justice issued a citation to Whitcomb to appear before him on the 7th June then next, and shew cause why he should not be held to pay the Am^t of said execution with damages interest & costs agreeably to the statute.

And it further appears, that both parties appeared before the Justice on the said 7th day of June—Whitcomb admitted that he had rec^d the execution for collection and that he had not levied the same—Collected the money thereon, nor committed the debtor, Chamberlin to prison, and showed no cause satisfactory to the Justice, why judg^t should not be entered against him for the Am^t of the execution &c.

Whereupon the said Justice entered a judg^t against said Whitcomb for the said $88.20 the Am^t of said ex^n with twenty five per cent. damages on the original judg^t interest & costs—computed at $32.06, Amounting in the whole to $120.36—

To these proceedings the Plf. in Error objects—First—That the execution alluded to, had been renewed by the Justice on the 22^d day of May 1837 & consequently had not expired at the time the judg^t was entered against him—

It does not appear by the return, that any evidence was offered on the hearing before the Justice, upon the said motion— of such renewal of the ex^n the Justice certifies that on the s^d 22^d of May a renewal was endorsed on the ex^n at the *instance* of Whitcomb, without the request or consent of the creditor.

Had that fact been proved before the justice it could not have availed the party—

When the execution expired in the hands of the officer, without a levy or return being made, the right of the creditor to a judg^t against the officer or his sureties, immediately vested & could not be defeated or delayed by a renewal of the ex^n made by the procurement of the officer himself—

Again it is insisted the proceeding is erroneous, because the Am^t of the judg^t entered against the officer exceeds the sum $100. beyond which, it is contended a Justice's jurisdiction does not extend—

We think this objection is not well founded, the Statute provides a two fold remedy for the creditor, in case the officer neglect to serve or return the execution—he may bring an action of debt against the officer himself, or his securities in which case he must resort to a court having jurisdiction of the *Amount,* of the judg^t sought to be recovered. Or, if he choose to rely on the responsibility of the officer alone, on his own motion, the justice may cite the officer before him, to shew cause why he should not be held to pay the Am^t of the Ex^n And unless good cause be shewn execution shall issue against him for the Am^t of the original ex^n with 25 pr. ct. dam^s interest & costs.

This is a summary proceeding provided for this class of cases alone, the justice derives his power to act in the matter, from the particular section of the Act creating this remedy, not from the first section which confers his general jurisdiction.

It can hardly be said that the magistrate performs a judicial act in these cases, the facts of which he is to enquire are whether the ex^n has been served & returned, or discharged by the creditor, which must generally appear by his own files & records—he is the mere agent thro. which the law declares its judg^t—the measure by which the Am^t of the judg^t is determined, is fixed by the statute—the justice is simply to make the computation.

The judg^t below must be confirmed with costs.

EDITOR's NOTE: The above opinion, in the handwriting of Justice Ransom, was found in file No. 88, Supreme Court, First Circuit—Law. A draft of a report by Harrington is also in the file. Volume I of the Journal of the Supreme Court, First Circuit, contains the following entries: p. 35 (Jan. 9, 1838) argued and submitted; p. 41 (Jan. 13, 1838) judgment affirmed. Also see- Calendar, First Circuit—Law, Vol. I, case No. 88.

ISAAC BURHANS *versus* ABNER REYNOLDS
January 19, 1838

1. *Where labor is performed under a subsisting special agreement, recovery may not be had under the common counts. But if the agreement has been fully performed by the plaintiff or rescinded by mutual consent, the rule is otherwise. From the contradictory evidence in this case it is difficult to determine whether the labor was performed under a special agreement, but it is unnecessary to decide because of other error.*

2. *In justices' courts jurors are judges of the law as well as of the facts. The justice in this case erred in directing the jury that inasmuch as the defendant had proved that the plaintiff had received one-half of certain crops, the jurors were bound by their oaths to allow credit for the same.*

3. *The above direction was not harmless as being in favor of the plaintiff in error (defendant below) because the jury might not have found against the defendant at all but for such direction.*

Supreme Court, Second Circuit. Certiorari to a justice of the peace, Washtenaw County. Opinion by Ransom, J. Judgment reversed.

O. Hawkins, attorney for plaintiff in certiorari.

J. Kingsley, attorney for defendant in certiorari.

[INDORSEMENT]
Isaac Burhans Plf. in Error
vs—
Abner Reynolds Deft Er.

[OPINION]

Isaac Burhans
vs—
Abner Reynolds
} Sup. Ct. Sec^d Cir. Jan. Tr. 1838.

Certio. to Justice of the Peace.

1. By return of Justice, it appears that the parties some years since entered into an agree^t to work together on Burhans land, in clearing & raising grain—were to continue to work there, *three* or six years— and were to divide all grain raised, equally between them—That the parties went on under s^d agree^t until they had cleared twenty eight acres of land— about one & half years—

That Reynolds performed other labor for Burhans in erecting log houses & upon the highway—

Disagreements arose between the parties, and the contract to clear land &^c together, was abandoned   Reynolds then brought his action against Burhans to recover pay for his labor in clearing the land together with other services performed by himself & boys for Burhans, and for money lent Burhans—Reynolds declared in gen^l indebitatus Assumpsit for work & labor, & money lent—

Burhans plead gen^l issue & gave notice of set off

The cause was tried by jury in May 1834.

Counsel of Burhans insisted & requested court to charge the jury, that, it appeared in evidence that the labor performed by Reynolds was done under a special agree^t—and that he could not recover upon the Common Counts should have declared on special agree^t.

Justice refused so to charge the jury—

After the cause was submitted to jury & they had retired —the justice was sent for by jury, and his opinion asked, upon a point of evidence—viz: Whether they could allow

Burhans anything for corn & wheat which Reynolds had rec^d
Justice told jury "that inasmuch as Burhans did prove that
Reynolds had one half the crops they were bound by their
oath to allow him for the same according to the testimony
given them in Court"

Jury returned a verdict of $129.60—
Remititer [Remittitur] was entered by Reynolds to $29.60
—Judg^t rendered for $100—
To these proceedings, two objections are urged—
1. That, inasmuch as it appeared on the trial that the labor
of Reynolds was performed under special agree^t should have
declared upon it—cannot recover in the gen^1 counts—
2. That the Justice erred in going into jury room & giving
his opinion in a matter of fact, after cause was submitted—
It is a general rule of law, that when labor is performed,
under a special agreement the terms of which at the time of
action brought, subsist in full force, a recovery cannot be
had under the Common Counts—the party performing the
labor, cannot waive the contract & resort to to an implied
assumpsit—the special agree^t should be set forth in the
declaration, that the Deft. may be apprised of the contract
he is charged with violating, and may have an opportunity
to shew the want of performance, on the part of the Plf. of
those stipulations, which may have been the consideration
of the promise made by the Deft. But if the terms of a special
agree^t have been fully performed on part of the Plf. or if
the contract be rescinded by mutual consent, after part
performance by Plf.—he may recover the value of the work,
in an action of gen^1 indeb. Assumpsit, and need not set forth
the special contract—

In this case it is insisted by Plf. in Error, that there was a
subsisting contract, between the parties, under which the
labor was performed—

Deft. in Error, contends that the contract was mutually rescinded & abandoned by both parties—

The testimony returned by the justice is so contradictory & uncertain, that it is difficult to determine, what the precise facts of the case were, and we deem it unnecessary to decide upon this point, inasmuch as the case may be determined on the other point made by the Plf. in Error, which we think free from all difficulties.

—The justice committed manifest error, in directing the jury, as to matters of fact, after the cause was submitted to them by the parties—In justice's Courts, the jury are judges of the law as well as of facts, and the justice had no authority, whatever, after the cause was submitted, to direct the jury how to find—we think it would be dangerous to tolerate such a practice—

It was urged in argument at bar, that what was said to the jury, by the Justice was in favor of the Plf. in Error, & that therefore he cannot take exceptions to it—but that was well answered by Plfs. Counsel, "that the jury might not have agreed upon a verdict, at all, against the Plf. but for the direction of the justice—

The judg^t of the justice must be reversed & the Plf. in Error recover his costs—

EDITOR'S NOTE: The above opinion, in the handwriting of Justice Ransom, was found in an unnumbered file of the Supreme Court, Second Circuit. A draft of a report by Harrington is also in the file. The case was transferred to the Supreme Court from the territorial Superior Circuit Court, Washtenaw County. The Judgment Record of the Supreme Court, Second Circuit, contains: p. 132 (Oct. 27, 1834) writ of certiorari; p. 133 (July 13, 1835) return of J. P.; p. 138 (Jan. 19, 1838) judgment of reversal. The writ of certiorari and other papers will be found in File 1160 (as renumbered in 1902).

MARK NORRIS *versus* CEPHAS HAWKS, JAMES HUTCHINSON and MARCUS LANE.
January 19, 1838

1. *Payment of rent to one of three joint owners is a discharge of the joint claim.*
2. *Where a justice of the peace had been informed by one joint owner that rent sued for in the names of three joint owners had been paid, the justice erred in rendering judgment against the defendant in his absence at the instance of another of the joint owners.*

Supreme Court, Second Circuit. Certiorari to a justice of the peace, Washtenaw County. Opinion by Ransom, J. Judgment Reversed.

O. Hawkins, attorney for plaintiff in certiorari.

M. Lane, attorney for defendants in certiorari.

[INDORSEMENT]

Norris
vs
Lane et al.

[OPINION]

Mark Norris
vs.
Marcus Lane et al.
} Sup. Ct. Sec^d Cir. Jan. Tr. 1838

Certio. to Justice of the Peace.
Plf. in Er. & Defts. Lane & Hawks

By a stipulation of the parties, the affidavit is substituted for the return—it is agreed that the facts set forth in the affid^t shall be the facts in the case on which the court decide—

By affi[t] it appears, that Defts. in Error, were joint owners of certain real estate, called Brewery property—that Plf. in Er. occupied said Brew. prop. under a lease or agree[t] of the Defts.—

Plf. in Er. paid the rent, amounting to about $10.00 to Lane one of joint owners—

In July last, Hutchinson, one of the joint owners of the s[d] property, commenced an action ags[t] Plf. in Er. in name of all the Defts. in Er. for recovery of the rents, which had accrued—

After the commence[t] of the suit, & before the return day of the writ—Lane informed Plf. in Er. that the suit should be discont[d] & that he need not give himself any trouble about it—

In pursuance of this agree[t] Lane, before the return day of the summons—directed the Justice to discontinue the suit—informed the Justice that the suit was brought in his name contrary to his wishes, and that the Plf. in Er. had fully accounted to him for the rents, to recover which the action was brought—

The Plf. in Er. did not appear before the justice, to defend the suit, in consequence of the agree[t] of Lane to discontinue—At the instance of Hutchinson, one of the Defts. in Er. Justice proceeded to hear the cause and rendered Judg[t] for Plfs. to recover $9.85 Dam[s] & their costs That there was no evidence of a privity of contract, between the parties, on the hearing before the Justice

Plf. in Er. excepts to this proceeding, insisting, that the rents for which the action was brought having been paid to one of the joint owners of the leased property, that Plf. was thereby forever discharged from liability to either & all the Defts—

And that this fact having been made known to the Justice,

& he directed to discontinue suit committed Error, in proceeding afterwards to render judg^t in the case—especially in absence of Plf. and without proof of privity of contract, between parties—

The pay^ts of the rents by the Plf. to *one* of the joint owners, was unquestionably a finale & complete discharge of the Plf's. liability to the joint claim of the Defts—

Judg^t being rendered for Defts. to recover am^t of debt, after the lease had been fully paid & discharged—is erroneous —& the judg^t must be reversed & the Plf. in Er. recover his costs—

EDITOR'S NOTE: The above opinion, in the handwriting of Justice Ransom, was found in file No. 66 (Nos. 1153 and 1157 as renumbered in 1902) of the Supreme Court, Second Circuit. A draft of a report by Harrington is also in the file. The Judgment Record of the Supreme Court, Second Circuit, contains: p. 158 (Aug. 9, 1837) writ of certiorari; p. 159 (Jan. 16, 1838) return of J. P.; p. 160 (Jan. 19, 1838) judgment of reversal.

JOSIAH R. DORR, WILLIAM B. ALVORD, and JAMES STETSON *versus* CHRISTIAN W. DREYER
August 30, 1839

1. *All objections to process are waived by a general appearance.*

2. *Testimony by a person claiming to be agent that he was "authorized by the* DEFENDANTS *to . . . employ workmen for them" is sufficient basis for inferring that the defendants, sued as "traders under the style of the Detroit Iron Co.," constituted such company. Furthermore, it does not appear that the point was raised in the lower court.*

3. *Where there is "some evidence" to support the judgment of a justice of the peace, the supreme court "will not stop to enquire whether it was so full or ample as to render the case entirely free from doubt."*

Supreme Court, First Circuit. Certiorari to a justice of the peace, Wayne County. Opinion by Whipple, J. Judgment affirmed.

G. E. Hand, attorney for plaintiffs in certiorari.

B. F. H. Witherell & Buel, attornies for defendant in certiorari.

[INDORSEMENT]

Dorr, Alvord &
Stetson
vs.
Dreyer.

[OPINION]

Josiah R Dorr
William B Alvord &
James Stetson
vs
Christian W Dreyer
} Sup Court: 1ˢᵗ Circuit
July term 1839—

Certiorari:

The plaintiff below sued out process against the defendants as "traders under the style of the Detroit Iron Cᵒ" in a plea of Trespass on the case, and declared generally for "work, labor, damages &c" & at the same time filed a bill of particulars: the defendants, as appears by the return of the Justice appeared by Hand their Attorney" and plead "non-assumpsit." The Justice after hearing and considering the cause rendered judgment in favor of the plff for $52.25 damages & $2.56 costs of suit; to reverse which judgment a certiorari was sued out by the plffs' in Error:

The following are the principal points relied upon by the plffs to reverse the judgment. (here insert brief) Nᵒˑˢ 1—2—

1:    It is a well settled rule that objections of the nature suggested in the first point must be taken advantage of on the return of the process by a motion to quash or by plea in abatement: the defendants below having appeared by an agent and pleaded generally to the declaration waived all objections to the process.

2:    Upon an examination of the return of the Justice, it appears, that the Detroit Iron C° pr F A Willis by a written authority authorized one A. W Wood "to engage two or three good, steady, faithful & temperate men, to work at finishing in their establishment, and that to such men constant employment and good wages payable every Saturday night would be given." Wood produced & proved the execution of the authority, which he states was given to him by Willis by the direction of Alvord, one of the plffs in error, who remarked that it (the authority) was correct: Wood further testified that by virtue of this authority he engaged the plff below, Dreyer, at Rochester, N Y; that he was such a man as he was authorized to employ, having been recommended to him as a temperate man and a good workman: that Dreyer came to Detroit with his wife & two children, the latter part of August 1837, pursuant to the engagement: and further that he had seen Dreyer at work, and that $2 per day were the wages paid for finishers:—The witness also testified that the charges for travelling expenses were reasonable, altho' there was no understanding that such expenses would be paid: Another witness Gorman, testifies that Dreyer was a good workman, that he was discharged sometime in the beginning of Oct 1837—and that he knew no reason for his discharge: Upon being recalled Wood further stated that Dreyer's work was trimming & filing: that he saw him at brass work, & that it was well done: The plff below having rested his case, the defendants below introduced one George Brundit, who testified that Dreyer worked at the foundry at finishing; that he was no chipper & ignorant of the use of the lathe: did not know why he was discharged—that he was good enough at filing and further, that workmen are paid $2 per day: Ge° A Fletcher another witness testified, that he worked at the foundry & in the same room with Dreyer; "that his filing was done very well," but that it might have been done sooner:—thinks his services worth 12 or 13s per day; and that he did not seem to understand the use of the lathe."

Upon a review of the above, which seems to have been all the testimony introduced on the trial below, it is difficult to perceive how this court can sustain the objection taken by the plff in error that the evidence does not shew any undertaking or assumpsit on their part: The testimony of Wood is conclusive on this point: he exhibited the authority by virtue of which he had hired Dreyer which authority was subsequently recognized by permitting Dreyer to enter & work in the foundry: he further states that he commenced work the latter part of August and it is in proof that he continued until some[time] in the beginning of Oct. when he was discharged, but for what cause, none of the witnesses were enabled to state: There is an apparent discrepancy in the testimony of the witness with respect to the skill of Dreyer as a finisher, but all concur that his work was well done: But it is objected, thirdly, that there was no evidence to establish the fact that the defendants below constituted the Detroit Iron C°. The return of the Justice by which we are bound, does not support this allegation, for it is expressly stated by Wood, that he was "authorized by the *defendants* to go to New York and employ workmen for them:" from this testimony the Justice had a right to infer that the C° was constituted of the plff's in Error. Besides it does not appear from the return that the objections stated in the brief of the plff's were made at the trial of the cause below: it has been repeatedly decided by this Court, that in order to avail himself of irregularities or errors in the court below, objection must be made at the proper time during the progress of the trial, otherwise this Court will not give a party the benefit of such irregularities or error.

Upon the whole, it appears that there was, to say the least, some evidence to support the judgment, & this Court will not stop to enquire whether it was so full or ample as to render the case entirely free from doubt.

Judgment affirmed—

Hand for plff in Error.
Buel for deft in Error.

EDITOR'S NOTE: The above opinion, in the handwriting of Justice Whipple, was found in file No. 106, Supreme Court, First Circuit— Law. Volume I of the Journal, First Circuit, contains the following entries: p. 47 (Jan. 2, 1839) motion to quash certiorari; p. 57 (Jan. 9, 1839) continued; p. 84 (Aug. 30, 1839) judgment affirmed. Also see Calendar, First Circuit—Law, Vol. I, case No. 106.

JOSEPH W. BROWN *versus* EZEKIEL G. MOORE and AMASA JACKSON
September 4, 1839.

1. *In an action against an indorser of a promissory note, the certificate of a notary public that he presented the note for payment, that payment was refused, and that he mailed notice of protest, is not admissible under the common law to prove these facts.*

2. *The statutes relative to notaries public (Terr. Laws of 1833, p. 244; Revised Statutes of 1838, p. 50) have not changed the common law in the above respect.*

Supreme Court, First Circuit. Error to Circuit Court, Wayne County. Opinion by Fletcher, Ch. J. Judgment reversed.

Daniel Goodwin, attorney for plaintiff in error.
H. N. Walker, attorney for defendants in error.

[INDORSEMENT]

Sup Court 1 Cir. Aug. 1839

Brown	Mem° of Opinion
vs.	Aug. 1839—Judg' reversed and
Moore	*venire de novo ordered*—

Goodwin for Plff in Error
H N. Walker—Deft.

[OPINION]

Joseph W. Brown	
vs.	Writ of Error to Wayne Circuit.
Ezekiel J. Moore	
& Amasa Jackson	

The Bill of exceptions, forming a part of the record in this cause, sets forth the only ground, upon which error is now alleged—

The Plff in error was the Deft below, and was sued as the indorser of Fargo & Boughton on their promisory note dated 14 July '37 for $1223.14 payable in 6 mo at the Bank of Tecumseh

To prove presentment for payment and refusal thereof at the Bank, and notice thereof to the Deft below as indorser—The plaintiff below offered in evidence an official certificate in due form of Geo. W. Jermain, a notary public of the County of Lenawee setting forth that on the day &c he duly presented the said note to the Bank for payment and that the same was refused; and that he caused notice of said protest to be put in the post office at Tecumseh, directed to the Deft &c— The attorney for the Deft below objected to the [a]dmissibility to prove these facts—, but the objection was overruled, and the evidence received.

There was no other evidence to prove these facts—The only question therefore is whether the evidence was properly admitted?

It was contended by the counsel for the Defts in Error that by the provisions of our Statute relative to Notaries public have enlarged the authority of a Notary public, and that his official certificate is made competent evidence in other cases than those recognized by the Com. Law. The only provision relied on for this purpose is that which declares due faith shall be given to all the protestations, attestations and other instruments of publication of notaries public—

(The Rev. Stat. is in other words—ack. of deed, adm. oaths, and perform such other official acts as have been customarily performed by N. P.

6 Wheat. 146. Young vs. Bryan
id. 572 Union Bank vs. Hyde
8 id. 326. Nicholas vs. Webb } A protest of an inland bill of ex. & pro. note is not necessary, nor is it evidence.

Chit. Bills 405. Rule at Com. law, only in case of Foreign—
        "But a protest made in England must be proved
        by the notary who made it, and by the subscribing
        wit., if any["].
6 Serg & R. 484 Brown vs. Philadelphia Bank
"   "   324 Stewart vs. Allison

Where it was held that under the act of the Leg. of Penn. of 1815 the official certificate of a notary was competent evid. to prove notice of non pay^t to the indorser of an inland note— By the act referred to it is declared that the official acts, protests and attestations of notaries public certified according to law under their respective hands and seals of office may be received in evidence.

The Stat. of Penn. goes farther than our own, it makes the official acts &c evidence generally when duly certified

But the safer course, and indeed the only, is to follow the established rule—unless &c &c—

EDITOR's NOTE: The above opinion, in the handwriting of Ch. J. Fletcher, was found in file No. 137, Supreme Court, First Circuit—Law. Volume I of the Journal, First Circuit, contains the following entry: p. 89 (Sept. 4, 1839) judgment reversed. Also see Calendar, First Circuit—Law, Vol. I, case 137.

OLIVER ROSE *versus* SOLOMON SIBLEY
September 4, 1839.

1. *Where a case is submitted to a trial court on an agreed statement of facts which does not "contain all the facts necessary to turn the case into a question of law," the trial court's determination of the facts is conclusive if the statement contains evidence tending to prove the facts found.*

2. *In this case the evidence tended to prove that the plaintiff's agent knew that the money claimed by the plaintiff was being collected by the defendant's former partner after the defendant had retired from the practice of law, hence the finding for the defendant is conclusive.*

3. *In the absence of statutory authority, an agreed statement of facts is not a part of the court's record and, therefore, cannot be considered on a writ of error.*

Supreme Court, First Circuit. Error to Circuit Court, Wayne County. Opinion by Fletcher, Ch. J. Judgment affirmed.

H. S. Cole & A. S. Porter, attornies for plaintiff in error.

E. Farnsworth & D. Goodwin, attornies for defendant in error.

[INDORSEMENT]

Rose
vs.
Sibley

$\left.\right\}$ 1st Circuit
Mem° of opinion—
Aug. 1839—
Jug^t affirmed

[OPINION]

Oliver Rose
vs.
Sol. Sibley Survivor
of himself & A. G. Whitney

$\left.\right\}$

This cause is before this court on Writ of Error brought to reverse a Judg^t rendered in the Circuit Court for the County of Wayne.

The suit was originally brought in the Circuit Court by Rose the present Plff in Error against the Deft, Survivor of himself, and Andrew G. Whitney, deceased, late partners,— in the profession and practice of law.—

The Plff declared specially on the undertaking of Deft, and also on the common money counts, and an account stated, to which the Deft pleaded the general issue. The Counsel for the parties afterwards waived the trial by jury, and upon the facts set forth in a case made and stated between them, submitted the whole matter to the decision of the Court.

The material facts stated in the case are the following:

Mark H. Sibley of Canandaigua, the Attorney of Oliver Rose transmitted to Sol. Sibley in Jany 1819 an exemplification of a Judg^t rendered in the State of New York in favor of Rose vs. Wm G. Taylor—When this claim was rec^d by Sol. Sibley he was in partnership with Mr. Whitney—Sibley and Whitney in their joint names prosecuted the claim to and obtained judg^t thereon in the Sup. Court in October 1822, for the sum of 452.56:

—On the 10 Sept. 1823, a fi. fa. was issued by S. & W., but nothing was made thereon.

The Deft. Sol. Sibley was appointed a Judge of the Sup. Court of the Territory of Michigan on the 11th Feby 1824, and continued in commission until after the Judg^t in this Suit below, and wholly ceased practice as an Att^y & Counsellor at law during that time. Sibley and Whitney, as between themselves settled their partnership business, leaving all unclosed business of their clients in the hands of Whitney, who was generally considered a good lawyer, a vigilant collector, responsible and punctual in paying over money.

By the agreement between them, the fees which had accrued up to the time of the appointment of Sibley as judge were to be equally divided between them, all fees accruing on any unfinished business after the said appointment, were to accrue to the benefit of Whitney.

On the 12 April, 1824, Whitney filed a praecipe for a Ca. Sa. on the said judg^t signed by himself for the late firm of Sibley & Whitney which was issued, which was returned non est. Mark H. Sibley was the agent of Rose, and had an interest in the judg^t obtained in the State of N. Y. against Taylor.

On the 25 Nov. 1824 Whitney filed a praecipe signed by himself alone, for an alias fi. fa.—upon which there was made the sum of $263.88, which was paid over to Whitney in November 1825, and after deducting fees, costs, and charges, there remained in Whitney's hands $216.73, which was deposited by him in Bank to his individual credit. Mark H. Sibley was in the City of Detroit in the Summer of 1825 on a visit. Mr. Whitney died in September 1826—and the money collected as above stated, was never paid over.

No other money was collected on the original judg^t of Rose vs. Taylor. Mr. Whitney's estate was represented insolvent—and no claim on the part of Rose was ever exhibited against the estate, and the time for presenting claims against the estate expired before the commencement of this suit below.

There are also several letters from Sibley and Whitney to Mark H. Sibley reporting the progress of the suit against Taylor, and a letter from Mark H. Sibley, all of which are annexed to, and made a part of the case submitted, but to which it is not necessary particularly to advert at present.

Upon this statement of facts it was submitted to the judges of the Circuit Court, whether the Deft Sol. Sibley was liable in this action for the Pay^t of the [$]216.73 collected by Whitney.—if the court should be of the opinion that he was liable then judg^t to be entered against him for that sum & interest thereon.—And if not judg^t was to be entered for the Deft for costs.

The arguments before this court, as to the liability of the Deft, have been, by the Counsel of both sides, based upon the facts set forth in the case submitted to the Circuit Court.—

The principles of law relating to copartners, and their liabilities, have been adverted to, as applicable to the present case; but the view which we have taken of this case renders it unnecessary to determine any of the points raised upon this subject. The case agreed upon, and submitted to the judges of the Circuit Court, did not contain all the facts necessary to turn the case into a question of law.

Some facts were required to be found by the Court, before it could be determined whether the Deft was liable in this case as a retiring partner, and as there was evidence contained in the case submitted, tending to prove those facts, the determination of such facts by the Court to which the cause was submitted, must be final and conclusive.

On looking over the evidence submitted it is manifest

that it tended to prove that Mark H. Sibley had a knowledge that the Deft had wholly retired from the practice of the law, and that Mr. Whitney was proceeding in his own name to collect the money on execution, and although it does not appear upon what grounds the Court below decided the case, yet there can be no doubt that the evidence submitted had a material bearing upon the merits of the case and the decision of the Court. Upon this part of the case this court cannot decide, having no authority, as a court of errors, to review the determination of the Court below settling the facts upon the evidence submitted—

But there was another objection taken by the counsel for the Deft, that this court, on a writ of error, has no authority to revise the decision of the court below on a statement of facts submitted to that court; however clearly and well ascertained the facts may be which are contained in the case, and properly presenting a case, to which the rules of law may be conveniently and well applied. It was contended that by no principles of the Common [Law] could this court take jurisdiction of such a case on writ of error: that it was like a submission to arbitration, where the arbitrators determine the facts and the law, and whose decis[ion] is final and conclusive—In support of this position no authorities were cited by the Deft's counsel,—But on examining the authorities many case[s] are found sustaining the objection.

a. 3 Peters 369.   b. 2 Greenl. R. 336.   c. 7 Mass. R. 380.   d. 9 do. 329.

These decisions go to establish the proposition, that where the facts are not determined and spread upon the record in virtue [of] some Statutory regulations, or according to the principles and usages of Courts proceeding according to the course of the common law, they cannot be reviewed on writ of error, by reason that the court into which the record is removed has no jurisdiction of such matters of fact, or the determination thereon. The statement of facts agreed on in the court below was sufficient to give jurisdiction to that Court of the matters submitted, but it forms no part of the record so as to authorise its removal to this court on a writ of error. It is not therefore so much the undoubted certainty of the facts, as it is the mode and manner of authentication which will confer jurisdiction upon this court to revise and correct the proceedings of subordinate courts on writ of error. This was the assumed principle in the case in 3 Peters, —The point of difference between the judges of the Circuit Court which alone gave the Sup. Court of the U. S. jurisdiction, not being certified according to the Act of Congress, although it might easily have been ascertained by inspection of the whole record—the Court refused to entertain jurisdiction So also in 2 Greenleaf, where the parties assented to the facts stated in a Bill of Exceptions, but which was not regularly certified by the judge who tried the cause. And in the 9 Mass, where in the statement of facts submitted to the Court of Com. Pleas, the parties further agreed that it should form a part of the record, and be removed by either party, to the Sup. Court on writ of error, the Sup. Court say that the consent of parties cannot give that court jurisdiction in a case where it is not conferred by law—and that if either party intends or expects to bring a writ of error and wishes the facts spread upon the record it will be necessary to have the facts found by the jury in a special verdict, according to the English practice.

5 Cowan R. 587 Rensselaer Glass Factory vs. Reid in Court of Error. Case referred by the Court to Refferees, and on their report being made, objections were made and a statement of facts agreed upon by the Atty and certified and signed by the presiding Judge—and by writ of error

was removed to the Court of Errors, it was then objected by the Counsel for Deft in Error that the case made and certified was no part of the record, and could not therefore be removed and revised on writ of error.

Sanford, Chancellor and Colden & Spencer Senators in giving their opinions tacitly admitted that if the case were voluntarily made by the parties that the objection would have been valid—But they overruled the objection solely on the ground that the reference of the cause was directed by the court under the Act of the Legislature and not by consent of parties—and that the Legislature did not intend in this mode to put it out of the power of either party to have his case reviewed in the Sup. Court of Errors—

EDITOR'S NOTE: The above opinion, in the handwriting of Ch. J. Fletcher, was found in file No. 1451 (as renumbered for *Transactions of the Supreme Court of the Territory of Michigan*, Blume ed.). The case was transferred to the state Supreme Court from the Supreme Court of Michigan Territory. Volume I of the Journal, First Circuit, contains the following entries: p. 38 (Jan. 12, 1838) continued by consent; p. 49 (Jan. 3, 1839) argued and submitted; p. 89 (Sept. 4, 1839) judgment affirmed. Also see *Transactions of the Supreme Court of the Territory of Michigan 1825-1836*, Blume ed., Vol. I, p. 148.

FRANCIS HENRETTY *versus* CITY OF DETROIT
September 28, 1839.

Section 2 of the ordinance under which the defendant was convicted (providing that "no person shall sell meat except in the stalls rented from the corporation") is invalid, being unreasonable and in restraint of trade.
(Opinion of one judge).

Supreme Court, First Circuit. Certiorari to Mayor's Court, City of Detroit. Opinion (not found) by Fletcher, Ch. J. Dissenting opinion by Whipple, J. Judgment affirmed insofar as it imposed fine and costs; reversed insofar as it ordered that plaintiff in certiorari be imprisoned until fine and costs are paid.

C. Tryon, W. Woodbridge & Backus, attornies for plaintiff in certiorari.

J. A. Van Dyke & A. D. Fraser, attornies for defendant in certiorari.

[INDORSEMENT]

First Circuit

Francis Henrietty

vs

City of Detroit

Opinion of
C W Whipple,

DISSENTING:

[DISSENTING OPINION]

Francis Henretty
vs
The People   } Supreme Court: First Circuit.

Cer¹ to Mayors Court of the City of Detroit.

The plaintiff in error was prosecuted in the Mayor's Court of the City of Detroit for an alleged violation of an ordinance of said City entitled "A law to regulate public markets:" The complaint was founded upon the 1st & 2nd Sections of the ordinance, which provides in substance that *"all public markets in said city shall be held at the market houses therein"* and secondly; that *"no person shall sell meat except in the stalls rented from the corporation."* The 7th Section prescribes as a punishment for a violation of any of the provisions of the ordinance, *"a fine not exceeding $50, and imprisonment not exceeding ten days, or either."* Upon a plea of not guilty being interposed a jury was empannelled, who after hearing the evidence returned a *general* verdict, of guilty: whereupon a judgment was entered in the words following: "*Said Mayor's Court then & there fined the said Francis Henretty, for said offence, of which he was found guilty by the jury, as aforesaid in the sum of fifty dollars and the costs of prosecution and ordered that he should stand committed until the fine and costs should be paid.*" The defendant feeling himself aggrieved by the judgment & proceedings in the Mayor's Court, made the necessary affidavit, upon which a certiorari was allowed and subsequently issued to remove the cause to this court.

The points made by the Counsel for the plff. in error and upon which they rely for a reversal of the judgment below are of the gravest character, involving questions which have never before been adjudicated upon by the judicial tribunals of this State or of the late Territory of Michigan; and which, if sustained by this court would affect most vitally the interests not only of the City of Detroit in its corporate capacity, but a very large class of private individuals. The importance, therefore, of the question at issue taken in connection with the magnitude of public & private interests at stake, have induced me to give to the cause, a careful and deliberate examination, the results of which I shall now proceed to state; and I may here remark that the opinion now to be expressed will contain little else than the conclusions of my mind upon the various points argued at the bar, without entering very much at large into the course of reasoning by which I have been conducted to these conclusions: contenting myself for the present, with a statement of such reasons in support of my conclusions as appear to me most obvious and striking, without referring to others which may have influenced but not controlled my judgment.

I shall consider the various points argued by the Counsel for the plff. nearly in the order in which they are stated in the very elaborate brief with which I have been furnished.

1: It is contended that the Legislative Council of the late Territory of Michigan had no authority to pass the law entitled "*An Act relative to the City of Detroit.*" This proposition tho' the same in substance, is different in terms from that stated in the very ingenious written argument of one of the Counsel, where the word charter is frequently adopted and as I think misapplied: In the argument of this question a much wider scope was indulged in, than was necessary for its determination; which depends upon the true construction to be given to the powers granted to the Legislative Council by the Act of Congress of March 3rd, 1823: What then were the powers conferred upon that body? In the Second Sec of the Act it is provided "that the same powers which were granted to the governor, Legislative Council, the House of representatives, of the North Western territory, by the ordinance of Congress, passed on the 13th day of July 1787, &c are hereby conferred upon, and shall be exercised by the governor and Legislative Council." What, then, were these powers? By reference to the ordinance it appears that "*the Governor, Legislative Council, and House of Representatives*" had "*authority to make laws, in all cases, for the good government of the district, not repugnant to the principles and articles in this ordinance established and declared.*" The question now recurs had that body, by virtue of the broad powers conferred upon them "*to make laws, in all cases, for the good government of the district,*" authority to pass the Act cited in the proposition I am now considering: To solve this question it will be necessary to define what is to be understood by a municipal or public corporation: Without discussing the propriety of the metaphysical and quaint definitions given by some of the ancient legal authors, I propose to adopt one which for simplicity and comprehensiveness, appears to me to be the best I have met with: I refer to the one given by Willcock who defines a public corporation to be "the investing of the inhabitants of a particular place with its local government." From this definition the nature & objects of such a corporation may be ascertained: Its nature & general characteristics are familiar to every lawyer; its objects the government of a portion of the state, & to this end it is endowed with a portion of political power: Is it not then manifest that the general authority to make laws for the government of the District includes the authority to incorporate subordinate communities for the government of a portion of that District?: I think it does: In expressing the opinion that the Legislative Council were invested with authority to pass the law in question, I desire it to be understood that it is not my purpose to affirm or disaffirm the views expressed by Counsel respecting the powers conferred upon the Govr & judges while performing the functions of a Legislative body: that question is not involved in this case, and does not, therefore call for a decision.

Secondly: admitting the authority of the Legislature to incorporate the City of Detroit, it is contended that all rights acquired by the City, ceased on the formation of the State Government unless expressly preserved:

The erection by Congress, of the Territorial Government, was certainly for temporary purposes: the ordinance of 1787, which was the fundamental law of the whole Northwestern Territory, contemplated a state of things when the people of the several Territories, which were to be carved out of that immense extent of Country, should throw off the Colonial condition, and assume the more imposing attitude of a state of the Confederacy, clothed with all the attributes of sovereignty & independence which belonged to the original

states: The people of the Territory of Michigan availing
themselves of the rights secured by the ordinance, did, in the
month of June, 1835, meet together, by their representatives,
in Convention, and formed a Constitution & state government, which was to take effect upon its ratification by the
people: that the Legislative Council could not establish or
ordain *political or public corporations,* which should outlive
the temporary government, is very true, and that the Convention which formed the state Constitution representing the
people in their sovereign capacity had ample authority to
annul all charters of the nature referred to is equally true:
The question then arises was the act incorporating the City
of Detroit preserved by the Constitution of the State: This
question turns upon the construction to be given to the 2^d Sec
of the schedule which ordains that "all laws now in force in
the Territory of Michigan, which are not repugnant to this
Constitution, shall remain in force until they expire by their
own limitations, or be altered or repealed by the Legislature."
Was then, the law incorporating the City of Detroit in
"force" at the time of the adoption of the Constitution? It
certainly was: Were any of the provisions of that law *"repugnant"* to the Constitution? It is contended by the counsel for
the plff in error, that the act of incorporation was repugnant
to the Constitution in this that the members of the Council
Council are clothed with Legislative & Judicial powers,
whereas the Constitution declares that *"The powers of the
government shall be divided into three distinct departments:
the legislative, the executive, and the judicial; and one de-
partment shall never exercise the powers of another, except
in such cases as are expressly provided for in this Constitution."* This provision, it is believed, is incorporated not only
in the Constitution of the United States, but in the Constitu-
tions of the several States of the Union: indeed it has become
a settled maxim in the science of government, that it is

essential to liberty, and to the harmonious action of the whole to keep separate the three great departments by which the government is administered & that each should move within the sphere prescribed by the fundamental law and never assume to exercise power granted exclusively to the others. Does then, the authority conferred upon the Common Council of the City of Detroit in their legislative capacity to enact laws, and then to sit as judges when their validity is drawn in question, and also try those charged with their infraction, involve a violation of the article of the Constitution just quoted? I think it does not: The "government" mentioned in the Article, means the STATE GOVERNMENT; the three "departments" referred to, means the three *great departments* of this *state government:* The Constitution prescribes and limits the powers of each of these three great departments, and in the article above quoted, it was the intention of the framers of the Constitution to guard against the Exercise by one of these three departments, of the powers conferred upon either of the other departments: To illustrate this position: Sec 1, art VI of the Constitution provides that *"The Judicial power shall be vested in one Supreme Court, and in such other Courts as the legislature may from time to time establish."* Pursuant to the powers conferred upon the Legislature by this Article, they proceeded to establish a Supreme Court, a Court of Chancery, and a Circuit Court: These Courts are the administrators of the Judicial authority of the State, or of one of the three great departments of which I have been speaking: Now: if one or the other of these courts should attempt the exercise of legislative power, their act [would] be void, because it would violate the fundamental principle to which I have adverted: If I have succeeded in giving to the Constitution a just construction it will follow, that the exercise of a limited legislative and judicial authority by a body constituted like the Common Council of the City of Detroit, is not repugnant to the Constitution: Like powers have been conferred by almost every Legislature in the Union, and the highest evidence of the validity of such a grant of power, is to be found in the fact that it never has been seriously questioned; and that if invalid, it should to this day have escaped the observation of the most eminent judges and lawyers who have adorned the Bench and the Bar in this Country. But while I admit the validity of the law conferring legislative and judicial powers on the persons composing the Common Council of the City of Detroit, I cannot permit the occasion to pass, without the expression of an opinion that such a combination of power in the same persons, violates in spirit, the very principle recognized in our Constitution, which I have endeavored to illustrate: If it is impolitic & dangerous and contrary to all our notions of government, to invest the Supreme Judicial Tribunal of the State with legislative powers, why should it be thought politic, safe, and consistent with correct principles to permit such powers to be exercised by an inferior jurisdiction? It is impossible that a body of men clothed with such authority, can gain that confidence & conciliate that respect so necessary to impart to their adjudications that moral influence without which judicial decisions are of little value: To grant legislative powers to a body of men, and at the same time invest them with the authority of judges to decide on their validity and to enforce obedience to them is putting into their hands an instrument of power which may be wielded for the worst purposes: In voting for the passage of law, it is fair to presume that the law maker is satisfied with respect to its validity, for his mind up to this period is open to conviction,—he weighs with impartiality all the arguments in favor & against it: Let the same lawmaker sit in the capacity of a judge, and let arguments drawn from the Constitution be directed against the very law *of his own creation,*—his pride of opinion is at once awakened,—he construes the argument into an attack upon the correctness of his judgment,—upon his wisdom as a legislator,—these combined produce a state of mind unsuited to the character of a judge:—who should be free from all influences but such as may tend to clear the way for a full, fair, impartial, and enlightened administration of law & justice: The views I have thus expressed, it must be understood, are directed against the structure of the Tribunal called the Mayor's Court, and not against the individuals who have heretofore, or who now, constitute that tribunal: the best evidence of their respectability and character is to be found in the fact that their fellow citizens have called them to the discharge of duties, so honorable & responsible.

Having, thus far, endeavored to prove that the Legislative Council had the authority to pass the law incorporating the city of Detroit, and that it has not been expressly or impliedly repealed, I shall now proceed to consider whether the enactment of the by law in question was a competent exercise of power on the part of the Common Council. It was urged with becoming zeal, and much ability that the by law is void because: 1st There is no authority for prescribing that "all public markets in said city shall be held at the market houses therein" and 2ly, "That no person shall sell meat except in the stalls rented from the corporation"

To determine these questions we must look at the act incorporating the City of Detroit, which is its constitution. By that act the Common Council are empowered to "establish keep & regulate one or more public markets" and "to make by laws relative to the public markets." Under this grant of power had the Com Council authority to ordain that all public markets should be held at the market houses in the City of Detroit; Corporations have such powers and no others than those given them by the laws which give them a legal existence: they can take nothing by implication. Applying this rigid & inflexible rule to the present case I yet think the power claimed for the Com Council can be sustained: The public health, & the public convenience, two objects of primary importance, especially in a populous town or city imperiously demand some regulation as to the time & place when & where public markets should be held: These facts which are unquestionable, should be looked to in giving a construction to a power granted in terms so general as those employed in the act of incorporation. But it is insisted upon with much force that the grant of power set forth does not authorize the corporation to restrain all persons from selling meat *"except in the stalls rented from the corporation."*

It was argued that such a regulation is *in restraint of trade,* and that, as a consequence the authority to pass such a by law cannot be fairly inferred. After giving to this question the most patient investigation I have come to the conclusion, founded on principle and authority that the second section of the by law which imposes the restraint I have just suggested is *void:* It is void because it is both unreasonable, and in restraint of trade: To test the correctness of this opinion let us look to the practical effects of such a restriction if rigidly enforced. And firstly: It precludes all persons from selling meat except such as the Common Council may choose to rent a stall, and to such only as have the ability to pay the rent that may be exacted: Secondly: the effect of such a restriction is to create a monopoly, and if the act was rigidly enforced such a monopoly as would preclude many at some seasons of the year from obtaining animal food: Thirdly: it is, in effect prohibiting the inhabitants of the City from purchasing meats, except from the few who may have been so fortunate as to obtain a stall, & fourthly, it puts the whole community in the power of the few who have rented stalls so far as regards the supply of meats and the price to be paid: For these reasons I think the by law so far [set] forth unreasonable, unnecessary and I must say oppressive: It will follow from what I have already stated that according to my conception, the Second Sec of the by-law, is also in restraint of trade. It was argued by the able counsel for the defts, that the restraint imposed was not general but particular: that it merely *fixed the place* where meats were to be sold; this is very true, but is it not apparent that such regulations both with regard to time & place may be so restrictive in their character as to be obnoxious to the general principle that all laws in restraint of trade are void: To illustrate my meaning: let us suppose that the Common Council should pass a law prohibiting the sale of meats except in *one* of the stalls of the public market, and that such sale should be made but *once* a week: now this regulation would regard *time & place*, yet it would hardly be contended that it could be sustained, because of its unreasonableness, and because the *effect* would be to restrain trade: But let us suppose a case which frequently occurs, & to which I took the liberty of directing the attention of the Senior Counsel for the defendants during the progress of his argument: Farmers residing out of the limits of the city and in adjoining counties are daily seen in our streets during the winter season with wagons laden with fresh beef, pork, mutton, veal & venison: Now according to the 2^d Sec of the by-law in question, they could not sell their meats unless in the stalls rented from the Common Council:—without subjecting themselves to fine and perhaps imprisonment: But it may be said, that no notice would be taken of such a violation of law, or that the law was not

intended to apply to such cases: The learned Counsel is the
Recorder of the City of Detroit, and usually presides at the
Mayor's Court and I should do injustice to his ability as a
judge, if with the plain provision staring him in the face
declaring that "no person shall sell meat except in the stalls
rented from the Corporation," he should charge the jury
impannelled to try the case that the law was not intended to
apply to such cases: Would he not rather say, that the law
was so plain as to admit of but one construction: that where
the meaning of a law was obvious & apparent, it was not the
province of a judge or jury to *intend*, that the law makers
did not mean what they have clearly expressed: This would
undoubtedly be the language of the Recorder, unless like
myself he should think the law unreasonable & in restraint
of trade:

The suggestion that the provision of the by law I am
considering would never be enforced, cannot influence the
decision of the case: I am bound to suppose that it is enforced:
But without resorting any further to those principles by
which the validity of by laws of corporations are tested, I
shall conclude this branch of the case by referring to one
reported in the 10 of Wendell p 99: I shall notice it with
some particularity as it not only sustains the views I have
expressed upon the point under consideration, but fully con-
firms some of the positions I have laid down in the progress
of this opinion: One Webster was sued for a violation of one
of the by laws of the Village of Buffalo, which made it un-
lawful for any person during certain months to hawk about
or sell by retail any kind of fresh beef, pork, lamb or mutton
for the consumption of the inhabitants of the Village, except
at the public markets, or within certain limits around the
same: The defendant agreed with a grocer to let him have
a quarter of lamb and to receive in payment goods out of his

grocery, and the sale & payment accordingly took place: On this evidence the Justice who tried the case imposed a penalty of five dollars; The judgment was removed to the Court of Common Pleas where the judgment of the Justice was reversed. Whereupon the Trustees of the Village sued out a writ of error from the Sup Court: Chief Justice Savage delivered the opinion of the Court as follows: "By the act incorporating the Village of Buffalo the trustees are authorized to make such prudential by-laws, as they may deem proper, relative to the public markets &ᶜ and the only question is whether the by-law is valid: At the Common Law corporations have power to make by-laws for the general good of the corporation. they must be reasonable & for the Common benefit: They must not be in restraint of trade, nor impose a burden without an apparent benefit. A by-law for the restriction of trade and imposing particular restraints as to time & place is good, but general restraints are bad: For example, a by-law that no meat should be sold in the Village would be bad, being a general restraint; but that meat should not be sold except in a particular [place] is good, not being a restraint of the right to sell meat, but a regulation of that right: Laws relating to public markets must necessarily embrace the power to require all meats to be sold there, *not that every man who sells meat shall rent a stall; nor is there any such objection to the present law; any one may sell meat in the street adjacent to the markets.*" This opinion which I have quoted literally establishes the following proposition: 1ˢᵗ: That the power to regulate public markets embraces the power to require all meats to be sold there: so far this decision affirms the right I have claimed on behalf of the Com Coun. to require all public markets in the City of Detroit to be held at the market houses: 2ˡʸ: By-laws must be reasonable & for the common benefit: 3ˡʸ: that general restraints are bad,—particular ones good: 4^{ly}: that a by-law requiring every man who sells meat to hire a stall would be bad:

Now the 2^d Sec of the by law of the City of Detroit prohibits any man to sell meats except in the stalls rented from the corporation: If so, it follows that in order to enable a man to sell meat he must first hire a stall from the corporation: Such a by law, altho' a mere regulation of trade, a particular restraint is according [to] Chief Justice Savage bad, & for the plain reason, that it is manifestly *unreasonable and not for the common benefit:* It being *essential* to the validity of a by law that it should be reasonable, and for the common benefit—not for the benefit of the few.

The counsel for the defts cannot fail to perceive the analogy between the case I have just reviewed, and that which I propounded to him during the argument of the present case: the right of the trustees of Buffaloe to pass the law was affirmed on the principle that it was reasonable to require the farmer who brot' his quarter of lamb to the Village to repair to the public market and there dispose of it, but disaffirmed the right to require those who thus sold meat to hire a stall.

EDITOR'S NOTE: The above dissenting opinion, in the handwriting of Justice Whipple, was found in file No. 159, First Circuit—Law. A memo. by Harrington, stating that Ch. J. Fletcher delivered the majority opinion, is also in the file. Volume I of the Journal, First Circuit, contains the following entries: p. 73 (Aug. 6, 1839) motion to set aside writ of supersedeas; p. 76 (Aug. 8, 1839) order that writ of supersedeas be set aside unless bond filed; p. 83 (Aug. 15, 1839) argued and submitted; p. 91 (Sept. 28, 1839) judgment affirmed in part; reversed in part. Also see Calendar, First Circuit—Law, Vol. I, case 159. Several papers pertaining to thise case will be found in Woodbridge Papers (Wallet for June—Sept., 1839, August Folder), Burton Historical Collection, Public Library, Detroit.

CALEB F. DAVIS *versus* ISAAC W. INGERSOLL
January 18, 1840.

Supreme Court, First Circuit. Certiorari to three Justices of the peace, Wayne County. Opinion by Whipple, J. Judgment reversed.

J. A. Van Dyke, attorney for plaintiff.

EDITOR's NOTE: The opinion in this case appears in a footnote in 2 Douglass (Mich.) 372 (1849). It deals with the substantive allegations necessary in an action of forcible entry and detainer. Volume I of the Journal of the Supreme Court, First Circuit, contains the following entries: p. 73 (Aug. 6, 1839) motion that justices make a more complete return; p. 74 (Aug. 7, 1839) specific points given on which return should be made; p. 95 (Jan. 13, 1840) argued and submitted; p. 100 (Jan. 18, 1840) judgment reversed. Also see Calendar, First Circuit—Law, Vol. I, case 153. The original MS. opinion is not in the files.

JONAH BREWSTER, MARTHA BREWSTER, GEORGE BREWSTER, MARY BREWSTER, and BENJAMIN BREWSTER *versus* EUROTAS P. HASTINGS, SHUBAEL CONANT, and HENRY S. COLE, Executors, etc., of FRANKLIN BREWSTER, Deceased.
March 7, 1840.

1. *A declaration made by a person in his last sickness, which was read over to him, approved by him, and declared by him to be his will in the presence of five persons who signed as witnesses at his request, is a* NUNCUPATIVE *will under section 3 of the statute of 1818 (Terr. Laws of 1820, p. 20) not a* WRITTEN *will which is defective because not signed by the testator.*

2. *A valid* NUNCUPATIVE *will which purports to dispose of both real and personal property does not come within the terms of section 9 of the above statute (providing that a*

defective will in WRITING *which purports to dispose of both real and personal property "shall not be allowed and approved as a testament of personal estate only"), hence may be allowed to stand as to personalty.*

Supreme Court, First Circuit. Appeal from the Probate Court, Wayne County. Opinion by Fletcher, Ch. J. Decree affirmed.

  A. D. Fraser, attorney for appellants.
  D. Goodwin, attorney for respondants.

[INDORSEMENT]

Sup. Court 1 Circuit
Brewster et al ⎞
vs. ⎟
Hastings et al ⎠

Opinion—
delivered March 7, 1840—
By Fletcher Ch. Jus.

Fraser for Appellants—
Goodwin for Respondants—

[OPINION]

Jonah Brewster et al ⎞
vs. ⎟
Eurotas P. Hastings ⎟
& Shub¹ Conant ⎠

  This was an appeal from the decree of the Judge of Probate for the County of Wayne, passed the 2ᵈ Feby 1835, by which an instrument purporting to be the last will and Testament of Franklin Brewster, deceased, was approved and allowed.

The Appellants are heirs at law of the testator, and the Respondants are the executors named in the will.

Several reasons for the appeal were duly filed by the appellants, but only one of them is now relied on, which is that the will purporting to be a disposition of Real and Personal property, and not being executed and attested so as to operate as a devise of the real estate, cannot be allowed as to the personal.

The will was a nuncupative will made by the testator in the Summer of 1834 in his last sickness—It was reduced to writing according to his directions, and read over to him, and approved. He then declared it to be his last will and testament in the presence of five persons who subscribed the same at the time, as witnesses by request of testator. The testator did not sign the will.

(*Read copy of the will*)

It is contended by the Counsel for the Appellants that this will, purporting to be a disposition of real and personal estate, comes within the provisions of the 9th Section of the ["] Act Prescribing the manner of devising land, tenements and hereditaments," adopted July 27. 1818.

The preamble to the 9th Sect. of that act is in these words "And as it may sometimes happen that a will respecting "lands and tenements and personal estate, through inattention "or otherwise, may be attested or subscribed by a less number "of credible witnesses than this act directs for devising land "tenements and hereditaments, which if approved and al-"lowed as a testament of the personal estate only, might de-"feat the original intention of the devisor respecting the "settlement of his estate"—Then follows the enacting clause, "—Be it further enacted that any will *in writing* hereafter "offered for probate, which purports a disposition of both "real and personal estate, that shall not be attested and sub-

"scribed as this act directs for the devising of lands, tenements
"and hereditaments, shall not be allowed and approved as a
"testament of personal estate only."—

By the 1ˢ Sect. of this act it is declared that any person
lawfully seized of any lands, tenements or hereditaments in
the Territory, being of the age of 21 years, and of Sane mind,
shall have power to devise the same by last will and testament in writing—And by the 2ᵈ Sect. it is declared that all
devises and bequests of any lands or tenements shall be in
writing and *signed* by the party *devising* or by some person
in his presence, and by his express direction; and shall be attested and subscribed in the presence of the devisor by three
or more credible witnesses, or otherwise shall be void—This
will is not executed so as to operate as a devise of real estate,
not being signed by the testator nor by any other person for
him in his presence and by his express direction.

But the counsel for the appellants contend, [1] that although the will is not executed & signed as required by the
Statute, still it is a will *in writing* and comes strictly within
the prohibition contained in the 9ᵗʰ Section of the Act; and 2.
That if it is not within the strict terms of that Section, it
comes clearly within the scope of the remedy intended by the
Legislature—and ought to be considered as within the equity
of the prohibition—and that it cannot, therefore be allowed
as a will of the personal estate.

1. Is it a will in *writing* within the terms of the Statute?

By the 3ᵈ 4ᵗʰ & 5ᵗʰ Sections of the same Stat. the right
to make nuncupative wills is recognized under certain restric-
tions and regulations therein provided.

A nuncupative will is a testamentary disposition of property made by verbal or oral declaration, of the testator—And
are uniformly contradistinguished from written wills, signed
and executed by the testator—The term nuncupative imports

merely verbal or oral declarations—And although such declarations should at the time be reduced to writing, and read over to the testator, and fully approved by him, yet if he should not sign it himself or by some other under his direction it would be a nuncupative will only, and not a will in writing—

This distinction between a will in writing, and a nuncupative will is expressly recognized in the Stat. 29 Ch. II. Chap. 3. commonly called the Stat. frauds, and also in our own Statute before referred to—By the 29 Ch. II. it is enacted that no written will shall be revoked or altered by a subsequent nuncupative will except the same be, in the life time of the testator, reduced to writing, and read over to him and approved. By the 6th Section of our own Stat. it is enacted, "that no will in writing concerning any goods, chattels or personal estate, shall be repealed, nor shall any clause or bequest therein be altered or changed by any *words* or *will*, by word of mouth only, except the same be committed to writing, and read to the testator and allowed by him." &c—

This distinction has been uniformly made or recognized— It is quite clear that this is not strictly a written will within the express terms of the Statute.

2. But, although not strictly within the express words of the Stat. it is further contended that it comes within the scope of the mischief intended to be remedied by the Stat., and that the same reasons and principles apply to it, and that therefore it should be held to be within the equity of the Stat.—

In the construction of Statutes the first object is to ascertain the intention and meaning of the Legislature. When from the terms used by the Legislature the intention is plainly expressed, there is no room for construction. But when the intention is not manifest, every part of the Stat: other Statutes upon the same subject—the general scope and object of the Act; the preamble & the title may be resorted to for the purpose of ascertaining the intention of the Legislature—

Is the Statute in question, therefore, as to the intent of the Legislature, plain and obvious, or doubtful, and still to be ascertained by judicial construction?

In the first place "a statute is the best expositor of itself."—

The 1ˢᵗ & 2ᵈ Sections of the Act declare who may devise lands—and direct that the will shall be in *writing* and signed by the devisor and be attested or subscribed in his presence by 3 or more witnesses—or else shall be utterly void, and of no effect.

The 3ᵈ 4ᵗʰ & 5ᵗʰ Sections relate to nuncupative wills. The 3ᵈ Section declares that no nuncupative will shall be good, when the estate thereby *bequeathed,* shall exceed the value of $150, that is not proved by the oath of 3 witnesses at least, that were present at the making thereof, nor unless it be proved that the testator at the time of pronouncing the same did bid the persons present, or some of them, to bear witness &c &c.

The 4th & 5 Sections regulate the time and manner of proving and allowing such nuncupative wills—

By these provisions the right to dispose of personal property by a nuncupative will is most expressly recognized, the mind of the Legislature was directly employed in providing against the evils which might attend such a testamentary disposition, either from accident or fraud—and all these regulations respecting the circumstances under which such a will may be made, how it may be made, the time and manner of the proof and the probate and allowance, are essentially different from those which are provided for a devise of real estate—

Having made these separate and distinctive regulations

upon these different subjects, the Legislature further provided in the 9th Sect. that a will *in writing purporting* a *disposition* of both *real* and *personal estate,* that should not be *attested* and *subscribed* as directed by that act for devising of lands, tenements and hereditaments, should not be approved and allowed as a testament of personal estate only. The will in question certainly purports to dispose of real, as well as personal estate—But in what part of the Stat. can it be discovered that the Legislature intend to subject an unwritten will to the operation of the 9th Section?

There is nothing in the terms employed by the Legislature indicating such intention—

But it is contended in general terms by the Counsel for the appellants that the mischief is the same in permitting an unwritten will purporting a disposition of real and personal estate, to stand as to the personal only, as in case of a written will, and as the Legislature intended to prevent the mischief in the case of a written will; the court will extend the remedy beyond the strict letter of the Stat. so as to reach and correct the same evil which will be occasioned by the allowance of a nuncupative will—

Whether the evil is the same in each case it may not be necessary now to determine, but it is manifest that the Legislature did not intend to put them on the same footing or subject them to the same rules and the reasons for this distinction are obvious.

Greater formality has always been required in the disposition of real property than of personal.

In the case of written will the testator may and most generally perhaps does make it in health, upon mature deliberation and by the assistance of Counsel—whereas in the case of a nuncupative will—it must be made in sickness and frequently without time for advice or the formal execution of written instruments—It is quite natural therefore that the Legislature should intentionally make a difference as to the regulations and rules respecting a nuncupative will which must be made *in extremis,* and those respecting a formal instrument intended to operate as a devise of real estate—

It seems to me therefore as well from the apparent intention of the Legislature as ascertained from the terms and manifest object of the Statute, as also from the obvious reasons arising from the subject matter respecting which the statutory regulations are made, that by extending the provisions of the 9th Sect. to an unwritten will, we should be directly contravening the express will of the Legislature.

But it is further contended by the Counsel for the appellants, that the Stat. in question was adopted from Mass^{ts}—that it has rec^d a construction in that state, that principles have there been established which if applied to this case would fully support their objection to this will—And that such adjudications should be adopted here as good authority, upon the principle that when a statute is adopted from another state, the construction of the Stat. which had obtained in such state—is also adopted—

The rule contended for is a sound and salutary rule, so far as it relates to open and well ascertained adjudications—

The case of *Brown vs. Thorndike* 15 Pick 388 has been relied upon as sustaining fully the position taken by the Counsel for the appellants, that the will in question should be held to [be] within the spirit and equity of the 9th Sect. of the Stat.—

Brown vs. Thorndike 15 Pick 388—C. Thorndike made his will on the 28 Feby 1825, duly excuted and attested to pass real estate, and purporting on the face of it to dispose of both real & personal estate—In June, 1829 he wrote and signed upon the will the following declaration.

"It is my intention at some future time to alter the tenor
"of the above will, or rather to make another will; therefore
"be it known that if I should die before another will is made,
"I desire that the foregoing be considered as revoked, and of
"no effect"—

There was no subscribing wit to this memorandum.
The testator afterwards died without having made any other
will.

It was contended by the counsel for the Appellant in
support of the will that a revocation of a will although not
expressly named in the 9th Sect. of a Statute of that State,
(which Section is precisely like our own) yet that revocations
are within the mischief—the same reason and principle applying to them, and therefore that they ought to be held to be
within the equity of the Stat.

But before this question was decided the Counsel for the
Respondants contended that at the time of the revocation the
testator had no real property upon which the will could
operate, and offered to show this fact by evidence,—This evid.
was admitted by the Court by which it appeared that all the
real estate held by the testator at the time of making his will,
had been aliened before the revocation. And the Court then
say that, as the testator at the time of the revocation, had
only personal property upon which the will could operate, the
will should be regarded as a will of personal property only,
and might be revoked without any attestation of subscribing
witnesses—They also say that the testator is to be presumed
to have a knowledge of the situation of his own property, and
being in fact only possessed of personal property, and the
effect of a revocation executed in the manner that one was,
must be presumed to be known to the testator,—and that to
give effect as a revocation of a will of personal property only,
would advance, and not defeat the general intent and purpose
of the testator—

—The Court then remark in relation to the equitable construction of the statute as claimed by the Appellants, that "to apply the provisions of the statute by any supposed equity "of construction, to such a case, would, we think, be going "contrary to the reason and purpose of the Statute, and would "be not only defeating the intent of the testator, but the in-"tent of the Legislature."—How any principle established in this case can be properly be urged as tending to bring the will under consideration within the equity of the Stat. it is difficult to preceive, because in that case the revocation was held not to be within the words or spirit of the statute.

There is another case cited from Mass^{ts} by the Counsel for the Respondants, the case of Deane vs. Littlefield, 1 Pick. R. 239.

In that case a minor made a will duly signed by him and attested and subscribed as required to a devise of real estate, and purporting a disposition of both real and personal estate. It was contended in opposition to the will, that it came equitably within the 9th Section of the Stat.—

But the Court say, "At common law a will which was good to dispose of personal estate, but not for real, might be set up for the former, though not for the latter; and the 9th Section of the Stat. was intended to repeal the Common Law; it must therefore be limited in its operation to the case intended by the Legislature; and it is very clear that the *provision had respect* only to such wills as should be *insufficient* to *dispose* of real estate only because they were not *attested and subscribed* in the manner required by the Stat.

— In that case the will was duly attested and subscribed to pass real estate, which the court decide took it out of the 9th Sect. of the Statute—and declare that it neither came within the words nor spirit of the Stat.

That case is quite similar to the one before us, and depending upon the same principles—

In that case a will of a *minor* purporting to dispose of real and personal estate, was not provided for by the Legislature—and was considered as standing as at the Com. Law— In this a *nuncupative will* purporting to dispose of real & personal estate does not come within the provision of the 9th Section, because a written will only is mentioned, and that made inoperative by the Stat. only because not attested and subscribed as required to devise real estate. The objection to the will in either case is not on the ground that it was *not* thus *attested* and *subscribed,* but on an *intirely different ground*—in the case of Deane vs. Littlefield on the ground that the testator was not 21 *years* of age, and in the present case because it is a nuncupative will, and cannot therefore operate as a devise of real estate.

In the case of Deane & Littlefield the Court laid some stress on the circumstance that as the testator had by his will given the whole of his estate to his mother, who was his heir at Law, an allowance of the will as to the personal estate could not defeat the intention of the testator. And in the present case if the will should be disallowed, the whole intention of the testator will be defeated, for then it will all pass to the father, to whom he has given nothing by the will— It is not necessary however for us in this case to give any weight to this consideration in this case.

There is another difference between the two cases which shows still more clearly that this case ought not to be considered as coming within the equity of the Stat. In the case of the minor, the will was not considered as within the Statute because the ground of the objection did not relate to the insufficiency of the attestation and subscription, and the Court say they must limit the operation of the 9th Sect. to the case specified by the Legislature.

In the case at bar the same rule must be applied because

the reason is the same—and in addition to this, there is another reason in this case equally conclusive, the fact heretofore alluded to, that the legislature have made specific regulations in the same Statute and entirely different in character, respecting written and unwritten wills, and have limited the operation of the 9th Section expressly to *written* wills.

On this ground therefore the present case is more clearly left to stand as at Com. Law, than the case in 1 Pick.—

But is was further insisted by the Counsel for the appellants that at Com. Law a will purporting to dispose of real and personal estate, and not executed so as to operate upon the real estate, could not be allowed to stand as to the personal.

This position, however, cannot be maintained. The rule that the will may be set up as to the personal estate, has been to long established to [and] too generally recognized, I think, to [be] now disturbed—

With these views I am of the opinion that this will be approved and allowed as to the personal estate only of which to testator died possessed—

EDITOR'S NOTE: The above opinion, in the handwriting of Chief Justice Fletcher, was found in file No. 112, First Circuit—Law. The case was transferred to the Supreme Court from Wayne Circuit Court, Michigan Territory. Volume I of the Journal, First Circuit, contains the following entries: p. 11 (Jan. 10, 1837) argued and submitted; p. 42 (March 1, 1838) moved by appellants that a real or feigned issue be formed and sent to Wayne Circuit Court for trial; p. 43 (March 2, 1838) ordered that a real or feigned issue be formed and tried by jury in Wayne Circuit Court; p. 54 (Jan. 8, 1839) moved that decree of probate court be affirmed; p. 58 (Jan. 10, 1839) argument opened; p. 101 (March 7, 1840) will of Franklin Brewster allowed and established as a good and valid nuncupative will; decree of probate court affirmed. Also see Calendar, First Circuit—Law, Vol. I, case 112.

GEORGE HILL *versus* DAVID PADDOCK and GIDEON O. WHITTEMORE
January 23, 1841.

1. *In the absence of evidence, a court cannot presume that a memorandum at the foot of a promissory note ("At 12 per cent int D. P.") was made when the note was made or that the letters "D. P." meant David Paddock, one of the makers of the note.*

2. *Where it does not appear that a memorandum at the foot of a note is a substantial part of the note, proof of the note and memorandum is not a material variance from a pleading ·which describes the note without mentioning the memorandum.*

Supreme Court, Fourth Circuit. Question reserved by the Circuit Court, Oakland County; certified to the Supreme Court. Opinion by Fletcher, Ch. J. Certified by Supreme Court that objection to note as evidence on the ground of variance was properly overruled.

John P. Richardson, attorney for plaintiff.

William Draper, attorney for defendants.

[INDORSEMENT]

Sup. Court. Pontiac
Jany 1841

Hill
vs.
Paddock et al

Mem° of opinion
Same term—

[OPINION]

George Hill
vs.
David Paddock &
Gid. O. Whittemore

On a question of law reserved & certified to this Court by the Pres. Judge of the Circuit for the County of Oakland.

The action below was assumpsit on a promissory note, drawn in the following manner

"One year from date for value rec^d we jointly and severally [promise] to pay George Hill or bearer four hundred dollars & interest.

Pontiac Feby 11, 1837

Signed D. Paddock

G. O. Whittemore

At 12 per cent int

D.P."

The Plff declared upon the note without noticing the mem° at the foot of the note.

On the Trial the Plff proved the execution of the note by the Defts, and offered the same in evid. in support of his said action. To this the Defts Att^y objected on the ground of variance between the note offered in evid. and that described & set forth in Plffs declaration, in this, that the mem° at the bottom of the note offered in evid. formed a part of the note, and that it was therefore materially variant from that described in the declaration.

This objection was overruled by the Circuit Court, and the note was given in evid. A verdict found thereon for the Plff.

The Defts moved the Circuit Court for a new trial, and as a reason in support of their motion insisted that the Circuit Court erred in permitting the note to go to the jury. And the question now is whether there was a material variance.

On the part of the Defts it [was] urged that there was a variance, because the mem° formed a part of the note, and should therefore have been declared on—and that having omitted to declare on the note according to the terms of the note itself, there is a misdescription of the note in the declaration.

On the part of the Plff it is insisted that the mem° upon the note is unmeaning or insensible in the absence of any evid. explanatory of its meaning. that neither the Circuit Court nor this Court can undertake to affix a meaning to the mem° for the purpose of affecting the plain and manifest terms of the note—

1. Can the Court in the absence of all evid. intend or presume that the letters D. P. mean David Paddock one of the makers of the note? or

2. that the mem° was made at the time of the execution of the note by the Defts—?

This Court certainly cannot, in the absence of proof, affix any meaning to the letters D. P. nor can they say that the mem° was made at the time of making the note, or was a part of the contract. We cannot therefore regard it as a substantive part of the note.

What affect might be given to this mem° upon the assess^t of dam^s, whether the Plff producing the note with this mem° upon it would not be bound by it—and thereby bring himself within the penal stat., giving a forfeiture where usury has been reserved it is not necessary now to determine—

We are of the opinion that the objection was properly overruled—certified accordingly—

Editor's Note: The above opinion, in the handwriting of Chief Justice Fletcher, was found in file No. 19, Fourth Circuit. The Journal, Fourth Circuit, contains the following entries: p. 6 (Jan. 21, 1841) argued and submitted; p. 10 (Jan. 23, 1841) certified that objection to note was properly overruled. Also see Calendar, Fourth Circuit, Case No. 19.

CORNELIUS ROOSEVELT *versus* SAMUEL GANTT
January 23, 1841.

1. *In an action for libel (that plaintiff and three others had "robbed" a ballot box by taking out ballots for Crary and putting in ballots for Wells, leaving only 157 for Crary), evidence that 200 persons had voted for Crary was inadmissible in mitigation of damages in the absence of evidence connecting the plaintiff with the "robbery."*
2. *The fact that plaintiff was clerk at the polls and had lawful custody of the ballots at the time of the alleged "robbery" does not connect the plaintiff with the "robbery."*

Supreme Court, Fourth Circuit. Question reserved by the Circuit Court, Oakland County; certified to the Supreme Court. Opinion by Fletcher, Ch. J. Certified by Supreme Court that the proposed evidence was properly rejected.

G. W. Wisner, attorney for plaintiff.

A. H. Hanscome, attorney for defendant.

[INDORSEMENT]

Sup. Court 4th Circuit

Jany 1841.
Pontiac—

Rosevelt
vs.
Gantt

} Qu. reserved
Oakland Circuit.

Mem° of *Opinion*

[OPINION]

Sup. Court 4th Circuit Jany T. 1841.

Cornelius Rosevelt }
    vs.
Saml N. Gantt }

This case comes before this court on a question reserved and certified by Hon. C. W. Whipple the Presiding Judge of the Oakland Circuit Court.

The Plff sued the Deft below in an action on the case for a libel.

The publication charged the Plff and 3 others with having robbed the ballot box, and taking therefrom ballots for Isaac E. Crary, and putting in other ballots for Hez. Wells, at the Special election for Member of Congress, in the Town of Pontiac.

The publication further stated that Plff was clerk at the Polls and kept the ballot box on the night after the first days ballotting, and charged that the robbery was committed at that time. It further stated that most of the principal persons in Pontiac believed that Plff and the others had committed the robbery. The Publication was signed by Benj. Irish—The Deft was charged with having put the papers in circulation—

The Deft pleaded only the general issue.

After the Plff had rested his case, Deft called a Mr Henderson to prove that 200 persons had made affid^{ts} before a Justice that they voted for Crary, (then having only 157 ballots found for him on the canvass) and that this fact was known to the Deft before his publication of the libel—for the purpose of mitigating the damages—To this evid. the Plffs counsel objected, as inadmissable—The court below rejected the evid. and the only question made here is whether that rejection was proper.

We are of the opinion that the evidence was properly re-jected—The facts offered to be proved by the witness furnish no excuse or palliation to the Deft, for having charged the Plff with the robbery—The proposed evid. does not connect the Plff with the robbery, and if the Deft will from such facts select out the Plff as the person who committed the al-leged offence, he is certainly without excuse, so far as his knowledge of these facts is concerned. It is stated in the publication that the Plff had charge of the ballot box as clerk, the night on which it was alleged that it had been robbed, and what reason has the Deft to charge Plff with being the robber, merely because 200 men swear that they voted for Crary.

The Plff lawfully had a lawful custody of the ballot box, during the time, and the proposed evid. lays no foundation for a charge upon him.

The utmost latitude which has been allowed under the most liberal rule as to mitigation in slander or libel, never has been carried to the extent here contended for. The report current or information of the Deft respecting the guilt of the party slandered, has been allowed in mitigation, because there is a reasonable ground upon which the Deft may urge his excuse by way of rebutting the presumption of malice, and it has been properly submitted to the jury in such cases, to say how far the Deft in making the charge has acted *bona fide* upon such report or information—

But in this case the information of the Deft that a greater number of persons had sworn that they had voted for Crary, than there were ballots found for that candidate, has no bear-ing whatever upon the fact that the Plff committed the robbery—nor can I perceive how the evid. if it had been rec^d could have warranted the jury in presuming an absence of malice.

The charge was not that somebody had robbed the ballot

box—the evid. offered might have been a reasonable ground to suppose that the box had been robbed—but it does not warrant the Deft in fixing it upon the Plff.

Upon such information, if the Deft will of his own accord charge the act of [to] the Plff he must justify or abide the result—

It is the opinion of this Court that the evid. was properly rejected—and it is ordered that this opinion be certified [to] the Circuit Court.

The above was the substance of the opinion—

On looking over the case after argument Judge Whipple stated that some material facts had been omitted in making up the case, which he thought might have a material bearing upon the question submitted—

After I had given the opinion of the Court he assented [to] it as the case was made—

EDITOR'S NOTE: The above opinion, in the handwriting of Chief Justice Fletcher, was found in file No. 15, Fourth Circuit. The Journal, Fourth Circuit, contains the following entries: p. 5 (Jan. 20, 1841) argued and submitted; p. 10 (Jan. 23, 1841) certified that proposed evidence was properly rejected. Also see Calendar, Fourth Circuit, case No. 15.

D. W. OWEN and I. OWEN *versus* the PRESIDENT, DIRECTORS and COMPANY of the FARMERS' BANK of SANDSTONE
January [?], 1841.

Supreme Court, Second Circuit. Error to the Circuit Court, Lenawee County. Opinion by Ransom, J. Judgment reversed.

A. D. Fraser, attorney for plaintiffs in error.

P. R. Adams, attorney for defendants in error.

EDITOR'S NOTE: The opinion in this case appears in a footnote in 2 Douglass (Mich.), 134 (1849). It deals with the necessity of proving corporate existence. Several papers pertaining to this case will be found in file No. 57, Second Circuit. The original MS. is not in the file.

MONIQUE GODFREY *versus* AMBROSE BEACH
March 4, 1841.

The clearing of wild land not being waste, it is proper to endow a widow in wild land.

Supreme Court, First Circuit. Questions reserved by Circuit Court, Monroe County; certified to Supreme Court. Opinion by Whipple, J. Certified by Supreme Court that Circuit Court correctly overruled objections to certain evidence, etc., and properly instructed the jury on the case.

McClelland & Christiancy, attornies for plaintiff.

Wing, Noble, Felch, Romeyn, attornies for defendant.

EDITOR'S NOTE: In *Campbell, Appellant*, 2 Douglass (Mich.) 141 (at p. 144), Justice Ransom quoted from an opinion said to have been delivered in 1841 by Whipple, J., in *Godfroy v. Brooks*. The case referred to was, no doubt, *Godfrey v. Beach*, which was an action of ejectment for dower. The MS. opinion has not been found. Volume I of the Journal, First Circuit, contains the following entries: p. 105 (Jan. 7, 1841) argued; p. 119 (March 4, 1841) certified that Circuit Court correctly overruled objections made by defendant to the introduction of a certain deposition, evidence, etc., and properly instructed the jury on the case. Also see Calendar, First Circuit, Vol. I, case 188.

A. B. CALHOUN *versus* DAVID CABLE,
A. H. STOWELL, and CALEB CROSS.
March 4, 1841.

1. *A bill in equity which alleges that the plaintiff assigned a land contract to one of the defendants to secure him and another defendant against liability as indorsers on certain notes is not demurrable on the ground that it appears the assignment was made in fraud of creditors, although the bill also speaks of securing a retreat for the plaintiff and his family, refers to a nominal consideration, and alleges that the assignee was to hold the contract subject to the plaintiff's directions.*

2. *A bill in equity which directly charges that a person to whom a land contract was assigned for a particular purpose violated his trust by disposing of the contract in a manner not warranted by the terms of the assignment alleges enough to show an equity between the plaintiff and the assignee.*

3. *A bill in equity which alleges that the maker of a land contract procured from a trustee, to whom the contract had been assigned for particular purpose, a wrongful assignment so as to destroy the plaintiff's interest in the land, and then conveyed the land to a third person, alleges enough to show an equity between the plaintiff and the maker of the contract.*

4. *A bill in equity which alleges that the purchaser of certain land knew that it had been sold to the plaintiff under a land contract states an equitable claim against said purchaser.*

5. *A bill in equity which claims a general right in which all the defendants are interested is not multifarious although each defendant has a separate and distinct interest.*

Supreme Court, First Circuit. In chancery. Demurrer to bill of complaint. Opinion by Fletcher, Ch. J. Demurrer overruled.

H. Chipman, for the demurrer.

H. N. Walker, contra.

[INDORSEMENT]

Sup. Court 1 Circuit.

Calhoun
vs.
Cable et al
⎱ In Chancery

Dem^r to Bill—
Mem^o bill-argument.
& opinion—

[STATEMENT]

Sup. Court 1 Circuit.

A. B. Calhoun
vs.
David Cable et al
⎱ In Chancery.

The Bill sets forth
1. That on the 26 March '33 Cable sold to Plff a certain lot of Land of 40 acres, and gave him an agr^t in writing— The consideration $250., $100 to be paid down, and the bal^s in 90 days—Cable to give a deed when the whole am^t was paid, or as soon thereafter as Plff should direct—
2. That Plff paid the whole amount of the purchase money according to the agr^t—but did not take a deed, as he had full confidence in Cable being his brother in law—
3. That Plff took poss. of the land, and with the knowledge and consent of Cable, and expended 7 or $800 thereon in building, and improving the land—
4. That Plff and Peter N. Girardin in the Spring of '34 being in partnership—procured Cable and A. H. Stowell to indorse for them in their Co business 2 notes for

$309.49 each pay⁰ at the Bank of Michigan, dated the 16 Ap. '34, one payᵉ in 6 and the other in 8 months—

5. That in the fall of '34 some of the Creditors of Plff and Girardin becoming alarmed, they made an assignᵗ of of their joint debts, effects and stock, to the Stowell and Garry Spencer, in trust to secure the said Stowell and Spencer in the first instance, and also the said Cable and others for their liabilities as indorsers—, and others to whom they were indebted—dated 3 Nov '34

6. That to secure a retreat for himself and family, and to prevent a sacrifice of his individual property, for the payᵗ of the Copartnership debts, in case of attempts by said indorsers and creditors to enforce payᵗˢ at an earlier period than would have been practicable to raise funds out of the joint effects assigned—The Plff upon the suggestion of Stowell, was induced, for a mere nominal consideration, to assign all his right and interest in the said written agrᵗ of Cable to convey the said land to said Stowell—That Stowell took the said assignᵗ in strict trust and confidence for the sole benefit of Plff.—and solemnly promised that he would use the instrument assigned in such manner as Plff should direct, and particularly that it should be so used that in case the debts and effects of Plff and Girardin should be insufficient to pay the said notes indorsed by Cable and Stowell, the said Cable and Stowell should be fully indemnified out of the private property of Plff—That it was agreed between Plff and Stowell, and it was the only object Plff had in view in making the assignᵗ of the instrument to Stowell, to get an extension of time for the payᵗ of said Cable and Stowell, for any advances they might be under the necessity of making upon their liabilities as such indorsers—and the said Stowell agreed to act as trustee that object in

virtue of the said assign^t of said agr^t to him—All of which matters the Plff informed the said Cable—and put him upon his guard, previous to the assign^t of the said contract by said Stowell to said Cable as hereinafter mentioned—

7. That the said note indorsed by Cable and Stowell, pay^e in *6 months* was taken up after it became due, and by some arrangement between them, one half of the note was understood to have been paid in some way by Cable, and the other half by Stowell, as assignee of Plff and Girardin—And that Plff has reason to believe, altho he has not rec^d a strict a/c of the same, that the funds belonging to said trust in the hands of Stowell, are amply sufficient for the pay^t of the said note, and said Cable will be fully indemnified and paid for his advances on a/c of said note out of said funds.

   —That Stowell has actually credited himself and said Spencer with the pay^t of said note, as Trustees of Plff and Girardin.

8. That in Feby '35 Plff had a conversation with Cable in which C. intimated to Plff that Stowell was about to apply the interest in the contract assigned to him by Plff, to his own private use, and that he intended to get the land for nothing—And the said Cable told Plff, that as his contract for the sale of the land was made with Plff— he was not bound to make a deed to Stowell, and expressly agreed to make a deed to Plff and take back a mortgage to secure him for pay^{ts} on said notes as indorser —and agreed to give Plff one year in which to pay the mortgage—That in pursuance of this agr^t Cable and Plff went to a Lawyer, to whom C. gave directions to prepare the deed and mortgage, which deed and mortgage were duly prepared and dated in the 23 Febry '35. That

the mortgage was for $470, which was to indemnify the said Cable as well for the full am^t paid by him on the first note, as for the whole am^t of the liability of the said Cable & Stowell on the Second note, then outstanding, and which Cable agreed to take up in consideration of the said mortgage—

9. That Plff executed said mortgage and delivered the same together with the deed so prepared to Caleb F. Davis, to be taken to Cable—

That Davis delivered the same to Cable, who with his wife executed the said deed and delivered it to said Davis

10. That Plff has always been, and still is ready under the direction of this Court, to pay and satisfy the sum so secured by the said mortgage to Cable—

11. That soon after Cable executed the said deed and while it was in the poss. of Davis, the said Cable, without the knowledge or assent, of Plff, entered into negotiation with one Caleb Cross for the sale of said Land to Cross —That Cross being well informed of the Plffs rights to the land, and that he was in poss. of the same, refused to purchase, unless Cable would take up the agr^t of Cable to Plff

12. That thereupon Cable applied to Stowell to give up to him said agr^t—and that Stowell did deliver up the agr^t to Stowell [Cable], and that in consideration thereof, it was agreed between them, that Cable would assume the pay^t of one or both of said notes, that Cable should take up one or both of said notes, and deliver the same to Stowell after Cable's name should be erased therefrom

—(Setting forth written agr^t of Stowell to this effect, —That Stowell assigned the said agr^t to Cable without the knowledge or assent of Plff—)

13. That the notes have not been given up to Plff, or cancelled, but are still outstanding against him.

14. That Stowell has treated the said notes as his private property—And has turned out, and actually passed away, one or both of said notes in pay^t of his private debts—and that Plff is still liable on said notes—

15. That Cable clandestinely obtained from Davis, and without his knowledge or assent, the said deed given by Cable to Plff, and exhibited the same to said Cross who had a full knowledge of all the circumstances,—That Cross purchased the said land of Cable who executed to him a deed therefor dated the 12 June '35—but which was not delivered until Sept. '35—

That the consideration paid by Cross to Cable on such purchase was $600—That that sum was greatly below the value of said land.

—That Cross took poss. of the said land and still retains the same—

16. The Bill concludes with prayer for relief—

—1. That the deed from Cable to Cross be cancelled and given up to Plff.—

2. That Cable be compelled to perform his agr^t with Plff upon such conditions as the Court shall deem proper &c.

3^d That the Defts be decreed severally to make and to execute all necessary receipts and releases and assurances—and 4th to account to Plff and pay & satisfy him for any monies which shall be found due Plff from the Defts or either of them—

And for such other & further relief &c &c.

To this bill all the Defts have demurred generally—

1. To the equity of the Bill, &

2. Multifariousness—

1. As to the Equity

—The Defts in support of their demurrer contend.

    1. That the assign[t] of the contract for the land, to Stowell—was made to secure the property from the reach of Plffs Creditors—

        (a)—Bill says to secure a retreat [for], from himself and family—

        (b)   A mere nominal consideration—

1 Story, Eq. 364
7 Johns. R. 163.
16 id.
12 Ves. 103.
4 Mass. 354
Roberts fraud. Con. 593, 4.
Yelverton 197
4 Cow. 207. 216.
8 id. 406.
11 Wheat. 213
1 Cowan. 171.

That being a voluntary conveyance, it is good between the parties—Altho void as to creditors—

All showing that whether voluntary or fraudulent as against Creditors, it is nonetheless good as between the parties

—Plff should have set out the consideration, that the Court might see what it was &c.—not having done so the Court will presume that the consideration was sufficient—

2 Kents Com. 365. Valuable consideration—what—

    —Benefit to the promissor, or trouble or prejudice to the promissee—

    —The consideration as stated in Bill is vague & uncertain.

        (c)—But the Bill states that the contract was assigned to Stowell as collatteral security to pay certain notes indorsed by Cable & Stowell in the event that the funds arising from the stock and effects assigned for that purpose by Plff and Girardin, should not be sufficient —This was to protect the indorsers—

Why does he then complain.

—If the assign^t of the contract was made to Stowell in trust for this purpose—Stowell had a right to convey, whenever the contingency required it—It was optional with him to wait or not—

—Plff cannot take it away, or ask to have it taken away—and the only supervision which a Court of Equity would take of the matter, would be to see that the trust was carried into effect—That the collattery security was applied according to the agr^t of the parties—

4 Kents Com. 302
1 Equity Cases Abridg. 93
11 Ves. 12. 22

—The Bill does not ask to have the property applied to the purpose for which it was assigned—but, on the contrary, without tendering the am^t of the notes paid by Cable, seeks to compel Cable to convey the land to Plff.

(d.) In addition to all this, the Bill sets out, That the *Leading* and ONLY object of the assignment of the contract to Stowell, was to get an extension of the time for the Plff to repay Cable and Stowell what they should pay on the two notes—

—And Bill states that Plff informed Cable of the assign^t to Stowell and "put him on his *guard*," against bargaining with him &c

—Clearly intending to prevent Stowell deriving any advantage from the assign^t to him—as the assign^t only could be available to Stowell by obtaining from Cable a deed of the land under the contract—

Bill States

1. That a mere *nominal* consideration was given by Stowell

on the ass^t and that S. rec^d the assign^t for the benefit of Plff—and that S. was to hold the contract, subject to Plffs direction—

2. That the object of the assign^t was to secure Cable and Stowell for pay^{ts} made and to be made by them on the 2 notes in case certain funds should not be sufficient for the purpose—
and

3. That the *leading* and *only object* of the assign^t was to get further time for Plff to repay C. & S. for the am^t paid by them on the notes—

Which of these 3 considerations here mentioned is the true one?—2 out of the 3 must be false.

—Plff not only intended to cheat his creditors, but also his confidential friend—

—The Bill next sets forth an agr^t made by Cable with Plff. in Feby '35, several months after the assign^t to Stowell, by which Cable agreed to make a deed to Plff—and states that the deed was accordingly made and put into the Hands of Davis, together with a mortgage back by Plff to secure Cable for payment of the notes—

—Now by Plffs showing what equitable interest in the land had Cable?

By the Bill itself this was clearly an attempt to defraud Stowell of the benefit of the assign^t as a collatteral security &c—

Stat. '33   —But the deed was never delivered to Plff—
P. 342—   and as there was no mem° in writing it is within the Stat. of frauds—

—The Relief prayed is that the deed from Cable to Cross may be cancelled—

That Cable be compelled to perform his agr^t
with Plff, upon such conditions &c In other
words his assign^t to Stowell be Cancelled, and
that the property be conveyed to Plff—

But if the Bill shows any equity to entitle Plff to Relief

2. It is bad for *multifariousness*

Storys Com. on Eq. Pleading. p. 224 §271—definition—

id. p. 226.
Cooper Pl. 182
Mitf. Pl. 181
18 Ves. 80
2 Masons R. 181.—

"The improperly joining in
one bill distinct matters, and
thereby confounding them, as
for example, the uniting in
one bill perfectly distinct matters against several defts in
the same bill" &c

2 Sch. & Lefr. 371.
Story Com. Eq. Pl. p. 226—
(id. 231)

"So if a Bill be bought for
a specific performance upon
a sale of an estate, it would be multifariousness to include
in such a bill a prayer for relief against third persons who
should claim an interest in it, and who are unconnected
with the sale which is sought to be inforced"—

—If the Plff seeks to recover upon his contract made
with Cable in Feby '35—then the bill is bad, because
Stowell & Cross who had nothing to do with the sale, are
made parties—

—If he seeks to recover on the ground that Stowell
is a trustee, and ought to account for his doings as such,
then it is bad as Cross never had any thing to do with him
in any manner—neither paid him money or received any
title from him,—neither had Cable any connection with
Stowell that would make him liable.—

—The same result would flow if Stowell violated his
trusts, as Cable and Cross could not be made to account.—

If he seeks to recover the land upon the first agr^t by Cable, then it is bad for multifariousness, as Cross, who had nothing to do with that contract, is made a party—

In support of the Bill the Counsel for the Plff. contends— That the objections of Defts to the equity of the Bill are not warranted by the case made by the Bill—

—Plff does not seek to have the assign^t to Stowell rescinded —He seeks to enforce it, according to the agr^t of the parties—

He charges Stowell with a breach of trust in disposing of the contract assigned, before the happening of the contingency, upon which alone he had any right to dispose of, by the express terms of the assign^t—alleging that the proceeds of the copartnership effects were amply sufficient to pay the notes indorsed by Cable and Stowell,—And therefore instead of seeking to avoid the assign^t—He asks this Court to supervise the doings of the trustee, and that he may be compelled to execute the trust—

This is certainly apparent upon the whole face of the bill—

2. It is also objected by the Defts, that Plff intended by the assign^t to Stowell to defraud, or delay his creditors, and that this design is expressed in the bill—

—But this objection has been already answered, on the ground that Plff does not seek to rescind the assign^t—but to enforce its terms and the trust connected with it—and therefore it does not lie with Stowell to urge this objection, when he is ask[ed] to execute the trust—

—Besides the interest assigned, is not such to subject the Plff to such a charge—

1 Story, Eq Com. 361.—"To make a voluntary conveyance *property* which would be liable to be taken in Execution for void as to Creditors, it is indispensable that it should transfer the pay^t of debts"

The assign^t was not absolute, but conditional coupled with a trust—

In making the assign^t to Stowell as a collatteral indemnity, Plff merely preferred two creditors to others, if indeed he had any others—

1 Story, Eq. Com 370.
Id. 364.   And a debtor may do
11 Wheat. 48 or 78.   this without fraud—
5 Term R. 424—Lord Kenyon—

1 John Ch. R. 119.—"Collatteral securities to creditors are considered as trusts, for the better protection of their debts, and equity will see that their intention is fulfilled."
2 John Ch. R. 283
15 John Ch. R. 571—Assign^{ts} in trust with a power of revocation is considered fraudulent *only as* regards judg^t creditors, or such as are taking measures to obtain pay^t of their debts.

—So far therefore, is [as] the charge of fraud is concerned, it is directly against the facts stated in the bill.— The assign^t was meritorious on the part of Plff—to secure his indorsers, in the event the co-partnership fund should prove insufficient to pay and indemnify them &c.

—As to multifariousness—

—The Deft are properly made parties to the Bill, and it would have been demurrable if either had been omitted—

They have each participated—

1. Stowell in disposing [of] the contract assigned in breach of his trust,
2. Cable, with a full knowledge of the object of the assign^t, in obtaining the contract assigned, and in executing a deed to Cross of the premises —also in violation of Plff rights—

3. Cross in taking the deed, having a full knowl-
    edge of all the equities of the Plff—

—As to the Relief prayed for—

—Plff not limited to the special relief prayed but under
the general prayer for relief, may have such specific relief as
his case calls for—

2 Madd. Ch. 138—"the practice now is to pray particular
relief, though if the particular relief prayed by the bill cannot
be given exactly as prayed, the Court will assist the particular
prayer under the general prayer; but relief *inconsistent* with
the specific relief prayed, cannot be given under the general
prayer."—

—Mem° of Opinion—

1. Ground of Dem^r Want of Equity in the Bill.
    1. That the assign^t of Contract for Deed, by Plff to
       Stowell, was fraudulent, intended to delay or hinder
       creditors of Plff

—I think the allegations in the Bill do not show a case
which will sustain this objection—

—There is a vagueness and looseness in that part of the
bill setting for[th] the assignment and the reasons and
inducement prompting the Plff to make the assignment—It
speaks of securing a retreat for Plff and his family—about a
mere nominal consideration—

That Stowell was to hold it subject to Plffs directions—
all which upon the first perusal seems to look as though the
Plff was putting his property beyond the reach of creditors—

But it expressly states that it was assigned for the purpose
of indemnifying Stowell and Cable for their liabilities as
his indorsers on the notes, in the event that the joint effects

of Plff and Girardin should not be sufficient for that purpose—

—And besides the Plff does not seek to set aside the assign^t—

He charges that the contract was assigned in trust to Stowell for a particular purpose—and that S. has violated that trust, by disposing of the contract in a manner and under circumstances not warranted by the terms of the assign^t— That the contingency had not happened upon which S. might have disposed of the contract, to wit, the insufficiency of the funds arising from the joint property and effects of Plff & Girardin to meet the liabilities of Cable & Stowell as such indorsers—And he avers that those funds were sufficient for that purpose—

Here then is a direct charge of misapplication of the equitable interest assigned.

—And the Plff seeks the aid of the supervisory power of this court, to compel the execution of the agr^t between the parties —and to correct a violation of the trust by Stowell—

—And that such a power is among the ordinary powers of a court of Equity will not be doubted—

Upon this part of the bill I think there is enough alleged to show an Equity between the Plff and Stowell.

The Bill then alleges that Cable having a full knowledge of the object of the assign^t and of the understanding and agr^t between Plff and Stowell respecting the use and application of the equitable interest assigned, procured the contract, so assigned to Stowell, to be assigned to him, for the purpose of destroying all evidence as to the equitable interest of Plff, in the lands agreed to be conveyed by said contract to the Plff—

Cable had thus taken up his own obligation to convey—and then conveyed the land to Cross.

—Upon this alleged participation with Stowell in the breach

of trust by Stowell, and the getting up his contract to convey the land to Plff—

—And then conveying the land to Cross—there is an equity between Plff and Cable—

The Bill further alleges that Cross, at the time he purchased the land and rec^d the deed from Cable, had full knowledge of all the equitable interest of Plff in the premises—

This allegation, upon its face, subjects Cross to the equitable claim of the Plff—

I think, therefore that the first ground of Dem^r that there is no equity in the Bill, is not sustained—

And as to the 2^d ground, *Multifariousness*—I think, that, for reasons already given, the Defts are all properly made parties, to the suit—The Bill claims a general right, that the legal title to the premises be delivered up to be cancelled, and that the same be conveyed to the Plff upon terms—And although the defts have each separate and distinct interests, each of them is interested in the general claim—And are therefore properly made parties—

Dem^r overruled—

EDITOR'S NOTE: The above opinion, in the handwriting of Chief Justice Fletcher, was found in file No. 1491 (as renumbered for *Transactions of the Supreme Court of the Territory of Michigan*, Blume ed.). Volume I of the Journal of the Supreme Court, First Circuit, contains the following entry: p. 120 (March 4, 1841) demurrer overruled. Entries showing later proceedings in this case will be found on pp. 121, 123, 140, 149, 157, 304. For earlier proceedings, see p. 4, *supra*. Also see Chancery Calendar, Supreme Court, First Circuit, Case No. 13, p. 25.

STEPHEN RAYMOND *versus* GEORGE WALES, MATTHEW HOWARD WEBSTER, and EDWARD WARNER.
March 4, 1841.

1. *Prior to the adoption of the Revised Statutes of 1838, a summary judgment by a justice of the peace against an officer for failure to return an execution could be reviewed by the supreme court on certiorari, even though the statute authorizing the summary judgment expressly prohibited an appeal.*

2. *The section of the Revised Statutes which declares that no proceeding before a justice of the peace shall be removed to the supreme court by certiorari or otherwise, but may be reviewed on appeal to the circuit court (R. S. 1838, p. 399), is in conflict with the above express prohibition (R. S. 1838, p. 397).*

3. *As it can hardly be supposed that the legislature intended to take away all modes of reviewing such a judgment, the circuit court may review such a judgment on an appeal in the nature of certiorari.*

Supreme Court, First Circuit. Motion for mandamus to Circuit Court, Wayne County. Opinion by Fletcher, Ch. J. Dissenting opinion by Whipple, J. Motion overruled.

J. A. Van Dyke, attorney for petitioner.

G. Bates, H. N. Walker, and Douglass, attorneys for respondants.

[Paper 1]
[INDORSEMENT]

Sup. Court 1ˢᵗ Circuit.

Raymond
vs.
Warner Junʳ
et al.

Memᵒ of opinion—

[OPINION]

Sup. Court 1st Circuit.

Stephen Raymond
vs.
Edward Warner Junr
George Wales &
Matthew H. Webster

In this case a motion is made by the Counsel for the Plff
for a mandamus to be directed to the Judges of the Circuit
Court for the County of Wayne commanding them to dismiss
a suit entered in that court by the above named Defts. on
appeal from the $Judg^{t}$ of a justice of the peace.

The affidavit of the Plff upon which the motion is made,
sets forth that the Plff sued Warner, as constable, and the
other two Defts his sureties in an action of debt, and declared
against them, & alleged that the Plff had delivered to the
said Warner, as such constable, a certain execution issued on
a $judg^{t}$ rendered by J. W. Strong Esq. a Justice, in favor
of the Plff and against Abraham Starks—And that the
said constable had failed to return the execution within the
life of the same.—

That on the trial of that suit $judg^{t}$ was rendered in favor
of the Plff and against the Defts for $97.50. That the Defts
appealed from said $judg^{t}$ to the said Circuit Court, and caused
the appeal to be entered in the Circuit Court at the last May
term—That his attorney at the same term moved the Circuit
[Court] to dismiss the appeal, and that his motion was
denied, and that the appeal in is now pending in that Court.
That a supersedeas to the Ex^{n} on the $judg^{t}$ rendered by the
Justice, has been issued by the Presiding Judge at the
Circuit Court.

In support of the Mo. it is contended that the Circuit
Court has no jurisdiction of the cause, on the ground that,

in such a case the Rev. Stat. expressly prohibit an appeal by the constable and his sureties in actions against them for such default of the constable—

The 25 Section of the Stat. relating to Justice's Courts, gives an action of debt against a constable and his sureties for the neglect of the constable in serving an execution, and authorizes the justice who shall try the case to give judg^t for the amount of the ex^n and 25 per cent damages thereon, with interest and costs; and expressly declares that, in such case, "neither the constable not his sureties shall be entitled to any stay of ex^n or *an appeal*, but ex^n shall issue forthwith."—

In opposition to the Motion it is urged, that by the 33^d Sect. it is expressly declared that no order, or proceedings whatsoever had or made by any justice of the peace, under the authority of any law of this State shall be removed to the Supreme Court by certiorari or otherwise—, but may be reviewed and corrected only by appeal to the Circuit Court according to the provisions of that Chapter—And that by the 34th Section, being a part of that Chapter it is provided that either may have an appeal to the Circuit Court, in all matters and proceedings before a Justice, upon which heretofore, according to the laws and usages of this State, a writ of certiorari might have been allowed and taken, to remove the same to the Supreme Court, and that upon inspection and ex^n of such proceedings the Circuit Court shall give such judg^t or make such order, as law and justice, and the rights of the parties shall require.—

There is certainly a mainfest inconsistency in these provisions—one prohibiting an appeal in a given case from the judg^t of a justice—and the other giving a party in all cases a right to appeal when by the laws and usages of this State, prior to adoption of the Revised Stat. the case might have been removed by certiorari to the Sup. Court. and when in the given cases, where by the 25 Sect. the appeal is prohibited, a certiorari to the Sup. Court did lay under those prior laws and usages.

Up to the time of the taking effect of the Rev. Stat. a Judg^t against a constable and his sureties for the neglect mentioned, could be removed to the Sup. Court by certiorari only—the appeal to the Circuit [Court] was then also expressly forbidden. And by the laws in force at the time of the adoption of the Rev. Stat. either party to a Judg^t rendered by a Justice in all cases make [might] take his certiorari to the Sup. Court.

By the Rev. Stat. the right to remove to the Sup. Court was entirely abolished in the most general terms—not confining it to judg^{ts} rendered in the ordinary jurisdiction in civil cases at law, but including all orders or proceedings of a Justice whatever under the authority of the laws of the State—

And in the same Chapter it is also explicitly declared that in all cases when by the former laws and usages, a certiorari might have been taken to the Sup. Court, either party may appeal to the Circuit Court, and have the record inspected and decide by that Court, as upon certiorari—

The manifest intent of the legislature in this provision was to substitute an appeal to the Circuit Court in all cases where by the former laws a certiorari might be taken to the Sup. Court.

It was evidently an oversight, after making this general provision, that the prohibition of an appeal in the 25 Sect. was stricken not out.

This prohibition was in all the former Stat., but then the Defts could review the proceedings on certiorari—

It can hardly be supposed that the legislature intended to take away every mode of review or redress in cases of such summary proceedings before a Justice of the peace, and where too he was authorized to inflict a heavy penalty upon the officer and his sureties—25 per cent & interest upon the am^t of the ex^n

With these views of the subject, the provisions of the Stat. conflicting in terms directly, I think the Defts are entitled to the same remedy, to which they would have been entitled to in the Sup. Court on certiorari previous to the adoption of the Rev. Stat. only modifying it however, as to the form, by taking this special appeal in the nature of a certiorari to the Circuit Court, according to the provisions of the Rev. Stat.

Mo. denied—

[Paper 2]

[INDORSEMENT]

Sup Court: 1st Cir^t

Stephen Raymond
vs
Ed^{wd} Warner Et al

Opinion of C. W. W.
Van Dyke for pff.
Bates, Walker & Douglass
    for defendant.

[DISSENTING OPINION]

Ex parte Stephen Raymond &:

This is a motion made by Stephen Raymond, for a mandamus to the Circuit Court of Wayne County, directing that Court to vacate and order, & dismiss an appeal:

The application is grounded on the following statement of facts, which are admitted by Counsel on both sides to be true.

It appears that Raymond instituted an action of Debt before a Justice of the Peace against one Edward Warner & his sureties, under the provisions of the 25 Section of Chapter 5 title 2 part 3 of the Revised [Statutes]: Warner was a Constable to whom, it would seem, an execution in favor of Raymond was confided for the purpose of being collected: failing in the performance of his duty in this respect the action of Debt, provided for in the section above cited was commenced, as well against the Constable as his sureties George Wales & Matthew H. Webster: The Justice rendered a judgment in favor of the plaintiff, & from that judgment the parties defendants took an appeal to the Circuit Court: upon entering the appeal, the plaintiff appellee moved the Circuit Court to dismiss the appeal for want of jurisdiction: this motion was denied, & the plaintiff now applies to this Court for a mandamus to the Circuit Court, directing that tribunal to vacate the order overruling the motion to dismiss the appeal, and further directing the Court to dismiss the cause:

The decision of this Court upon the application, must depend upon the construction of the 25, 29, & 33 Sections of the Justice's Act: The 25 Section provides that "in case any sheriff or constable, to whom an execution shall be delivered, shall not levy the same on the goods & chattels of the person against whom such execution shall be granted, and on the return day thereof pay the debt or damages, with interest & costs &c levied, in the hands of the Justice who issued the same; the said Sheriff or Constable, and their sureties, shall be holden to pay the amount of such judgment, with interest & costs, to the person in whose favor such execution was granted, to be recovered by action of debt: in which case, & in cases where judgment is entered on motion against him, *neither the sheriff or constable, nor their sureties, shall be entitled to any stay of execution, or an appeal,* but execution shall issue forthwith": Section 29 provides, that "if any person shall conceive himself injured by any judgment of a Justice of the Peace, except in cases where judgment is rendered on the report of referees or arbitrators, such party, his agent or attorney, may appeal to the Circuit Court of the County" &c: Sec 33 provides that "no judgment or or proceeding whatever, to be had or made by any Justice of the Peace, under the authority of any law of this State, shall be removed to the Supreme Court by any writ of Error, false judgment, habeas Corpus Cum Causa, certiorari or by appeal; but may be reviewed only by appeal to the Circuit Court of the proper County, according to the provisions of this Chapter." Sec 34 provides, that "in all cases where either party shall appeal from the judgment of a Justice of the Peace pursuant to the provisions of this Chapter, the Circuit Court to which the appeal is taken, shall have authority to inspect & examine into the proceedings of the Justice" &c with respect to all matters which heretofore, according to the laws of the State, a writ of Certiorari might have been allowed & taken to remove a cause to the Supreme Court: and upon such inspection & examination the Circuit are authorized to make such order as law & justice & the right of the parties shall require.

The 25th Section is clear & explicit: it expressly denies the right of appeal to a sheriff or constable and their sureties in cases where judgment is rendered against them for a failure on the part of the Sheriff or Constable to perform the duties enjoined upon them by that Section:

The 29 Section is equally clear, & grants to any party who may consider himself injured by the judgment of a

Justice of the Peace, the right of appeal, except in certain cases:

The 33rd & 34th Sections prohibit the removal of judgments &c rendered by Justices of the peace to the Supreme Court, but provides a remedy by appeal to the Circuit Court, which is authorized to inspect the proceedings of the Court below, and generally, to exercise, both in reviewing the case & in giving judgment all the powers which the Supreme Court formerly exercised, when writs of certiorari were sued out for the removal of causes originating before Justices of the Peace:

The 25 & 29 Sections apparently conflict the one with the other, and we are called upon to give such a construction to these Sections, as will conform to the intentions of the Legislature, & if possible, to give such effect to each provision, as that the whole may stand well together:

The obvious intent of the Legislature in denying the right of appeal to ministerial officers who should fail in the performance of their duty, was to ensure faithfulness & fidelity on their part, & to provide a summary remedy for those who might be injured by reason of their unfaithfulness or infidelity The provision of law which denies the right of appeal, is well calculated to achieve the object the Legislature had in view: The proceding is in its nature summary, and the remedy somewhat stern, but not too summary or stern for a breach of trust & a violation of duty by a public officer, who should, in all cases, be held to a strict account.

How then can we reconcile the provisions of Sec 25 & 29. Simply by supposing that the legislature never intended in one breath and in direct & intelligable language to deny a right of appeal, & at the same time by a general provision, embracing all but one excepted case, affirm that right: The reasonable & only rational construction, evidently is, that the

general right of appeal was intended to be given in all cases
by the 29 Sec, except such as are either expressly excepted
in that Section, or in any other Section of the same Chapter.
By this construction, each provision is made to harmonize
with the other, & no violence is done to any rule of construction with which I am familiar.

But it is contended that the Legislature never intended
to deprive a party against whom a judgment may be rendered
by a Justice of the peace, of the right of having that judgment
reviewed either by appeal or Certiorari. As a general proposition it is true that a party ought not to be bound, conclusively,
by the judgment of a Justice; hence the Legislature has
provided an appropriate remedy by which such judgment
may be reviewed: Public policy, however, as in this case, may
suggest the propriety of denying to a public officer, a remedy,
which in his individual capacity he might be entitled to; and
such if [as] I am disposed to think was the motive in the
cases like that under consideration.—

But it is by no means certain that such a judgment may
not be removed to this Court by a writ of certiorari: the 33
Sec directs that no order or proceeding of a justice of the
Peace shall be removed to the Supreme Court by a writ
of certiorari, but that the remedy shall be by appeal to the
Circuit Court: The 3rd Sec of Chap 1 title 1 part 3 of the Revised Statutes, gives to this Court a general superintendence
over all inferior jurisdictions, to prevent & correct abuses
therein, *where no other remedy is provided by law:* The
remedy by appeal in a case like the present being expressly
denied, it may be a question whether this Court may not, by
a writ of certiorari, correct any "Error or abuse," that may
occur even in proceedings against sheriffs or constables who
may be charged with a dereliction of duty: The remedy by
appeal, however, is clearly prohibited by law, & it is not

necessary to the decision of the present question, whether any other remedy, than that by appeal has been provided.

I am, therefore, of opinion that the mandamus should issue as prayed for:

EDITOR'S NOTE: The above opinions, in the handwriting of Chief Justice Fletcher and Justice Whipple, respectively, were found in file No. 189, First Circuit—Law. Volume I of the Journal, First Circuit, contains the following entries: p. 107 (Jan. 8, 1841) motion for mandamus; p. 116 (Jan. 14, 1841) argued and submitted: p. 119 (March 4, 1841) motion overruled. Also see Calendar, First Circuit—Law, Vol. I, case 189.

JOHN BT. BOMIER *versus* THOMAS CALDWELL
March 6, 1841.

Supreme Court, First Circuit. Appeal from Court of Chancery. Opinion by Fletcher, Ch. J. Decree modified and affirmed.

J. A. Van Dyke, attorney for plaintiff.

F. Johnson, attorney for defendant.

EDITOR'S NOTE: The opinion in this case appears in 8 Mich., 463 (1860). It deals with specific performance, variance in pleading, statute of frauds, past performance, etc. The original MS. is not in the files. Volume I of the Journal, First Circuit, contains the following entries: p. 107 (Jan. 8, 1841) argued; p. 108 (Jan. 9, 1841) argued and submitted, Whipple not sitting; p. 121 (March 6, 1841) decree modified and affirmed. Also see Chancery Calendar, First Circuit, Case No. 19, p. 37. For opinion of chancellor, see Harrington, Chancery Reports p. 67.

EX PARTE BENJAMIN IRISH
July 12, 1841.

1. *A sheriff, being a ministerial officer, must obey the command of a writ of capias ad satisfaciendum with respect to the county in which the prisoner shall be confined.*
2. *A writ of capias ad satisfaciendum issued from the circuit court of Genesee county directing the sheriff of Oakland county to imprison a judgment debtor in Genesee county is void insofar as it fixes the place of imprisonment.*

Before Whipple, one of the justices of the Supreme Court, Fourth Circuit. Habeas corpus to Sheriff, Oakland County. Opinion by Whipple, speaking for himself as justice, not for Court. Prisoner released.

G. W. Wisner, attorney in person.

[INDORSEMENT]

Ex parte
Benj. Irish:
Filed July 12th 1841
A. Treadway Clerk
Sup Court 4th Circuit

[OPINION]

Ex parte   Habeas Corpus ad Sub[m]
Benjamin Irish

The party (Irish) was brought before me by virtue of a writ of Habeas Corpus: The writ was directed to the Sheriff of Oakland County, who returned, in obedience to the writ that he held Irish in custody by virtue of a capias ad Satisfaciendum issued out of the Circuit Court of the County of Genesee.

It appears that judgment was rendered in Genesee

County, in favor of Ge° W Wisner & against Irish for $50 & costs: that the action brought by Wisner was for a libel, which I take it for granted authorized the suing out of a ca sa, on the judgment:

The only objection to the writ is, that it directs the Sheriff of Oakland County to commit Irish to the *jail in Genesee,* in the event that no goods & chattels &c can be found to satisfy the execution: it is contended that if imprisoned at all, he must be imprisoned in the County in which he resides, & that, therefore, the writ should have directed the Sheriff accordingly.

Upon a review of the Statutory provisions on the subject, I am clearly of opinion that the objection to that part of the writ, which commands the Sheriff to commit the defendant to the Keeper of the jail in Genesee is well taken: It is a well established principle that the Sheriff must obey the command *in the writ:* by it he must be guided: If that officer, contrary to the command in the writ, should undertake to incarcerate Irish in this County, he would, I think, be liable in action for false imprisonment: this would result from the *disobedience* of the command in the writ, not withstanding the place of confinement is the one designated by law; for the Sheriff is a mere *ministerial* officer, & cannot of consequence exercise a discretion which is strictly *judicial:* So much, then, of the ca sa as directs the Sheriff to deliver Irish to the Keeper of the jail in Genesee, is irregular, & therefore void:

It is, therefore, ordered & adjudged, & I do accordingly order & adjudge that the Sheriff of Oakland County do release & discharge from his custody the said Benjamin Irish, provided he be held by none other than the writ of capias ad satisfaciendum aforesaid:

Chas W Whipple

Pontiac 12 July 1841.   Asso Jus Sup Court.

EDITOR's NOTE: The above opinion, in the handwriting of Jusice Whipple, was found in an unnumbered file of the Supreme Court, Fourth Circuit. Newspaper accounts of the case out of which the present proceedings arose will be found in *Detroit Daily Free Press,* Oct. 7, 1837, and *Pontiac Courier,* May 18, 1838.

PEOPLE *versus* PETER D. LABADIE, JR.
January 17, 1842.

1. *Although, in an indictment for perjury, it is not necessary to allege that issue was joined in the action in which the perjury is alleged to have been committed, such an allegation is descriptive and must be proved strictly.*

2. *Proof (a) that a plaintiff, in an action on a jail-limits bond before a justice of the peace, filed the bond as his declaration; (b) that the defendants filed no plea; (c) that, on appeal to the circuit court, the transcript of the justice stated "The plaintiff declares on a limit bond on file" which bond was attached to the transcript; (d) that defendants in the circuit court filed a plea of nil debit; and (e) that no similiter was added or other pleadings filed—is not proof that issue was joined in the circuit court.*

Supreme Court, First Circuit. Questions reserved by Circuit Court, Monroe County; certified to Supreme Court. Opinion by Fletcher, Ch. J. Verdict set aside; nolle prosequi entered.

Christiancy, prosecuting attorney.

H. T. Backus, attorney for defendant.

[Paper 1]
[INDORSEMENT]
The People &c
vs.
Peter D. Labadie Junr
On Questions Certified to Sup. Court—from
Monroe Circuit.

To the Hon⁰ the Judges of the Supreme Court of the State of Michigan.

The undersigned respectfully certifies and submits for the determination of the Supreme Court, certain questions of law which were reserved by him on the trial of Peter D. Labadie Junʳ on an Indictment charging the said Labadie with Perjury in the Circuit Court for the County of Monroe at the last December Term thereof—, a copy of which Indictment is hereto annexed.

On that trial two questions were raised and reserved by the undersigned.

First   Whether the averment in the Indictment, that a certain issue was joined in a plea of debt, between James Ellison Plaintiff and John D. Labadie Medard Labadie and Anthony B. Beaubien, as set forth in the Indictment, was duly proved on the trial of said Peter D. Labadie Junʳ?

and

Second—Whether the matter testified to by the said Peter D. Labadie Junʳ on the trial of such issue, upon which the Perjury was assigned as set forth in said Indictment, was duly proved to have been material on the trial of said issue?

The Evidence on the trial of said Labadie Junʳ on said Indictment which tended to prove the averment in the Indictment that an issue was joined between the parties as set forth in the Indictment; was as follows, that is to say: that an action of debt was originally commenced before a Justice of the Peace in favor of James Ellison Plaintiff, and against John D. Labadie, Medard Labadie and Anthony B. Beaubien Defendants—that the Plaintiff filed with the Justice of the peace as his declaration in the cause, a bond for the Prison limits executed by the Defendants to the Plaintiff conditioned that one of the Defendants John L. Labadie should remain within the prison limits in the usual form—that the Defendants did not file any plea before the Justice—that the cause was tried before the Justice and that all the Defendants were present at the trial, together with Peter D. Labadie Jun[r] as their attorney & Counsel—that the Justice gave judgment for the Plaintiffs, and thereupon the Defendants appealed to the Circuit Court aforesaid—and that such appeal was duly entered—that while the appeal was pending in the Circuit Court and before trial, the Defendants Attorney applied to the Court and obtained leave to plead in the cause and thereupon filed a plea of Nil debit—that there was no other declaration filed in the cause by the Plaintiff but the said bond which was sent up on the appeal by the Justice and examined in the Circuit Court, except the transcript of the Justice, which contained these words—"The Plaintiff declares on a limit bond on file—["]

Upon this State of the pleadings the parties went to trial in the Circuit Court before a Jury and the cause was tried in the same manner as though a regular and formal declaration upon the bond had been filed setting forth a breach of the condition by the Departure of the said John D. Labadie from the prison limits, and as though the Defendants plea of Nil debit had been filed to such formal declaration—and an issue had in due form been joined in the cause.

This was all the Evidence to show that an issue had been joined in the cause as alleged in the Indictment.

The second question is whether there was proper and sufficient evidence given on the trial of Labadie Jun[r] on the Indictment, that the matters testified to by him on the trial of said cause on appeal in the Circuit Court, upon which the Perjury was assigned, were material to the issue joined in the cause?

And upon this point there was no other evidence excepting that above stated, and that hereinafter stated—

The matters testified to by Labadie Junr and upon which the Perjury was assigned related to the admissions of John D. Labadie on the trial of the origination [original] action before the Justice of the Peace as stated in the Indictment and the Evidence corresponded with the Statement.

Upon the trial of the said Peter D. Labadie Junr—on the said Indictment, the above mentioned questions were raised by his Counsel and by the counsel of the said Labadie Junr the undersigned reserved the same for the decission of the Supreme Court; and thereafter left the cause to the Jury as if the Evidence in both respects was sufficient in the law,—and the Jury returned a verdict of guilty.

All which is respectfully submitted.

Ann Arbor Jany 1, 1842:

Wm A. Fletcher.

[Paper 2]

[INDORSEMENT]

People &c ⎫
vs.   ⎬ 1 Circuit—
Labady   ⎭

Opinion—

[OPINION]

The People   ⎫
vs.   ⎬
Peter D. Labadie Junr ⎭

This case comes before this Court on certain questions

reserved and certified by the Presiding Judge of the Circuit Court for the County of Monroe.

The Deft was indicted for Perjury—

The Indictment alleged that the Deft was sworn and testified as witness on the trial of a certain issue joined in a plea of debt in a certain action wherein James Allison was Plff and John D. Labadie, Medard Labadie and Anthony Beaubien were Defts—and assigned the perjury upon that Testimony.

On the trial of the Deft. upon this Indictment, the prosecutor proved that the cause between the above named parties, was originally commenced before a justice of the peace, in debt, and that the Plff in that cause filed, as his declaration before the Justice, a bond for the prison limits executed by the Defts to the Plff, conditioned that John D. Labadie should remain a prisoner within the limits of the County, in the usual form—And the Justice made upon his docket the following entry—"The Plff declares on a limit bond on file"—It was further proved that the Defts did not file any plea. That all the Defts were present before the Justice, and that a trial was had, and a Judg^t rendered against the Defts— And that the Defts thereupon appealed to the Circuit Court for the County of Monroe—It was further proved that the appeal was duly entered in the Circuit Court, and that no other declaration was filed in the cause, except that the transcript of the justice was filed on entering the appeal, in which it was stated that the Plff declared on a limit bond on file;— and the return and filing of the said bond—That after the appeal was entered and before trial, the attorney for the Defts moved for and obtained leave from the Circuit Court to file a plea—and thereupon filed *for all of the Defts a plea* of *Nil debit*—concluding to the country—No Similiter was added—*and there was no* other or further pleadings in the cause.

Upon this state of the pleadings the parties went to trial before a jury, and the cause was in fact tried in the same manner as if a formal declaration alleging a breach of the condition of such bond, by the departure of the said John D. Labadie from the prison limits—had been filed, and a Similiter had been added to the plea nil debit This was all the evidence given on the trial upon the Indictment, tending to prove the averment in the indictment that a certain issue was joined in a plea of debt. And the question is whether the evidence supports this averment?

In support of the prosecution, it has here been urged that the evid. substantially supports the allegation—on the ground that formal pleadings and a formal issue are not required in a suit before a Justice's Court, nor on the trial of such a suit on appeal to the Circuit Court. That the Stat. has declared that appealed causes shall be tried on the pleadings below, unless the Circuit Court shall otherwise direct, and that it was therefore competent and proper for the Circuit Court to try the cause in question, upon the state of the pleadings above set forth—in the same manner as if there had been regular pleadings and a formal issue joined to the country— —On the part of the Deft. it is contended, that whether it was or was not competent and regular for the Circuit Court to try the cause on appeal upon the State of the pleadings set forth, yet the evid. does not support the averment that an issue had been joined in the cause—That having made this averment the prosecutor is bound to prove it strictly—

There is a well settled dis[tinc]tion between descriptive allegations, which must be strictly proved, and other averments which must be substantially proved—Averments *descriptive* of records, writings, and property, must be supported by proof of every fact and circumstance which is necessary to establish the identity of the matters averred—In each of these descriptive allegations, the question, as to the sufficiency of the proof to support the allegation, is one of identity, and any substantial variance is fatal. The same rule upon this subject applies both in civil and criminal cases.

2 East P. C. 3 Stark. Ev. 2 Russ on Cr. Arch. cr. Pl. &c.

That the averment in question is descriptive can hardly be questioned—The subject matter of the allegation is the State of the pleadings, and when the Indictment alleges that an issue was joined in a plea of debt in a certain specified cause depending in a Court of Record of common law jurisdiction, and proceeding according to the course of the common law, we must intend, that there are sufficient pleadings and an issue joined in due form of law.

The pleadings are a part of the record, and when it is averred that an issue has been joined in a plea [of] debt, in a suit upon a bond for the prison limits, we must legally intend, that a declaration has been filed assigning a breach of the condition of the bond, and that such further pleadings have been filed as have resulted in the joining of an issue to the country in due form—of law.

Nor is it any answer to say that the Circuit Court, on such a State of pleadings, in an appealed case had a right to proceed in the trial of the cause in the same manner as if there had been formal pleadings and a formal issue. There was no necessity to aver in the indictment that an issue had been joined in the cause—

But although not necessary to have been averred, yet, as it is averred, the proper and strict proof must be made and can in no case of descriptive averments be dispensed with— Verdict set aside—And a nolle pros. entered—and that Deft be discharged from custody, unless detained on some other cause—

EDITOR'S NOTE: The above questions and opinion, in the hand-writing of Chief Justice Fletcher, were found in file No. 212, First Circuit—Law. Volume I of the Journal, First Circuit, contains the following entries: p. 128 (Jan. 5, 1842) case received and filed; p. 133 (Jan. 8, 1842) Labadie brought from jail in Monroe County by habeas corpus; ordered committed to jail in Wayne County; p. 134 (Jan. 10, 1842) argued; p. 135 (Jan. 11, 1842) argued and submitted; p. 139 (Jan. 17, 1842) verdict set aside; nolle prosequi entered. Also see Calendar, First Circuit—Law, Vol. I, case No. 212.

PEOPLE *versus* LURETT C. HARGER ET AL
January [?] 1842.

An indictment which charges that defendants killed certain hogs of one Davis and did "thereby" destroy the personal property of said Davis does not embrace two distinct offenses under Revised Statutes of 1838, p. 632 viz., (1) the killing of another's livestock, and (2) the destruction of another's personal property.

Supreme Court, Fourth Circuit. Question reserved by Circuit Court, Oakland County; certified to Supreme Court. Opinion by Fletcher, Ch. J. Certified by Supreme Court that motion in arrest of judgment should be overruled.

. . . . , prosecuting attorney.
. . . Hanscomb, attorney for defendant.

[INDORSEMENT]

Sup. Court 4th Cir. Jan^y '42

People
vs.   } Indict—
Harger et al

Mo. in arrest
of Judg^t

Mem° of opinion—

[OPINION]

The People
vs.
Harger et al

This case was tried at the last term of the Circuit Court of Oakland Co., a verdict of guilty was found against the Defts—and a motion was made in arrest of judg', and the questions arising on that motion were reserved and certified to this Court by the Presiding Judge of that Circuit.

The Defts were indicted for wilfully and maliciously killing certain hogs—and on the trial were found guilty—

A motion in arrest of judg' was made, on the ground that each of the 2 Counts in the Indict' embraces two distinct offences—

The first Count of the Indic' alleges that the Defts "did wilfully and maliciously kill *25 barrow hogs of the value of $10 each, three sows* of the value of *$20 each,* the *Beasts* of one Phineas Davis, and did thereby then and there wilfully and maliciously destroy the personal property of him the said Phineas Davis, against the Peace," &c

The 2ᵈ Count is precisely like the first except that it alleges the property to be the property of N. T. Ludden and Alanson Shuley.—

The counsel for the Defts contend that two distinct offences are charged in each count—the charge of killing the hogs, as one, and the charge of destroying personal property as the other—

The statute under which this Indict' was found is in these words.

Rev. Stat, 632 §38—"Every person who shall wilfully and maliciously kill, maim or disfigure any horses, cattle, or other beasts of another person—or shall wilfully and mali-

ciously administer poison to such beasts, or expose any poison-
ous substance, with intent that the same should be taken or
swallowed by them,—or shall wilfully and maliciously destroy or injure the personal property of another person, in
any manner, or by any means, not particularly described or
mentioned in this chapter, shall be punished by imprisonment". &c &c

Several distinct offences are here created and enumer-
ated—and if any two of them are embraced in the same
Count it would be a valid objection to the Indict^t—

If after alleging that Defts. killed the hogs of Davis,
there was a distinct and independent allegation that the
Defts. destroyed the personal property of Davis, then the
objection is well taken—

But I think that the averment that the Defts. thereby
then and there destroyed the personal property cannot be
considered independent of the previous allegation that the
Defts. killed the hogs—

The charge altogether is that the Defts. killed 25 hogs,
the beasts of P. Davis, and did thereby destroy the personal
property of said Davis—

The language here used necessarily precludes any supposition that other personal property, than the hogs, were
intended—It is a mere conclusion of law that by killing the
hogs, they had thereby destroyed the personal property of
Davis—

This concluding averment that the Defts. thereby destroyed the personal property, is a mere inference or conclusion of the prosecutor, and can in no sense affect or qualify
the charge of killing, especially as the conclusion of law is
strictly true—

Mo. in arrest overruled—

To be certified—

EDITOR's NOTE: The above opinion, in the handwriting of Chief Justice Fletcher was found in file No. 19½, Fourth Circuit. The Journal, Fourth Circuit, contains the following entries: p. 13 (Jan. 19, 1842) question reserved filed; p. 15 (Jan. 20, 1842) argued and submitted. Also see Calendar, Fourth Circuit, case No. 19½. The question reserved will be found in file 1182 (as renumbered in 1902).

HENRY A. CASWELL *versus* SAMUEL WARD
February 18, 1842.

Supreme Court, First Circuit. Certiorari to two justices of the peace, St. Clair County. Opinion by Whipple, J. Judgment reversed.

A. & H. H. Emmons, attorneys for plaintiff.

J. F. Joy & G. E. Porter, attorneys for defendant.

EDITOR's NOTE: The opinion in this case appears in a footnote in 2 Douglass (Mich.) 374 (1849). It deals with procedure before justices of the peace in forcible entry and detainer. Volume I of the Journal of the Supreme Court, First Circuit, contains the following entries: p. 127 (Jan. 5, 1842) motion to quash certiorari and supersedeas; p. 146 (Feb. 4, 1842) argued; p. 147 (Feb. 5, 1842) argued; p. 150 (Feb. 9, 1842) argued; p. 151 (Feb. 10, 1842) argued and submitted; p. 155 (Feb. 18, 1842) judgment reversed. Also see Calendar, First Circuit, Vol. I, case No. 209. The original MS. opinion is not in the file.

WILLIAM BREWSTER *versus* JOHN DREW
March 29, 1842.

1. *The fact that an indorser of a promissory note received security from the maker to indemnify him against liability as an indorser does not make him absolutely liable without demand on the maker and notice to the indorser of non-payment.*

2. *In an action by an indorsee against the indorser of a promissory note, a declaration which alleges that the defendant received from the maker certain property to indemnify him as indorser and that the defendant has not "sustained any damage by reason of his not having received notice of the nonpayment of said note" is demurrable.*

Supreme Court, First Circuit. Question reserved by Circuit Court, Wayne County; certified to Supreme Court. Opinion by Fletcher, Ch. J. Certified by Supreme Court that demurrer to counts 3 and 4 of declaration should be sustained.

G. C. Bates, attorney for plaintiff.

A. D. Fraser, attorney for defendant.

[INDORSEMENT]

Sup Court: 1ˢᵗ Cir.
Janʸ 1842

Brewster
vs.
Drew

Mem° of Opinion
29 March '42
delivered—

[OPINION]

William Brewster
vs.
John Drew

This case was certified to this Court by the Presiding [Judge] of the 2ᵈ Circuit, from Wayne Cir. Court, and presents a question raised upon Demʳ to the 3ᵈ & 4ᵗʰ Count[s] of Plffs declaration—These two Counts are the same, only varied as to the description of two different notes—

Plff as the Indorsee sued the Deft as indorser of two notes made by E. Morse & Co, and payᵉ to the order of, and indorsed by the Deft—

In the 3ᵈ & 4 Counts, there are no averments of demand of payment of the maker, or notice of non payment to the indorser, but it is averred that the Deft, at the time of the indorsement recᵈ indemnity from the maker, and that Deft has not sustained any damage—

That part of the Count which avers these facts, is in these words

"And the said Plff avers that at the time of the making of said note as aforesaid, towit: on the 10ᵗʰ day of March 1838, at Detroit aforesaid, the said E. Morse & Co. *assigned, transferred* and *delivered* to the said John Drew a large amount of property to secure and indemnify him the said John Drew as indorser aforesaid, of great value, towit: of the value of $10,000, which said security, property, and indemnity, the said John Drew held and retained in his possession as security aforesaid at and from the time of the making of the said note until the time the said note became due, towit, on the 11ᵗʰ June 1838, at Detroit aforesaid, and the said Plff avers that the said Deft hath not *sustained any damage* by reason of his not having rec^d notice of the non payment of said note, all of which said several premises the said Deft had notice."—

To this Count the Deft demurs alleging for cause that these allegations do not dispense with the necessity of presentment and notice to the indorser

The only question, therefore, which is presented by the pleadings in this case is whether an indorser of a promissory note taking an assignment of property from the maker at the time of indorsing as collateral security to indemnify him against his liability as indorser, is entitled to the usual notice of non payment?

The liability of an indorser, being conditional, and not absolute in the first instance, the general rule is that, in order to charge him, there must be a demand upon the maker, and notice to the indorser of non payment.

But, on the part of the Plff, it is insisted that the facts averred in the Count in question, bring this case within a recognized and well established exception to the general rule. And to maintain this proposition, several authorities have been cited—

Those principally relied [upon], however, are Corney vs. Da Costa 1 Esp. R. 302. 3 Kents Com. 79. Bond et al vs. Farnham, 5 Mass. R. 170. Mead vs. Small, 2 Greenleaf, R. 207. Barton vs. Baker, 1 Serg. & R. R. 334. Prentiss vs. Danielson, 5 Conn. R. 175. & The Merchants Bank of N. Y. vs. Griswold, 7 Wend. R. 165.

It will be necessary, therefore to examine these authorities, with such others as relate to the question—In the case of *Corney* vs. *Da Costa,* the Deft was not held liable, on the ground of his liability as an indorser merely. Da Costa & Co.

compounded with their creditors, and drew notes payable to the Deft, and at the same time put property to the am^t of the composition into the hands of the Deft. And it was held that Deft was not entitled to notice—he having no remedy over; and having in his hands the fund with which to pay the notes.

—The Court held there that the Deft was liable at all events, not upon any condition—And it would be a fraud for the Deft to call upon the maker, who had provided and left in his hand property to meet the note—

In the 3 Kents Com. 79, it is laid down that "if the in-dorser has protected himself from loss by taking collateral security of the maker of the note, or an assignment of his property, it is a waiver of his legal right to require proof of demand & notice."

—And in support of this proposition, the learned commen-tator cites Bond vs. Farnham—5 Mass R. Mead vs. Small 2 Greenleaf R. & Prentiss vs. Danielson 5 Conn. R. 175.

In the case of Bond et al vs. Farnham—Deft was sued as indorser of a note made by Barker—Before the note became due, Barker became insolvent, and the Deft having indorsed other notes for him, he obtained from Barker an assign^t of all his property as security which was insufficient to meet the Defts liabilities—and it further appeared that the Deft had offered to pay the note to the Plffs if they would take foreign bank notes.

Parsons Ch. J. in giving the opinion of the note [court] says that "under the circumstances of this case the Deft had no right to insist upon a demand upon the maker. It appears that he knew such a demand would be fruitless, as he had secured all the property the maker had. And as he secured it for the express purpose of meeting this and his other indorsements, he must be considered as having waived the condition of his liability, and as having engaged with the maker, on receiving all his property, to take up his notes. And the nature or terms of the engagement cannot be varied by an eventual deficiency in the property, because he received all that there was. This intent of the parties is further supported by the offer of the Deft to the Plffs to take up this note if they would receive foreign bank notes in payment —We do not mean to be understood that when an indorser receives security to meet particular indorsements, it is to be concluded that he waives a demand or notice as to any other indorsements." "But we are of opinion that if he will apply to the maker, and representing himself liable for the pay^t of any particular indorsements, receives a security to meet them, he shall not afterwards insist on a fruitless demand on the maker, or on a useless notice to himself, to avoid pay^t of demands, which, on receiving security, he has undertaken to pay."

The Ch. Jus. further adds "The case most analogous to this is, where the drawer of a bill had no effects in the drawee's hands. He cannot insist on a demand upon the drawee, for he could not expect an acceptance, and he suffers no injury for the want of it. The indorser of a note resembles the drawer of a bill—Although once having effects, as he had a demand on the maker, yet he has afterwards withdrawn from the maker all his property, to enable himself to meet his own indorsements, and had not, when the bill was payable, any remedy, unless perhaps the miserable one of seizing the body of a man worth nothing: and that remedy he has never lost."

It will be seen that the decision in this case, does not support the rule laid down in 3 Kents—The ground of this decision was not that the indorser had merely taken security, or an assignment by way of indemnity against his conditional liability as indorser—But that the indorser had taken all the means of the maker, to enable the indorser to meet the liability—

The Court say the nature of the transaction is such, that the indorser must be considered as having engaged with the maker to take up the note— —That having taken all the means which the maker had to meet the note, the indorser is to be regarded as having the fund to provide for the payment, and is therefore, himself the principal debtor—

The case of *Prentiss* vs. *Danielson* 5 Conn. R. 175. is next refered to. This case I have not been able to find—

Mead vs. Small, 2 Greenleaf R. 207. is also cited to support the doctrine in 3 Kent Com.

That is the only case which, in terms, goes to support the doctrine. In that case the indorser held a mortgage from the maker as collateral and sufficient security for the am^t of the note. The case was decided upon the authority of Bond vs. Farnham. 5 Mass. R.

Mellen Ch. J. in delivering the opinion of the Court says—

"These facts present a stronger case in favor of the Plff, than those in the case of Bond vs. Farnham. There the property pledged was not a *sufficient* indemnity, to the indorser, but it was all the maker had. Here it is proved to be sufficient. If the indorser has protected himself from eventual loss by his own act in taking security from the maker, such conduct must be considered as a waiver of the legal right to require proof of demand and notice."—

Now with all deference for this very respectable authority, I must say that, the true ground upon which the case of Bond vs. Farnham was decided, was entirely misapprehended or overlooked—Ch. J. Mellen says the case of Bond vs. Farnham was not so strong a case as the one before the Court, because the security in that case was insufficient to meet the Defts liability, When Ch. J. Parsons expressly says the nature & terms of the engagement cannot be varied by a deficiency in the property.—The true ground in 5 Mass. was that the indorser had *got all* the makers property, and like a drawer of a bill who had no funds in the hands of the drawee, and had no reasonable expectations that the bill would be excepted—was himself the proper party to provide for pay^t.—

So that so far from the case in 2 Greenleaf being a stronger case for the Plff than the 5 Mass. R., they have nothing in common and cannot be compared together.

The *am^t* of the *security* was considered the strong ground in favor of the Plff, in the one case—but in the other the *nature* of the *transaction* between the maker and the indorser was the ground upon which the Plff recovered—

The case of Barton vs. Baker, 1 Serg. & R. 334, was also cited by the Counsel for the Plff—In that case, as in the case of Bond vs. Farnham, the maker had assigned *all his property* to the indorser to indemnify him for his advances and indorsements, it was held that the holder of the note was excused from proving a regular demand & notice in order to charge the indorser.

In that case, and in the case of *Bond* vs. *Farnham*, the decisions seem to have been made upon the supposition that the indorser of a promissory note, and the drawer of a bill of exchange, are placed in the same situation as to their liabilities, and their right to insist upon notice—So far as this right may be affected by the want of funds in the hands of the drawee of the bill, and a want of reasonable expectation of acceptance by the drawee, and a reasonable expectation by the indorser that the note would be or has been paid by the maker.

And this supposed analogy has occasioned some inconvenience in several of the English cases, respecting the rights of indorsers of promissory notes—

—A distinction seems first to have been taken in the argument of Counsel in the case of Nicholson vs. Gouthit, 2 H. Bl. 609, where it was contended, that altho notice of the dishonor of a bill drawn without funds in the hands of drawee, need not be given, yet that the rule in the case of promissory notes is totally different, and notice must in all cases be given to the indorser—

And in delivering the opinion of the Court Lord Ch. J. Eyre assented to this distinction, and admitted the rule with respect to notice to the indorser, to be as stated. He therefore reversed his own decision at Nisi Prius, and granted a new trial upon the strict law, contrary to his ideas of the Justice of the case.

That was a very strong case, because the indorsement was made in consequence of a previous engagement on the. part of the indorser to guaranty the payment of a debt due from the maker of the note, who appears from the transaction to have been in bad circumstances at the time, and who became insolvent before the note was payable.

From his connection with the maker, and from other circumstances, the indorser must have known that the maker would not pay the note, and it was the understanding of all parties that it should be paid by the indorser.

The justice of the case was said to be clearly with the Plff., and under the impression that the want of notice could not injure the Deft, the Lord Ch. J. *had at the trial* instructed the jury that it was unnecessary, and indeed that it might be considered as received by anticipation—

In the case of French vs. The Bank of Georgetown 4 Cranch R. 141—where the decisions of the subject were reviewed, Marshall Ch. J. in delivering the opinion of the Court, says "However, then, the law may be with regard to the drawer of a bill of exchange, who from other circumstances may fairly draw, but who has no funds in the hands of the drawer; it seems settled in England, by the case of Nicholson vs. Gouthit, that the law with regard to a promissory note is different, and that if, in any case, where the note is made for the benefit of the maker, notice to the indorser can be dispensed with, it is only in the case of an insolvency known at the time of indorsement." And he adds—

"In point of reason, justice and the nature of the undertaking, there is no case in which the indorser is better entitled to demand strict notice than in the case of indorsement for accommodation, the maker having received the value."—

Several other cases are found where the same doctrine has been laid down in respect to the indorser of a note, which go further to establish the distinction between the right of a drawer of bill to demand notice, when he had no funds in the hands of the drawee, and no reasonable expec[ta]tion that the bill would be accepted, and the right of an indorser of a note to require notice, notwith[stand]ing there was the strongest evidence to show that the indorser must have known that the maker would not, or had not paid the note—

In Dwight vs. Scovill, 2 Conn. R. 654 it was held that notice to the indorser was necessary under the following circumstances—

A person was a member in each of two copartnerships—one of which made the note and the other indorsed it—Swift Ch. J. in delivering the opinion of the Court, says, "It is true one of the Defts must, in legal consideration, have known that the note was not paid; but he equally well knew that the note when it became due had not been presented to the makers, and pay^t demanded. He knew the fact that exonerated the Defts from all liability on their indorsement; and it would be strange logic to say that this knowledge rendered the Defts liable."

In the case of Ireland et al. vs. Kip, 11 Johns 231, the Plff offered to prove on the trial, for the purpose [of] holding the Deft liable as indorser of a note, that the maker of the note had failed before it became due, and that he had conveyed his property in trust, to secure and indemnify the Deft against his indorsement, and that the trust fund was amply sufficient to indemnify him. This evid. was a rejected and a non-suit entered—and on motion to set aside the non-suit, the motion was denied.

But the strongest case upon this point is that of Magruder vs. The Union Bank of Georgetown, 3 Peters R. 87.

There the maker of the note died before it became due, and the indorser was appointed administrator to this estate.

On the part of the Defts in Error, the Plffs below, it was contended in argument—that the indorser having taken adminis[tra]tion of the estate of the maker, was to be considered as the payer of the note—and as such was bound to pay without demand—& no demand on him being required, it was useless to give him notice that he had not done what he well knew he had omitted. That the purpose of the rule as to notice did not exist in that case, if notice was required to enable the indorser to secure himself by calling on the drawer, this could not be done; and that as he had the estate of the maker of the note in his hands for his indemnity, no demand or notice was necessary. That the law never requires that to done which is useless: and therefore the Deft in Error, who could not by the notice or by its omission have affected the rights of the indorser, or his means of protecting himself from loss, was not required to give it.

In giving the opinion of the Court Marshall Ch. J. says "The general rule that pay^t must be demanded from the maker of a note, and notice of non pay^t to the indorser, in order to render him liable, is so firmly settled that no authority need be cited in support of it. The Deft in Error does not controvert it, but insists that this case does not come within it; because demand of pay^t, and notice of non pay^t are totally useless, since the indorser has become the personal representative of the maker. He has not, however cited any case in support of this opinion, nor has he shown that the principle has ever been laid down in any treatise on promissory notes or bills.

The Court ought to be well satisfied of the correctness of the principle, before it sanctions so essential a departure from established usage." "The fact that the indorser is the representative of the maker does not oppose any obstacle to proceeding in the regular course"—"If this unusual mode of proceeding can be sustained, it must be on the principle that, as the indorser must have known that he had not paid the note, as the representative of the maker, notice to him was useless. Could this be admitted, does it dispense with the necessity of demanding pay^t? It is *possible* that assets which might have been applied in satisfaction of this debt, had pay^t been demanded, may have received a different direction. It is possible that the note may have been paid before it fell due.

Be this as it may, no principle is better settled in commercial transactions, than that the undertaking of the indorser is *conditional*. If due diligence be used to obtain pay^t from the maker, without success, and notice of non pay^t be given to him in time, his undertaking becomes absolute; not otherwise.

Due diligence to obtain pay^t from the maker, is a condition precedent, on which the liability of the indorser depends. As no attempt to obtain pay^t from the maker, was made in this case, and no notice of non pay^t given to the indorser, we think the Circuit Court should have given the instructions prayed for by the Deft in that Court"—

This appears to me a very strong case. The indorser must have known that the maker had not paid the note—It was his duty to provide for and make the pay^t—He had the whole of the makers estate in his hands in trust to pay all his debts—Neither of these facts, nor all combined were considered sufficient to warrant the Court in departing from the general rule.

Not on the ground that the Indorser would suffer any injury—Ch. Jus. Marshall says it is possible that the maker had paid the note before it fell due—or that it was possible the assets which might have been applied in pay^t of the note in question, had notice been given, may have been otherwise applied—

After supposing these possible, but improbable results— He goes on to say "be this as it may."—as much as if he had said supposing even that there could be no possible loss or inconvenience to the indorser from want of notice, yet "no principle is better settled in commercial transactions, than that the undertaking of the indorser is conditional—And that due diligence to obtain pay^t &^{c} is a condition precedent, on which the liability of the indorser depends"—

Had such just views been taken by the Courts in some of the earlier cases, where exceptions [could] have been easily made to the general rule; and the Courts had looked at the *nature* of the *engagement* entered into by the indorser, and had endeavored to carry his undertaking into effect, instead of speculating upon the possible injury to the indorser in certain cases, where a departure from the general rule has been urged, much litigation would have been saved, and great inconvenience avoided—

Even if it were conceded that, as between the parties, in all those cases where notice has been dispensed with, justice had been done, yet a wide door has been opened for litigation, and the uncertainty of the rules by which commercial engagements are to be governed, has occasioned much greater mischief, than would have arisen from a failure of equitable justice in a few cases, by the uniform observance of a general rule of law, equally known to all.

That there are exceptions to the general rule is not intended to be questioned; but as observed by Marshall Ch. J., in the case of French vs. Bank of Georgetown, "The Court ought to be well satisfied with the correctness of the principle, before it sanctions so essential a departure from established usage."

In the case of Corney vs. Da Costa, the very nature of the undertaking on the part of the indorser, was not conditional, but absolute, and on that ground the case was decided—

This was not strictly an exception to the general rule, that an indorser is entitled to notice—

In the case of the Merchants Bank of N. Y. vs. Griswold, 7 Wend R. 165. the indorser after the making of the note, received in trust, an assign^t of property and outstanding debts from the maker, with a power to sell the property and collect the debts for the express purpose of meeting the note.

In other words he had consented to take funds to meet the payment of the note, and to act as the agent of the maker in making such payment. And it was as good ground upon which to dispense with notice to him, as if the maker had left the money with the Deft the day before the note became due, with instructions to take up his note the next day—

There is an averment in the Counts demurred to that the Deft has not sustained any damage by reason of his not having received notice of non pay^t of said note—

But this can avail nothing—no evidence could be received in support of this averment.

In the case of Dennis vs. Morrice, 3 Esp. R. 158, where to excuse the holder of a bill for not having given notice to the drawer of non pay^t by the acceptor, an offer was made to prove, in fact, that the Deft had not been prejudiced by the want of notice, Lord Kenyon said, "This would be extending the case [rule] still further than ever has been done, and opening new sources of litigation in investigating whether in fact the drawer did receive a prejudice from this want of notice or not"—and the evidence was rejected—

In the case now before the Court the property is alleged to have been assigned by the maker to the Deft to secure and indemnify him against his liability as indorser—There is no allegation that there was any authority on the part of the Deft to dispose of the property for the purpose of paying the holder—nothing showing that the Deft had undertaken to provide the means for the payment of the notes.

It was a transaction between the maker & the indorser, by which the indorser provided for security in case his conditional engagement should become absolute, and he be obliged to pay the money.

That the prudence of an indorser, in taking security from the maker, as indemnity against eventual and contingent liability on his conditional undertaking as indorser, should be construed as changing the nature of such an undertaking into an absolute undertaking, by which he would be liable in the first instance and at all events, without the holder's making any attempt to get pay^t of the maker, cannot, certainly, be sustained either upon principle or authority.

We are, therefore, of the opinion that the facts alleged in the 3^d & 4th Counts of Plffs declaration, do not present such a case as dispenses with a demand of pay^t upon the maker— and notice to the indorser—and that the Dem^r be sustained—

EDITOR'S NOTE: The above opinion, in the handwriting of Chief Justice Fletcher, was found in file No. 232, First Circuit—Law. Volume I of the Journal, First Circuit, contains the following entries: p. 141 (Feb. 2, 1842) argued and submitted; p. 160 (March 29, 1842) demurrer to counts 3 and 4 of declaration sustained. Also see Calendar, First Circuit, Vol. I. case 232.

WILLIAM E. DUNN *versus* JAMES MURRAY and J. CLEMENS
March 29, 1842.

1. *Where in an action for trespass there is any legal testimony, however slight, against one of the defendants, the court may not direct a verdict for that defendant in order that he may testify in behalf of a codefendant.*
2. *The fact that a witness called by the plaintiff on rebuttal testified that one of the defendants had declared during the trial "that he had no hand in taking the property" did not justify a conclusion by the court that the plaintiff had abandoned his action against that defendant.*
3. *Whether the declaration of a defendant sued for trespass can be used against a codefendant sued as a joint tortfeasor, quaere.*

Supreme Court, First Circuit. Questions reserved by Circuit Court, Washtenaw County; certified to Supreme Court. Opinion by Whipple, J.; Fletcher, Ch. J. dissenting. Certified by Supreme Court that court below erred in directing a verdict for Clemens.

E. Mundy, attorney for plaintiff.
O. Hawkins, attorney for defendants.

Supreme Court 1 Circuit

Dunn
vs
Murray & Clemens

Opinion of the Court
by Whipple, Justice.

Morell, Ransom
& Whipple

Chf Justice Dissenting.

2^d Circuit Jan^y
term 1842.
Hawkins for defts.
Mundy for plff.

[OPINION]

William E. Dunn   Sup. Court: 2nd Circuit
      vs.   Jany term 1842.
James H. Murray   Questions reserved:
and Clemens

This is an action of Trespass brought by the plaintiff
against the defendants for taking and carrying away a pair
of horses and a wagon: The declaration was in the common
form and the pleas were; 1st the general issue; 2^{ly}, a special
plea of justification setting forth that the property was in
Clemens &^{c} & that Murray acted by the request & under
his direction: The cause was tried at the   term of the
Circuit Court Court for the County of Livingston; From the
case as reported to this Court, it would seem that evidence

was introduced a[t] the trial tending to prove that Clemens
was present & assisted Murray in taking the property: It
also appears that after the defendants had concluded the
testimony for their part, the plaintiff introduced rebutting
evidence, & at this stage of the proceeding a witness was
introduced, who stated, in answer to a question propounded
to him by the attorney of the plaintiff, that he had heard
Clemens declare during the trial, "that he had no hand in
taking the property &ᶜ," this answer it is further stated
occassioned no surprise on the part of the Counsel of the
plff: aft. this declaration was elicited from Clemens the
Counsel for the defts' moved the Court to instruct the jury to
give a verdict of acquittal, forthwith, in favor of Clemens:
which motion was granted on the ground that the plaintiff's
Counsel had abandoned his action against him: the jury under
the instruction of the Court rendered a verdict of not guilty
in favor of Clemens, who was then called as a witness &
testified in behalf of his co-defendant Murray: The cause
was then submitted to the Jury, who were unable to agree
upon a verdict.

In the abstract of the cause with which I have been
furnished, it further appears that the Circuit Court decided,
during the trial that the declarations of one of the defendants could not be given in evidence against the other:

The questions which arise in this case, & which were
reserved for the consideration of this Court, by the Chief
Justice who presided at the Trial, are, 1ˢᵗ, whether the instruction asked by the Counsel of the Defts', should have been
granted; & 2ˡʸ, whether the declarations of one of the defendants should have been received as competent evidence
against the other:

Upon the argument of this cause, the Counsel for the
plaintiff insisted that the Circuit Court erred upon the first

point, for the reasons; That in an action of Trespass against
several, the Court cannot discharge any one of the Defendants, when there is the slightest evidence against him: The
proposition is undeniable that one of several persons charged
with the commission of a trespass cannot be discharged by
the Court, nor can the Court direct a nolle prosequi to be
entered, or the jury to render a verdict of acquittal, where
there is any legal testimony, however slight, against him:
The rule is of universal application, as is founded upon a
principle too firmly established by reason & authority to be
shaken at this day: that principle is, that, in civil causes, it
is the province of the Court to decide upon the questions of
law that govern the case, & of the jury to decide upon the
facts: the wisdom of the rule will not be questioned, & any
invasion of it would overthrow the constitutional & legal
rights of parties: Let us apply, then, this rule to the case
at bar, and ascertain whether under the circumstances the
instruction asked by the Counsel for the Defts should have
been given: It is admitted that there was some evidence
tending to shew that Clemens participated in the alledged
trespass: the *degree* of evidence introduced by the plff to
prove his guilt does not appear, nor is necessary that it
should under the strict rule I have laid down: But it was
contended upon the argument of the cause by the Counsel for
the defendants, that, the plaintiff having elicited from a
witness the declaration of Clemens that he was in no wise
concerned in the trespass, and especially as it was well known
to the plaintiff's Counsel whe[n] the question was put to the
witness, what the answer would be, that its effect was an
abandonment of the cause as to Clemens. It does not affirmatively appear in the case reported, whether the plaintiff's
Counsel was apprised what the answer of the witness would
be,—but it is suggested that when the answer was elicited

it occasioned no *surprise:* according to the view I take of the question, however, it is of no consequence whether the plff had a full *knowledge* of what the answer would be, or whether he manifested *surprise* when the answer was given. What then was the condition of the cause with respect to Clemens, after his declarations were given in evidence; It was as follows: the plaintiff had before the defendants entered upon their defence introduced evidence tending to prove that he participated in the alledged trespass, & after the defence had closed, he propounded a question to a witness which elicited a declaration made by Clemens that he had no hand in the matter: here, then, was conflicting evidence; a portion of that evidence tending to the proof of guilt, a portion tending to the proof of his innocence: which was, then, the tribunal to *weigh* this conflicting evidence & *decide upon its effect:* to my understanding the *jury* & *not* the *Court* was the appropriate tribunal to refer the question: unless there was an *"abandonment"* of the cause against Clemens: But in what consisted this "abandonment" of the cause? Why the Counsel would reply the "declaration of Clemens" voluntarily drawn by the plaintiff's Counsel, from a witness, that he was not guilty of the Trespass: this view of the case would be correct, if the declarations then elicited is to be regarded, as CONCLUSIVE evidence of the innocence of Clemens: whether it be *conclusive,* must depend upon the law of evidence, and my apprehension of the law upon this point, is, that, such declarations are not *conclusive,* however strongly they make against the party who thus voluntarily draws from a witness declarations, like that made by Clemens: To test the question: suppose that three or any other no. of witnesses of undoubted veracity had sworn that Clemens had confessed to them that he committed the trespass alledged against him; would it be contended that the declarations of Clemens given in evi-

dence as stated in the report, that he had nothing to do with
the matter, would be *conclusive* as to the fact of guilt or innocence, or that the *legal effect* would be an "abandonment" of
the cause by the plffs as regards him: the mere statement of
the question, exhibits the falacy of such a conclusion: The
whole testimony in the case, would necessarily be referred
to the jury, as the appropriate & constitutional body for
determining questions of fact:

Allusion was made by the Counsel for the defts upon
the argument of the case upon the extraordinary course
adopted by the Counsel of the plaintiffs in the trial, in intro-
ducing evidence of declarations, when he was well advised,
that those declarations would conduce to the proof of the
innocence of one of the defts: Such a course ought not, &
cannot vary or influence the legal rights of the plaintiff: he
had a right to elicit the declarations, and it was for him to
bear the consequences which might result from its exercise,
the defendants ought not to complain that the plaintiff elicited
facts which would go far towards establishing their claim to
a verdict of acquittal: If I have taken, a correct view of the
question under consideration, the Circuit Court erred in directing the jury to acquit Clemens:

I ought here to state, that reliance was had by the Counsel for the plff, in argument, upon the pleadings in the cause,
to establish error in the direction given by the Court to the
jury: Beside the plea of the general issue, it is said that there
was a *joint* plea of justification, & it was argued that if the
plea is not supported as to all, neither of the defendants can
be protected under it. The books recognize a distinction, in
this respect, between a case where several defendants, in
trespass, plead the gen[l] issue, and where a joint plea of justification is pleaded, but as it is not clear from an inspection of
the pleadings, whether in point of law the second plea

amounts to a joint plea of justification, and especially as this point was not urged upon the Circuit Court, an expression of opinion upon the question will not be given—

II: In the abstract of the case as reported it is alledged that the Circuit Court decided that the declarations of one of the defts was not competent evidence against the other: This opinion of the Circuit Court may have been right or wrong according to circumstances: and as the facts necessary to form an opinion have not been spread out in the case, any expression of opinion by this Court would be hypothetical: the general rule upon the subject I apprehend is this: that if there was any evidence connecting the defendants as joint trespassers, the declarations of one may be given [in] evidence against the others, in the same manner as the acts of one may be given in evidence, against all concerned: the foundation laid by connecting the defendants as being jointly concerned in a trespass, the declarations & acts of each become that of all:

EDITOR'S NOTE: The above opinion, in the handwriting of Justice Whipple, was found in file No. 235, First Circuit—Law. Volume I of the Journal, First Circuit, contains the following entry: p. 162 (March 29, 1842) court below erred in directing jury to render a verdict in favor of Clemens; with respect to other questions raised in the case the Court declined to express an opinion. Also see Calendar, First Circuit, Vol. I, case 235.

JOHN LARGY *versus* PATRICK HOLLAND
March 29, 1842.

1. *Delivery of an award of arbitrators (addressed to the court) to the clerk of the court in vacation is a delivery to the court within the meaning of the statute (Revised Statutes of 1838, p. 532.)*
2. *Although, ordinarily, an award made without notice of hearing is void, in this case the parties appeared before the arbitrators and agreed that they might, after viewing the land involved, make an award without notice and without hearing evidence.*
3. *Where an award is silent with respect to notice of hearing, it is fair and reasonable to intend that notice was given.*
4. *By making the agreement set forth in (2), supra, the parties did not annul the original agreement for arbitration. They merely agreed upon the means of giving effect to that agreement.*

Supreme Court, First Circuit. Certiorari to Circuit Court, Wayne County. Opinion by Whipple, J. Judgment affirmed.

D. Goodwin & Collins, attorney for plaintiff in certiorari.

J. A. Van Dyke & E. B. Harrington, attorneys for defendant in certiorari.

[INDORSEMENT]

Largy
vs
Holland

Sup Court: 1st Circuit
Jany term 1842.

Opinion of Court
by Whipple Justice.

Goodwin for Plff in Error
Van Dyke & Harrington for
Deft.—

[OPINION]

John Largy, plff in Er-   upon Certiorari to Wayne Cir-
ror,   cuit.

vs

Patrick Holland, deft in   Sup Court 1ˢᵗ Circuit
Error.   Jany term 1842.

From the return made to the Certiorari in this cause, it appears that the parties on the 15 day of Sept 1840, "agreed to submit, the demand, a Statement whereof was annexed to the agreement, to the determination of David Thompson, Edwin Jerome, & Joseph H. Steele, the award of whom, or the greater part of whom, being made & reported within one year from this day to the Court Court of the County of Wayne, the judgm. thereon should be final &'": this agreement was acknowledged pursuant to the statute, before a competent officer: the statement of the demand of Holland against Largy, is in the following words "On or about the 17th day of June 1839, John Largy purchased of Patrick Holland certain land in Livingston County described as the S E ¼ & S W frac¹ ¼ of the 28 town 2 N R 4 E being 251 81/100 acres; which land the said Holland has conveyed to Largy: The said Largy has paid Holland $100 on the purchase: the matter now in dispute is how much, if anything more, the said Largy ought to pay said Holland as a just & full consideration for said land." An award was made by the arbitrators in favor of Holland for the sum of $604: upon which judgment was rendered in the Circuit Court: To reverse this judgment a certiorari was sued out of this court by Largy.

Various grounds have been urged by the plff in Error why the judgm. below should be reversed: I shall consider them in the order in which they are set forth in the Plff's brief:

1: The award was not returned to the Court either by the arbitrators or under seal: Endorsed upon the award is the following memorandum made by the Clerk of the Circuit Court: "I do hereby certify that the within award was transmitted to the Court & remained sealed until opened by me in open Court on the 12 November 1840." The 7 Sec. of chapter 7 part 3 title IV of R. S provides that *"the award shall be delivered by one of the arbitrators to the Court designated in the agreement, or shall be enclosed and sealed by them, & transmitted to the Court & shall remain sealed until opened by the Clerk"* It is contended by the plff that in as much as the award was returned to the OFFICE OF THE CLERK & FILED UPON A DAY OUT OF TERM, and not TO THE COURT by whom the same *should be opened,* that the return was void, as being against the provisions of the 7th & 10th of the chapter ref^d to: It will be perceived that the 7th Section contemplates two modes by which an award may be returned; and if the return made by the arbitrators in this case is to be sustained it must be under the 2^d clause of the 7th Sec: was then 1^{ly} the award enclosed & sealed by the arbitrators; 2, was it transmitted to the Court; & 3^{ly} did it remain sealed until opened by the Clerk: The certificate of the Clerk endorsed on the award appears to me to be conclusive with respect to the 1st & 3rd requisitions of the statute: that the 2^d requirement was complied with is equally conclusive from a further endorsement on the award, which is in the following words: "To the Circuit Court for the County of Wayne" "Detroit" "award of arbitration." But it is insisted that the statute evidently contemplates that the return should be made to the *Court in term,* & *by the Court opened:* it would certainly be competent under the provisions of the 10th Sec. of the same chapter for arbitrators thus to return & for the Court thus to open the award, but it does not necessarily follow, that a return made in the manner pointed out by the 7 Sec. is nugatory: The language of the 7th Sec. is *imperative,* that of the 10th *permissive,* "The award *may* be returned at any term or session of the Court, that shall be held within the time limited in the submission" &°.

With respect to the objection that even under the 7 Sec. the award should be transmitted to the Court *in term,* I have only to remark, that in my opinion the language of that Sec does not justify such a construction: I regard a transmission of the award, enclosed & sealed, to the Clerk of the Court, as a transmission to the Court, and the fact that the award is to remain sealed until that seal is broken by the CLERK, indicates with sufficient certainty that the return may be made as well in vacation as during the term of the Court, for if the return was required to be made in term, it is probable that the language of the 7th Section would have been different, by containing an *express* provision to that effect, or directing that the COURT should break the seal: I might have stated that this construction was adopted by this Court at the last term in the case of the Black River Steam Mill Co vs Chadwick when the question was fully considered & decided.

2^{ly} another objection to the award is that Largy had no notice of the proceedings of the arbitrators; & that if notice was given it should appear, affirmatively, on the face of the award. The 5th Section of the Chapter already adverted to, contemplates notice to the parties to appear before the arbitrators: and altho' the language of the Section is does not contain an express direction to that effect, yet, a reasonable construction justifies the conclusion that notice in all cases is required to be given: indeed this would be the dictate of common justice, which will not justify a proceeding of this character, in which important interests are at stake, without notice to the parties immediately concerned: was there notice given to Largy? to ascertaine this fact we must resort to the affidavits which were filed in the Circuit Court, copies of which have been returned to this Court as part of the proceedings in the cause: The affidavit of Largy sets forth "that he had no notice of the time & place appointed for the meeting of the arbitrators, & that he had no opportunity of being heard by them nor of producing his witnesses on the investigation" &c. If this was the only testimony upon this point, the award could not be sustained; but the affidavits of Daniel Thompson, one of the arbitrators, & of one Thomas Gallagher, while they do not deny the facts stated by Largy, give such a version to this part of this cause, as are sufficient, in my view, to render notice unnecessary: They both state, "that both parties appeared before the arbitrators, & agreed they might, instead of giving notice, and hearing evidence respecting the matter submitted, go upon the lands & premises mentioned in the demand annexed to the agreement of submission, & from a personal view & examination make the award." But it is urged by the Counsel for the plff in Error, that the award is void, upon its face, for the reason 1st that it does not there appear that notice &c was given: & 2ly admitting the facts to be as is stated in the affidavits of Thompson & Gallagher they cannot avail, inasmuch as if true, they shew a *new* agreement between the parties, taking it out of the statute, & in that case the award could only be enforced by an action at law. It has been the policy of the law to sustain the adjudications of tribunals erected & chosen by the parties themselves. The award of arbitrators are always liberally & favorably construed, & every reasonable intendment will be made to support them: And there is reason in the rule: The submission to arbitrators is the voluntary Act of the parties—, the arbitrators are agreed upon by them—They are the

judges of their own choice, which implies great confidence
not only as respects their judgment but fairness & disinter-
estedness: It is a mode of adjusting differences which has
always been encouraged, as it prevents protracted litigation,
& the great expense which necessarily follows: with these
general rules in view, I think it a fair & reasonable to intend
that notice was given to the parties: & in this opinion I am
sustained by the whole current of American Authorities: The
reasoning of the Court in the case of Lutz vs Linthicum in
the 8th Peters 165, and in case of Ackley vs Finch, 7 Cowen
290 is strongly in point; in the latter case the Supreme Court
of N. Y. assert, (with respect to an objection to an award
that it did not appear whether all the arbitrators heard the
cause, or only two, a fact necessary to be determined) "that
no case could be adduced shewing the necessity of this fact
appearing on the face of the award itself." And in the case
first cited the Supreme Court of the United States, say:
"Without question due notice should be given to the parties
of the time & place, for hearing the cause, & if the award
was made without such notice, it ought, on the plainest principles of justice to be set aside: *But it is by no means necessary
that it should appear on the face of the award that such notice
was given.*"

I am next to consider whether the first agreement to refer
was annulled by the subsequent assent of both parties, that
instead of receiving evidence touching the matters in controversy, the arbitrators should by a personal view of the
premises determine its value, and make their award without
any further hearing: without an assent, expressed, or implied
it is certain that the arbitrators were confined in the examination of the case to legal evidence, but it was certainly competent for the parties to prescribe another rule for attaining
the same end: they did not make a new agreement, but

simply agreed upon the means of giving effect to the existing one: It was simply saying to the arbitrators, that they repose more or at least as much confidence in their judgment touching the value of the premises, after they should have viewed it, as they would in the testimony of witnesses who could have no better means of forming an opinion: This objection, then, to the award cannot be sustained:

With regard to the other objections, of a more formal & technical character, it is only necessary to say, that this Court cannot, for the alledged irregularity in receiving the affidavits as stated in the Exceptions, reverse the judgment below: whether they should have been received or not was a matter which rested in the discretion of the Circuit Court:

The other objections, if of any force, can be remedied, by the necessary amendments: they are of too technical a nature to authorize this Court to interfere with the judgment—

Judgm-affirmed

EDITOR's NOTE: The above opinion, in the handwriting of Justice Whipple, was found in file No. 200, First Circuit—Law. Volume I of the Journal, First Circuit, contains the following entries: p. 145 (Feb. 4, 1842) motion to set aside rule for return to certiorari; p. 149 (Feb. 8, 1842) rule for return; p. 154 (Feb. 14, 1842) argued and submitted; p. 161 (March 29, 1842) judgment affirmed. Also see Calendar, First Circuit, Vol. I, case 200.

DUNCAN McCALL et ux. *versus* SIMEON M.
HOUGH and PETER McPHERSON, Executors,
etc. of ROBERT FINDLEY, Deceased.

March 29, 1842.

*Although it appeared from testimony that a paper offered
for probate as a will had been signed by a person now deceased
and by three persons who signed as witnesses at his request,
in his presence, and in the presence of each other, one of whom
thought he had seen the decedent sign,* HELD *the supposed
will was not executed pursuant to statute (Laws of 1820,
p. 20) because "All must see the act of signing, or the
testator must acknowledge that he had signed it, or declare
that it is his will."*

Supreme Court, First Circuit, on transfer from Fourth
Circuit. Appeal from Probate Court, Oakland County.
Opinion by Fletcher, Ch. J. Decree reversed.

J. Goodrich & W. Draper, attorneys for appellants.
O. D. Richardson, attorney for respondents.

[INDORSEMENT]

Sup. Court 4th Cir. 1842

McCall et ux. }
vs.   } app. from
Hough et al   } Judge Probate

Mem° of Opinion—
29 March '42—

[OPINION]

Duncan McCall and
Janette McCall, his wife
    Appellants
Simeon M. Hough & Peter
McPherson, Ex^rs of the last
Will & Testament of Robt
Findley, deceased,
    Respondants

This is an appeal by Duncan McCall & wife heirs at law of Robt Findley, deceased, from the decree of the Judge of Probate for the County of Oakland, allowing probate, and establishing the last will and testament of the deceased, Robt Findley.

The cause, by the stipulation of the parties, was heard and argued at bar, at the last term of this Court in the 4th Circuit—

Several reasons were assigned for the appeal, but only one has been insisted upon before this Court, which is that the execution of the said will was not duly proved—

The will appears to have been executed on the 12 July 1838—and devised Real estate—

It was objected that there was no evidence that the Wit. saw the Testator sign his name to the will — — or that he declared in their prescence that it was his last will and testament —or in the last place that the Signature was his—

On the hearing before this Court, the three subscribing witnesses were produced & sworn on the part of the Repondants—

Theron T. Armstrong—one of these wit.—testified that on or about the date of the will—(12 Aug. '38) the testator came to the field where he, Le Roy Armstrong and Saml Clark, the other subscribing wit., were at work and requested them to go to Mr McPherson's house—said he would not detain them long—He did not say what he wanted of them—They went with him to McPherson—After they went into the house they were requested to witness a paper laying on the table—

Mr Hough, one of the Executors, and the person who drew the will, was there, and directed wit. and the others where to write their names—The paper was so folded up that wit. only saw the name of deceased to the paper——Wit. signed the paper & saw the other two wit.—Le Roy Armstrong and Sam¹ Clark sign it—The will produced and shown to wit. is the same paper signed by him and the other witnesses—The deceased was present in the same room near by when they all signed the will as witnesses—No one spoke of it as the will of deceased at that time—Wit. supposed he knew what it was, as the deceased had before spoken to him about making his will—The wit: states that he did not see the deceased sign the paper, nor him [hear] him say that it was signed by him—or that it was his last will & testimony—The paper had the signature of deceased to it, when wit. subscribed his name as a witness—

Le Roy Armstrong—testified nearly to the same facts—and says further, that when the three wit. went into McPhersons house with the deceased, Hough asked the deceased if those were his witnesses—Deceased nodded assent, and said they were—that he signed as a wit. with T. T. Armstrong and Sam¹ Clark—That the deceased was present, and looking on when the witnesses subscribed the paper—That after all the witnesses had signed Hough took up the paper and gave it to the deceased, who delivered it back to Hough at the same time saying something which witness did not notice or understand—Wit. does not recollect whether he saw deceased name written on the paper at the time witness signed it—did not hear him say that he had signed it—

Sam¹ Clark—was present and subscribed his name as a witness to the paper—same paper now shown him— — Before the witnesses signed, thinks deceased went to the table and sign something—Is not positive, but thinks such was the fact—Thinks that after Hough had done writing, the deceased went to the table took up the pen and signed the paper—After the witnesses had all signed Hough took the paper and handed it to deceased who immediately delivered it back to him, saying something which witness did not understand—

Hiram A. Hills—was called to prove that the signature to the will to be the hand writing of the deceased—and testified he had seen him write two or three times, and thinks the signature to the will is the hand writing of deceased—

Simeon Hough, one of the Ex^rs and one of the Respondants, was then offered as a wit. by the Respondants in support of the will—to show the due Execution &c—

Objection to the competency of this wit. was made by the appellants, on the ground of interest, being a party to the proceeding &, and liable under our Stat. for costs in case the decree of this Court should disaffirm the will—

The testimony was heard by the Court, subject however, to be rejected if on examination the Court should be of the opinion that the Ex^r was an incompetent wit.—

The view I have taken of this case, however, renders it unnecessary to decide this point, or to consider the testimony of the witness—

The Respondants also called Dan¹ Rowe as a witness to

prove the declarations of the deceased made after the date
of the will, that he had made a will and left it in the hands
of Mr Hough—Appellants objected to this evid. as inadmissable—but the Court received it subject to be rejected
and disregarded, in case they should be of opinion on ex^n that
it was not admissable

—But for the reason before given it is not necessary to decide
the question, or to take the testimony into consideration—
—Taking therefore only the testimony of the three subscribing witness[es] and the testimony of Mr Hills who [testi-
fied] to the signature of the Deceased to the will—Is the
Evidence sufficient to establish the due execution of the will
under the Statute?

On the part of the appellants it is contended that the
testator must sign the will in the presence of the subscribing
witnesses, or must declare in their presence and hearing that
he signed the same, or that it was his last will and testament—

The act of the 27 July 1818, entitled "An Act prescribing the manner of devising Land, Tenements and Hereditaments"—Which was in force at the time this will appears
to have been executed, enacts

"That all devises and bequests of any lands or tenements, shall be in writing and signed by the party so devising
the same, or by some person in his presence and by his
express direction, and shall be *attested* and *subscribed* in the
presence of the *said Devisor*, by three or more credible witnesses, or else shall be utterly void, and of no effect."—

This is a transcript of the 5 Sect of the Stat of 29 ch. II—,
and in relation to that Stat. the principles by which it is to
be construed, have long been settled in England, and also
in this country, where the same phraseology has been adopted
by the Legislature—

In England it was never questioned but that the attestation of the witnesses must be in the presence of the Devisor, or that the witnesses must either see him actually sign the Devise or that the Devisor must declare to them that it is his last will, or must acknowledge that he had signed the same—

6 Cr. Dig.   It was indeed for some time questioned
    p. 60.   whether such acknowledgement by the Devisor in the presence of wit. that he had signed the instrument, was a sufficient compliance with the Stat., or whether the witnesses ought not to attest to the very act of signing by the Devisor—

Stonehouse vs. Evelyn. 2 P. W^{ms} 264—[3 P. W^{ms} 252]
Grayson vs. Atkinson. 3 Ves. 454—[2 Ves. S^r 454]

But it was finally settled 1 Ves. Ju^r 10 [11] Ellis vs. Smith, when Ld Hardwicke, assisted by Sir John Strange, Ld. Ch. J. Willes and Ld Ch. B. Parker, in which it unanimously resolved that the declaration of a testator before 3 wit. that a paper was his will was equivalent to signing it before them, and constituted a good will within the 5th Section of the Stat. frauds—And there has never been any relaxation of this rule in England—

—Indeed how can any meaning be given to the act requiring that the 3 persons shall attest and subscribe as witnesses— unless this construction be adopted? what do they attest, or witness but the *execution* of the will by the testator?—If this act of the testator is not attested and witnessed by the three witnesses, to what do they attest, or witness?—

In this case one of the wit. was under the impression that he saw the testator sign a paper—but the other two think that the name was to the paper when they first saw it, and when they subscribed as witnesses— —All must see the act of signing, or the testator must acknowledge that he had signed it, or declare that it is his will &c—

The testimony therefore of the Executor Mr Hough, even if admissable, could not avail anything—nor does the testimony of Mr Hills who testified to the hand writing of the testator—

The three credible witness[es] are placed around the testator by the Legislature for the express purpose of proving the due execution of the will, and their testimony alone can support it—

This court therefore doth order adjudge and decree that the decree of the Judge of Probate be reversed, and that the said will and testament—be altogether held for nought—and void—

EDITOR'S NOTE: The above opinion, in the handwriting of Chief Justice Fletcher, was found in file No. 234, First Circuit—Law. Other papers will be found in file No. 12, Fourth Circuit. The Journal, Fourth Circuit, contains the following entries: p. 2 (June 25, 1839) rule for issues to try sanity and fraud; p. 5 (Jan. 20, 1841) continued; p. 5 (Jan. 20, 1841) motion for security for costs; p. 6 (Jan. 21, 1841) motion overruled; p. 14 (Jan. 19, 1842) argued and submitted. Volume I of the Journal, First Circuit, contains the following entry: p. 161 (March 29, 1842) judgment reversed. Also see Calendar, Fourth Circuit, case No. 12; Calendar, First Circuit, Vol. I, case No. 234.

PEOPLE *versus* VIRGIL M. ROSE
March 29, 1842.

1. *Repeal by the Revised Statutes of 1838 (p. 690) of the act for the punishment of crimes which was in force when the offence charged in the indictment in this case was committed did not exempt the defendant from the punishment previously prescribed for his alleged crime, the Revised Statutes having expressly provided against such exemption except to the extent that any punishment was mitigated by the Revised Statutes (p. 616).*

2. *Repeal of the punishment for larceny prescribed by the Revised Statutes of 1838 (p. 628) and provision that larceny of property worth less than $100 may be punished by imprisonment in the state prison (Pub. Acts, 1840, p. 42) "does not affect any criminal act committed under the act in force for the punishment of crimes previous to the taking effect of the Rev. Stat."*

3. *Repeal of the mitigating provisions of the Revised Statutes of 1838 (p. 628) leaves the defendant under the provisions of the act in force when the crime was committed.*

Supreme Court, First Circuit, on transfer from Fourth Circuit. Question reserved by Circuit Court, Oakland County; certified to Supreme Court. Opinion by Fletcher, Ch. J. Certified by Supreme Court that demurrer to indictment should be overruled.

. . . . , prosecuting attorney.

M. L. Drake, attorney for defendant.

[INDORSEMENT]

[Sup.] Court 4th Cir.
Jany 1842

The People
vs.
Rose

Mem° of Opinion
29 March '42
Dem^r overruled,
order that Deft
plead over—

[OPINION]

The People
    vs.
Virgil M. Rose

On questions reserved and certified from Oakland Circuit, by the Presiding Judge of that Circuit—

The Deft was indicted in the Court below for Larceny— Indict^t exhibited and filed 15 Oct. '39—Charging the offense to have been committed on the 6th March 1838—and alleging the property stolen to be of the value of $82.

—To this Indict^t the Deft demurred generally.

The grounds urged in support of the Dem^r are

1. The the act for the punishment of crimes, which was in force on the 6th of March 1838, the time when this offense was alleged to have been committed, was repealed when the Rev. Stat. went into operation on the 1 Sept 1838—

2. That if by the saving clause in the Rev. Stat. repealing the former act for the punishment of crimes the Deft might have been Indicted, notwithstanding such repeal, yet that by the act of the   of   1840, so much of the Rev. Stat. as prescribed the punishment in case of Larceny, was repealed, and therefore the Deft cannot be punished for the offense—

1. As to the repeal of the act for the punishment of crimes by the Rev. Stat.—

In the Repealing part of the Rev. Stat. there is an exception in the 6th Section respecting criminal offenses— It is in these words—"No offense committed, or penalty, or forfeiture incurred, under any of the acts hereby repealed, and before the time when such repeal shall take effect, shall be affected by such repeal, except that when any punishment, penalty or forfeiture shall have been mitigated by the provisions of this act, such provisions may be extended and applied to any judgment to be pronounced after the said repeal"—

Here then is an express provision that offenses committed under the former act which was repealed by the Rev. Stat. may be punished in the same manner, as if the former act had not been repealed, with this exception only, that in case the penalty under the formerly law were mitigated by the Rev. Stat. that such mitigated punishment should be applied—

—The repeal of the former act, by the Rev. Stat. does not therefore exempt the Deft from indictment, conviction and punishment for an offense committed before the Rev. Stat. took effect.

2. As to the effect of the act of the 14 of March 1840. upon this prosecution—

That part of the Rev. Stat. which prescribed the punishment for Larceny, was repealed by the act of March 14. 1840—And a new provision was made by that act for the punishment of Larceny—being the same as that in the Rev. Stat. except that it abolished the distinction made in the Rev. Stat. between Grand and Petit Larceny, and authorised the Court to sentence the offender to imprisonment in the State prison when the property stolen should be of less value than $100 But this does not affect any criminal act committed under the act in force for the punishment of crimes previous to the taking effect of the Rev. Stat.—

Because all that a party convicted could claim under the Rev. Stat. was that, if by the Rev. Stat. the punishment was mitigated, he should have the benefit of that mitigation—And if the mitigated provisions of the Rev. Stat. were subsequently repealed, he was left then under the provisions of the act, in force at the time the offense was committed—

For it will be observed, that the saving exception in the Rev. Stat. is, that—"No offense committed before the taking effect of the Rev. Stat. shall be affected by such repeal, except that the accused shall have the benefit of any mitigated punishment provided by the Rev. Stat.

The repeal of such mitigating provisions of the Rev. Stat. left the offender under the provisions of the act in force when the offense was committed—and wholly unaffected by the Repeal part of the Rev. Stat.—

The Dem' therefore is overruled—

EDITOR'S NOTE: The above opinion, in the handwriting of Chief Justice Fletcher, was found in file No. 239, First Circuit—Law. The Journal, Fourth Circuit, contains the following entries: p. 13 (Jan. 19, 1842) question filed; p. 18 (Jan. 21, 1842) submitted without argument. Volume I of the Journal, First Circuit, contains the following entry: p. 163 (March 29, 1842) Demurrer of defendant overruled; leave to plead anew. Also see Calendar, Fourth Circuit, case No. 20½; Calendar, First Circuit, case No. 239.

JUSTUS SIMONS *versus* ENOS PECK
March 29, 1842.

1. *Property was taken from B's possession on a writ of execution and sold to S on said writ while being held for P under a writ of replevin issued in an action by P against a receiptor who held under a prior writ of execution against B, which action of replevin was pending when the present action of replevin was commenced by S against P.* HELD, *such property was not in the custody of the law at the time the present action of replevin was commenced; hence it was error to instruct the jury that the property could not be replevied in the present action.*

2. *In an action of replevin brought under the circumstances set forth in (1), supra, the plaintiff should be permitted to prove that a prior sale, under which the defendant claims, was made in fraud of the seller's creditors.*

Supreme Court, First Circuit, on transfer from Fourth Circuit. Error to Circuit Court, Oakland County. Opinion by Fletcher, Ch. J. Judgment reversed.

M. L. Drake, attorney for plaintiff in error.

G. W. Wisner, attorney for defendant in error.

[INDORSEMENT]

Sup. Court 4 Cir. Jan^y '42

Simons
vs.
Peck

Mem° of Opinion
Judg^t reversed—
29 March 42—decided—

[OPINION]

Justus Simons
vs.
Enos Peck

This is a writ of Error directed to the Circuit Court of the County of Oakland, brought to reverse a Judgment rendered in the Court against the Plff below, who is also the Plff in error—

Simons sued Peck in the Court below in an action of Replevin for a yoke of oxen—

The Deft pleaded that he did not detain the property,

and gave notice that he would prove on the trial that the property, in question, was the Defts—

A bill of exceptions was allowed, and sets forth the matters upon the errors [which] have been assigned—

From the bill of exceptions it appears, that on the trial the Plff proved that he purchased the oxen at a public sale the 1 Feby '39, made by a constable in virtue of an execution in favor of Le Roy & Munson and against one Wᵐ C. Bowering, and that the oxen, by some means unknown to the Plff got into the possession of the Deft.

And the Plff brought this action—The Plff then rested—

The Deft proved that he bought the oxen of Bowering in Decʳ 1838, or about the 1 Janʸ '39—That afterwards they were levied upon by a constable on an Exⁿ against Bowering, and that the officer delivered them to a Receiptor—and that the Deft. Peck replevied them from the Receiptor, and gave bond in the usual manner—That after Peck had commenced his replevin against the Receiptor, the cattle were again taken by a constable on Exⁿ vs. Bowering, that the officer sold the cattle upon that Exⁿ to the Plff.

It was further proved the Replevin suit of Peck against the Receiptor had been tried in the same Term at which this suit was tried, and that Peck had recovered the property—

It was also in evidence that when the Exⁿ under which the Plff in this suit purchased the oxen was levied, the oxen were in the poss. of Bowering.

—And the Plff introduced testimony to show that the sale from Bowering to the Deft. was fraudulent, made with intent to keep the property from the creditors of Bowering—

Upon this evidence, the Court charged the Jury, that the oxen having been replevied by Peck in his suit against the Receiptor, and that suit then pending when they were levied upon and sold to the Plff in virtue of an Exⁿ, and the Replevin suit of Peck against the Receiptor being pending when this suit was commenced, that the property was in the custody of the law could not be sold to the Plff on the Ex^n or recovered by him in this action. The Court further instructed the Jury that they need not inquire whether the sale from Bowering to Peck was fraudulent, or not, and that the Deft. was intitled to a verdict.

—To this charge the Plff excepted—

On the part of the Plff in error it is insisted that the Court erred in giving the above instructions to the Jury.

1. In charging the Jury that inasmuch as the property in question had been replevied by Peck against the Receiptor, and that suit pending when this was commenced, that the property was in the custody of the law, and could not be replevied in this action—

2. That the Court also erred in charging the jury to disregard the evid. given by the Plff tending to prove that the original sale from Bowering to Deft. was fradulent and intended to defraud creditors—

I think both these objections are well taken—
In the case of Clark vs. Skinner 20 John. R. 467, there is a very full review of the cases showing under what circumstances property taken on Ex^n &c is in the custody of the law—

Platt says the Deft in Ex^n whose goods have been taken on a fi. fa, cannot bring trespass or Replevin against the officer—as *to him* the property is in the custody of the law—
But this rule has no application to the rights of a *Stranger* whose property has been wrongfully taken on Ex^n against another person—
Nor can a Deft in Replevin, replevy the property from the Plff—

But a third person may—
The first point being sustained, the 2^d is of course, because

if the Plff could maintain the action, he had a right to show that Deft claimed the property under a fraudulent sale—

Judg^t reversed—case reman^d with directions that a *venire de novo* be awarded—

EDITOR'S NOTE: The above opinion, in the handwriting of Chief Justice Fletcher, was found in file No. 231, First Circuit—Law. Other papers will be found in file No. 14, Fourth Circuit, and in file No. 201, First Circuit—Law. The Journal, Fourth Circuit, contains the following entry: p. 12 (Jan. 18, 1842) argued and submitted. Volume I of the Journal, First Circuit, contains the following entry: p. 160 (March 29, 1842) judgment reversed; venire de novo. Also see Calendar, Fourth Circuit, case No. 14; Calendar, First Circuit, Vol. I, case 231.

JAMES SLAUGHTER *versus* PEOPLE
March 29, 1842.

Supreme Court, First Circuit. Certiorari to Mayor's Court, Detroit. Opinion by Whipple, J. Judgment reversed.

G. A. O'Keeffe & G. C. Bates, attorneys for plaintiff.

J. A. Van Dyke, attorney for defendants.

EDITOR'S NOTE: The original MS. opinion in the above case is in file No. 201, First Circuit—Law. In printed form, it appears in a footnote in 2 Douglass (Mich.) 334 (1849); also, in *By-Laws and Ordinances of the City of Detroit, 1842* (Burton Historical Collection, Public Library, Detroit). It deals with the constitutionality of prosecutions by complaint instead of by indictment. Volume I of the Journal, First Circuit, contains the following entries: p. 75 (Aug. 7, 1839) motion to change name of defendant from *City of Detroit* to *People of the State of Michigan;* p. 76 (Aug. 8, 1839) motion granted; p. 138 (Jan. 14, 1842) motion to quash writ of certiorari; p. 140 (Feb. 2, 1842) argued and submitted; p. 158 (March 29, 1842) judgment reversed. Also, see Calendar, First Circuit—Law, Vol. I, case No. 201.

ELISHA TAYLOR *versus* ELISHA BEACH
and HARVEY PARKE
March 29, 1842.

Testimony by an employee of a bank that it was his uniform practice to demand payment of promissory notes held by the bank on their due dates, and, on the same dates, to give notice of nonpayment to each indorser either in person or by leaving notice at his place of business or dwelling house if residing in the village, or by mail if residing outside the village, plus testimony that the witness knew from a memorandum attached to the note sued on in this case that it was protested on the day it became due, is "no evidence at all" that notice of nonpayment was given to the defendants who are sued as indorsers of said note.

Supreme Court, First Circuit, on transfer from Fourth Circuit. Question reserved by Circuit Court, Oakland County; certified to Supreme Court. Opinion by Fletcher, Ch. J. Certified by Supreme Court that a new trial should be granted.

Hunt & Watson, attorneys for plaintiff.

M. L. Drake, attorney for defendants.

[INDORSEMENT]

Sup. Court. 4th Cir.

Jan^y '42

Taylor

vs.

Beach et al

Mem° of opinion
29 March '42
Verdict set aside &
venire de novo

[OPINION]

Elisha Taylor
vs.
Elisha Beach &
Harvey Parke

This case was reserved and certified to this Court from the Oakland Circuit by the Presiding Judge of that Court., and presents a single question whether the evidence given on the trial to prove notice to the Defts who were sued as Indorsers of a promissory note, of the non payment of the note by the maker.

A verdict was taken for the Plff, subject to the opinion of this Court on this question—

The note was discounted at the Bank of Pontiac, and was there at maturity—

The evidence to prove the notice, was the Deposition of Mr. Vandevanter, and is as follows.—"I cannot recollect particularly whether I did, or did not, give notice of the nonpayment of the note to the said Defendants—["]

["] There is no memorandum on said note by which I can tell positively whether I did, or did not give said notice to said indorsers—["]

—["]It was at the time the said note matured, the practices in said Bank of Pontiac, for me to demand payment, and give notice of the non payment to endorsers, on all notes which fell due at the said Bank—Sherman Stevens was at that time, an officer of the said Bank, and a Notary Public, and it was the common practice for said Stevens to leave with me certificates of protest, signed by him, to be annexed to notes which should fall due at said Bank in his absence from the Bank—And when notes so fell due in his absence, and not paid, it was the uniform practice for me to demand payment of said notes, and give notice of nonpayment to the indorsers on the day the note or notes matured—And whenever notice of nonpayment was served by me, it was done by delivering the same to the indorser personally, or by leaving the same at his place of business or dwelling house, if he resided in the village of Pontiac—and if he did not reside in said village, to deposit the said notice in the Post office, directed to the Post office nearest the residence of such indorser—From a memorandum on the back of the certificate of Protest, in my handwriting, it appears that the said note hereto annexed, was protested at said Bank; and from the practice prevailing in said Bank, at the time said note matured, my best impression is that the said note was protested by me, and that I gave notice of the non payment thereof to the Deft—E. Beach by delivering the same in writing to him personally, or at his dwelling house in Pontiac, on the day the said note mature; and to the Deft. H. Parke by leaving the said notice at the Post office at Pontiac, directed to said H. Parke at his place of residence"—

This is all the evidence of notice to the Defts—

For the Plff it is contended that this evidence was competent for the jury to pass upon, and they having found that notice was given, it is conclusive—

But whether the evidence was sufficient is not exclusively for the jury to determine—and as the question was reserved by the Judge on the trial, the question now is what direction this Court would give to the Jury if the case were now here on trial—

The witness's swearing to his belief, which belief is founded upon the practice in the Bank or the general course of business has never been held sufficient—Some act done is required to be shown before such general practice can be permitted to be allowed as a ground of belief—

Smedes vs. *Utica Bank*—20 John. 372.

Halliday vs. *Martinet* 20 John. 168—

Where the evid. of notice was quite similar to the evid. in this case—In that case a mem° of notice made by a person in the office of a Notary Public of notice left at post office—But the persons who made the mem° being called as a wit. could not recollect any thing upon the subject—Who put the letter in the post office, or how it was directed,—

—He further said that it was the custom of the office to leave notice at the residence of the indorser, if they could learn where it was, and if they could not discover it, to put a notice for him in the post office; and that he had no doubt that inquiry was made for the residence of the indorser, and that it could not be ascertained; but he could not say that such inquiry was made by him, or any other person.

The Judge who delivered the opinion of the Court says—"If the Notary has stated, that the indorser could not be found, he would have would have made out sufficient to entitle the Plff to recover; but to charge a party on a contract which is conditional in its nature, and creates no liability until certain precedent acts are performed, by merely proving the general practice of the office in other cases, accompanied by the opinion of a witness, not resting on any recollection or knowledge, but manifestly derived from such usual practice only, would, in my opinion, be dangerous and unjust. There could be no security in the administration or Justice, if such an innovation on the rules of evidence should receive the sanction of our Courts."

In the present case the evid. is even less than it was in the case of Halliday vs. Martinet, last cited—

The witness does not refer to a fact or circumstance within his knowledge or recollection respecting the notice to the Defts—He says that from a mem° which he found on the back of the certificate of Protest, in his own handwriting, it appears that the note was protested at the Bank, the day it became due—Even this does not relate to the notice to the indorsers—And the whole of his testimony in relation to the notice is his belief founded, and so stated by him to be, solely on the general practice prevailing in the Bank at the time—

There was no evidence at all upon the subject, and the jury could make no inference or presumption in the case—
—Verdict set aside—VENIRE DE NOVO

EDITOR's NOTE: The above opinion, in the handwriting of Chief Justice Fletcher was found in file No. 229, First Circuit—Law. The certificate of question reserved is in file No. 26½, Fourth Circuit. The Journal, Fourth Circuit, contains the following entries: p. 14 (Jan. 19, 1842) reserved question filed; p. 18 (Jan. 21, 1842) argued and submitted. Volume I of the Journal, First Circuit, contains the following entry: p. 159 (March 29, 1842) certified that the evidence was insufficient to support proof of notice and that a new trial should be awarded. Also, see Calendar, Fourth Circuit, case 26½; Calendar, First Circuit, Vol. I, case 229.

JOHN CHAMBERLIN *versus* CULLEN BROWN
March 31, 1842.

Supreme Court, First Circuit. Certiorari to two justices of the peace, Wayne County. Opinion by Fletcher, Ch. J. Judgment affirmed.

A. & H. H. Emmons, attorneys for plaintiff.

D. Stuart, attorney for defendant.

EDITOR's NOTE: A copy of the opinion in this case, in Harrington's handwriting, will be found in file No. 195, First Circuit—Law. In printed form, it appears in a footnote in 2 Douglass (Mich.) 120 (1849). It deals with notices to quit, forcible entry and detainer, function of juries in justices' courts, etc. Journal I, First Circuit, contains the following entries: p. 146 (Feb. 4, 1842) rule for further return; p. 152 (Feb. 11, 1842) motion to expunge part of return; p. 153 (Feb. 12, 1842); part of return ordered expunged; case argued and submitted; p. 167 (March 31, 1842) judgment affirmed. Also, see Calendar, First Circuit—Law, Vol. I, case 195.

JAMES L. LOCKWOOD and HIRAM BARRETT
versus JOHN SCUDDER and EDWIN WILCOX
March 31, 1842.

Although it appears that a writ of attachment directed to the sheriff of another county was levied by summoning a person of that country who appeared and admitted that he had money and effects belonging to the defendants, the court is without jurisdiction to render judgment unless it appears that a writ of attachment was first directed to the sheriff of the county in which the attachment suit was commenced and levied on property in that county. A suit in attachment must be "pending" before a writ may be issued to another county. (Revised Statutes of 1838, p. 511.)

Supreme Court, First Circuit. Question reserved by Circuit Court, Wayne County; certified to Supreme Court. Opinion by Fletcher, Ch. J. Certified by Supreme Court that motion to quash attachment and subsequent proceedings should be granted.

J. G. Atterbury, attorney for plaintiff.
A. D. Fraser, attorney for defendant.

[INDORSEMENT]

Sup. Court 1st Cir. Jany '42

Lockwood et al
vs.
Scudder et al }

Mo. to quash
Attachment—

Mem° of opinion
29 March '42

[OPINION]

James L. Lockwood &
Hiram Barrett
vs.
John H. Scudder &
Edwin Wilcox

Motion to quash and set aside proceedings on a writ of Attachment. Certified from Wayne Circuit, Court, on a statement of Facts agreed upon by the Attys of the parties.

From the facts agreed on it appears that the Plffs on the 2 Feby '41, obtained from the Clerk of the Cir. Court of Wayne Co. on the usual affid^t—of indebtness and that Defts were non residents a writ of Attach. against the Deft, returnable the next May term—And afterwards on the same day, filed an affid^t that Defts had property in the County of Hillsdale, and another affid^t that Henry A. Delavan of the Co. of Hillsdale, had monies & effects in his hands belonging to the Defts—And upon these affid^{ts}—obtained another writ of Attach^t directed to the Shff of Hillsdale County and returnable at the said May term. To the the first writ, directed to the Shff of Wayne County, the Shff returned that he could find no goods, &^{c}&^{c} in the County where onto levy the Attach^t—

Under the 2^d writ of Attach^t directed to the Shff of Hillsdale, H. A. Delavan was summoned as Garnishee, and on the return of the writ appeared and admitted that he had moneys and effects of Defts in his hands—

At the May Term '41 the Defts Atty moved the Court below to quash & set aside all the proceedings.

The grounds relied upon in support of this mo. are

1. That as the writ directed to the Shff of Wayne Co. was not levied on any property, the second writ directed to the Shff of Hillsdale Co. was issued without any authority of law—

2. That the Cir. Court for the County of Wayne could only
acquire jurisdiction of the cause by return of the writ of
Attach[t] upon property within that County, and as no property
was attached on that writ, or any other proceedings had upon
it, by which the Cir. Court could acquire jurisdiction, that
Court cannot take jurisdiction of the cause in virtue of the
issuing and service of the writ directed to Hillsdale Co.

3. That if the writ of Attach[t] issued to the County of Hillsdale was regularly issued, yet the Plffs could not on such
writ, proceed against the rights, credits &[c] in the hands of the
Garnishee, but could only proceed to attach the lands, tenements, goods or chattels of the Defts situate in that County—

In opposition to the motion, and in support of the proceedings it is contended

That the Stat. authorised the issuing of the second writ of
Attach[t], on the taking of the writ of Attach[t] in the proper
County; and that the jurisdiction of the Court over the cause
on the service of the 2[d] writ, was not dependent upon the taking of property on the original writ—And that inasmuch as
the Statutes directs that the same proceeding shall be had
upon the 2[d] writ as upon the original writ—The Plffs had a
right to Garnishee any one having moneys, credits or effects
in his hands belonging to the Defts—& that *choses* in *action,*
are properly included under terms "goods & chattels" mentioned in the Stat.—

The determination of the questions raised in this case will
depend upon the construction of the Stat. for—

It is not, and cannot be questioned, that the Legislature
may, if it deems proper, give jurisdiction to the Circuit Court
of any County in cases of Attach[t] by the service of a writ of
Attachment in any other County in the State—

The first seventeen Sections of Chap. 1, Title 4, Part 3[d]
of the Rev. Stat. provide for the issuing, and serving writs of
Attach[ts] and the manner of proceeding to judg[t]—

The 18th Sect., under which the 2^d writ of Attach^t, was issued in this case, provides, that "In all cases of Attachments in virtue of the provisions of this Chapter, if the Plff, or some other person in his behalf, shall make and file with the Clerk an affid^t, stating therein that he believes that the Deft in Attach^t, has lands, tenements, goods or chattels, situate in any other county in this state, naming therein the county, the clerk shall, on application in behalf of the Plff, make out and seal another writ of attach^t, directed to the Shff, or other proper officer of the County in which such property shall be, who shall serve and return the same in the same manner, and under the same liabilities and penalties, as if such writ had issued, and been made returnable in his own County: and on such writ being executed, the same proceedings shall be had, as hereinbefore prescribed—"

The contingency, declared by the Stat., upon which a second writ may be taken into another county, is the pendency of an attach^t in virtue of the previous provisions of that Chapter.

The words of the Statute are " in all cases of Attach^t" &c. seem to me to require that a suit in Attach^t be pending—that property has been attached on the original writ, or a Garnishee summoned, so as to give the Court jurisdiction, on the original writ, before another writ may be issued into another County—

It does not appear to have been the intention of the Legislature to give jurisdiction by the issuing of the second writ, but when jurisdiction has been acquired by an attach^t of property, or by summoning the Garnishee under the original writ, to give additional and further process, to perfect the remedy, and reach other property of the Defts.

Such, we should naturally suppose was the intention of the Legislature, and there is nothing in the Stat. which requires a different construction—On the contrary, the very language of the Stat. seems to require such a construction—

The very language employed seems to require, that, before the second writ shall isssue, an attachment shall be pending over which the Court has jurisdiction—

The language is "In *all cases of Attachment* in *virtue* of the *provisions* of this chapter" — —

This does not mean, merely the issuing of the writ—It includes also such proceedings on the writ, as to give the Court jurisdiction, and when that jurisdiction has attached, then the Plffs may proceed, under the 18th Section, to bring within the jurisdiction of the Court any property which may be found in another County—

—And besides, if jurisdiction may be acquired in virtue only of the service of the collatteral writ, a suit may be commenced in a Cir. Court in any County, when there is no property, and for the very purpose of attaching property in another County—For in order to obtain a writ of Attach[t] it is not necessary that an affid[t] should be made stating that the Deft has property in the County.—

Statutes of this description, giving a special remedy in derogation of Common law rights, are to be strictly construed

Mo. granted—&°

EDITOR'S NOTE: The above opinion, in the handwriting of Chief Justice Fletcher, was found in file No. 247, First Circuit—Law. Volume I of the Journal, First Circuit, contains the following entry: p. 168 (March 31 1842) writs of attachment issued in the courts below and all subsequent proceedings thereon, quashed. Also see Calendar, First Circuit, I, case No. 247.

LUTHER MOSES *versus* STEAM BOAT MISSOURI
March 31, 1842.

Supreme Court, First Circuit. Questions reserved by Circuit Court, Wayne County; certified to Supreme Court. Opinion per curiam. Certified by Supreme Court that demurrer to plea should be sustained.

. . . ., attorney for plaintiff.

. . . ., attorney for defendant.

EDITOR's NOTE: The original MS. opinion in this case has not been found. In printed form, it appears in 1 Mich. 507 (Appendix) (1852). It deals with application of statute giving liens on boats, causes of action arising outside of state, etc. Volume I of the Journal, First Circuit, contains the following entries: p. 147 (Feb. 5, 1842) argued and submitted; p. 169 (March 31, 1842) demurrer of plaintiff to defendant's plea sustained. Also see Calendar, First Circuit—Law, case No. 248.

MORRISON PAULDING *versus* ROSS WILKINS and JOHN S. BAGG impleaded with ELIJAH J. ROBERTS
March 31, 1842.

1. *A writ of error sued out in the names of two of three persons against whom a joint judgment was rendered should be quashed unless an amendment is allowed.*
2. *At common law a writ of error may not be amended by adding a party.*
3. *In Michigan the statute authorizing amendments in substance (Revised Statutes of 1838, p. 461) does not apply to proceedings in error. Such proceedings, in the absence of usage or court rules changing the common law (id., p. 522), may be amended only in form (id., p. 461.).*

Supreme Court, First Circuit. Error to Circuit Court, Wayne County. Opinion by Fletcher, Ch. J. Writ of error quashed.

D. E. Harbaugh & Rowland, attorneys for plaintiff in error.

D. Goodwin, attorney for defendant in error.

[INDORSEMENT]

Sup. Court 1ˢᵗ Cir.
Jany 1842

Paulding
vs.
Bagg et al ⎬ Writ of Error

Mo. to quash &
Mo. to amend.
29 March '42
Mem° of *Opinion.*

[OPINION]

Morrison Paulding
vs.
Ross Wilkins & John S. ⎬ Writ of Error to Wayne Circuit
Bagg, J^r impleaded with ⎬ Court
E. J. Roberts

A motion is made by the Defts. in Error that the Writ be set aside and quashed, on the ground that judg^t in the Court below was rendered against three Defts, to wit the present Defts in Error—Wilkins and Bagg, and also against Elijah J. Roberts.

From the return of the record to the writ of Error it appears that Judg^t was rendered against all the three Defts below.

The motion must be granted unless, the Court shall grant leave to amend the writ of Error, on the motion made by Plffs in Error.

The only question therefore is whether the amendment shall be allowed.

In support of the mo. to amend the counsel for the Plff relies upon the Sect. 20 & 21, Chap. 8, Title 2 part 3^d of the Rev. Stat. Sect. 20 declares that "The Court in which any civil action is pending, may at any time before judg^t rendered therein, allow amendments, either in form or substance, of any process, pleading or proceedings in such action, on such terms as shall be just and reasonable"—

The counsel for the Defts contend that this provision does not include Writs of Error, but only original suits pending in Court and before final judg^t therein—in as much as there is also in the Rev. Stat. express provision made for amendments in causes pending on Writ of Error. The Sect. 21 of the Chap. above cited, providing that defects or imperfections in matter of form found in the record, or proceedings, may be amended by the Court into which the record shall be removed by Writ of error.

And that by Chap. 4. Title 4. p^t 3 of the Rev. Stat. regulates the proceedings on writ of error.

Sect. 6 is in these words "The proceedings upon writs of error as to the assignment of error, and as to the appearance of the Deft in error, and the pleadings, judg^t and *all other matters* not herein provided for, shall be according to the Course of the Common law, as modified by the practice and usage in this State, and such general rules as shall be made by the Supreme Court."

We think the 20 Sect. does not relate to amendments on Writ of Error—The amendments there allowed are expressly limited to amendments before *final* judg^t and the Judg^t in the Circuit Court was a *final* judg^t—The judg^t denominated final, does not mean a judg^t on a writ of error in the appellate Court.

—And the statute having provided expressly for amendments in causes pending on Writs of Error, this court must be governed, in deciding this motion, by the course of the Com.

Law, and the practice and usage in this State—Because this court has not by any general rules provided for amendments—

Nor has any usage or practice obtained in this State except the course of the Com. law practice in this respect.

By the practice of the Com. law a writ of error cannot be amended by adding another party.

Nor is [it] allowed in England since the 5 G. 1 Ch. 13 which authorizes amendment in all writs of Error wherein there shall be *any variance from the original record, or other defect.*

One case is found (2 St. 682) where an amendment was allowed by adding other parties; but this has been overruled—2 Str. 1110—1 Lord Ray^m 71   2 Lord Ray^m 1403. & 8 T. R. 302.

In the case of Andrews & another, vs. Bostwich, 3 Mass R. where 2 only of those Defts against whom judg^t was rendered, brought error, the writ was quash^d.

The case of Clapp vs. Bromagham et al, 8 Cowan & 9 Cowan, in the Court of Errors, cited in support of the mo. to amend, does not apply to this question—That was a Writ of Error on a Judg^t of Partition of real estate—

The Petition was filed against Clapp, and others unknown, which was in conformity with the requirements of the Stat. respecting partition—

Clapp, the only one of the respondents named, or known, brought writ of error in his own name, omitting the words, "and others unknown["]—

—Deft in Error moved to quash on the ground that all the Respondants had not joined in bringing error—Plff in Error moved to amend by adding, and others unknown—The amendment was allowed, on the ground that it was a matter of form—merely descriptive of the proceedings—

And Spencer, Senator, in giving the opinion of the Court,

said the proceedings below were not according to the course of the Com. law, but peculiar, and given by the Stat. which declares that "any of the parties to such judg^t may bring writ of Error.—The judg^t determines nothing, nor can this court determine any thing respecting the persons "unknown."["]

The only question which can be agitated in this court relates to the rights of Clapp, the Plff in Error.

The practice of summons & severance does not apply. The reason given why all the Defts should join in a Writ of Error, is to prevent multiplicity of suits—that is, different suits presenting the same question, but if the judg^t in partition be final, the same question will not be presented on different writs of error—But in this case the record is not correctly described—and the amendment was allowed.—

It will be seen therefore that in the case of Clapp vs. Bromagham, the amendment was allowed not for the purpose of adding substantially other parties, but merely that the writ might correspond with the description of the cause in the record—and on the ground that the proceedings were not according to the course of the Com. law.

This same question was decided in this Court on the 5 March '41 in the case of Ives vs. Chaffee—that was originally a Suit appealed from a justice of the peace into the Cir. Court of Wayne Co.—

Judg^t was rendered in the Cir. Court against Ives the appellant, and Dubois his surety—Ives only sued out a Writ of Error—A mo. was made to quash on the ground that Dubois ought to have joined—and a Mo. by Plff to amend— The Mo. to amend was denied, on the authorities above cited —and the writ was quashed—Mo. to amend denied & the mo. to quash is granted—

EDITOR's NOTE: The above opinion, in the handwriting of Chief Justice Fletcher, was found in file No. 168, First Circuit—Law. Volume I of the Journal, First Circuit, contains the following entries: p. 104 (Jan. 6 1841) defendant in error ordered to file joinder; p. 108 (Jan. 9, 1841) motion to set aside above order; p. 109 (Jan. 11, 1841) order set aside; p. 127 (Jan. 5, 1842) motion to quash writ of error; p. 129 (Jan. 6, 1842) motion argued and submitted; p. 131 (Jan. 7, 1842) motion to amend writ of error; p. 135 (Jan. 11, 1842) motion argued; p. 167 (March 31, 1842) writ of error quashed. Also see Calendar, First Circuit—Law, Vol. I, case No. 168.

ALBERT H. PORTER and CHARLES PARSONS *versus* ARTHUR G. SPARHAWK and SAMUEL SHERWOOD
March 31, 1842.

A person sued as principal, who has defaulted and consents to testify, is a competent witness for the plaintiff against a codefendant sued as secondarily liable on the same contract.

Supreme Court, First Circuit, on transfer from Fourth Circuit. Question reserved by Circuit Court, Oakland County; certified to Supreme Court. Opinion by Fletcher, Ch. J. Certified by Supreme Court that Sparhawk is a competent witness for the plaintiffs.

............., attorney for plaintiffs.
............., attorney for defendants.

[INDORSEMENT]

Sup. Court 4 Cir. Jany 1842

Porter et al
vs
Sparhawk et al   } Mem° of Opinion

Aynur
vs.
Knowlton et al   } March 31—decided—

[OPINION]

Porter & Parsons
vs.
Sparhawk & Sherwood

This is a case certified to this court from the Oakland Circuit by the Presiding [Judge] of that Court, and presents only this question, Whether in assumpsit against two defts, and one of them, the principal in the Contract having suffered judgment against him by default, is a competent wit. for the Plff to support the action against the other deft, he the principal, consenting to testify?

The decisions upon this question have been somewhat con[tra]dictory both in England, and in the United States.

In the case of *Chapman vs Graves 2 Campb. R. 333* Le Blanc J. said "The general rule is that a party to the record is not admissible as a Witness"—and the evidence was rejected.

In Emmet vs. Bradley, 7 Taunton R. 599, 3 of 5 Defts pleaded Bankruptcy, and the evidence having established their plea, it was proposed to enter a verdict for them forthwith, and to call them as witnesses, to show that the other two were not joint contractors, but the evidence was rejected.

And in Mant vs. Mainwaring, 8 Taunt. 139, a co defendant who had suffered judg^t by default, was not allowed when called as a witness for the Plff to show that the other defts were his partners.

Dallas and Park Justices, on the ground that he was interested—But Burrough Justice, said "The general rule is, that no party to an action can be examined but by consent; and all the parties to the record must consent; and without such consent none can be called. In this case, he continues, the codefendants objected, and therefore the witness was properly rejected"—

Cited 8 Taunt.
139

In the case of Brown vs. Brown, 4 Taunt. 752 it was decided that a witness who had suffered judg^t by default, could not be called for the plff to prove the partnership between himself and the other Deft., because he had an interest in fixing the other Deft. with a proportion of the debt; inasmuch as, having suffered judg^t by default, if the Plff failed in the joint action, he the Witness would be liable for the whole in a separate action.

But in several other cases it has been held that when a party to the suit had suffered judg^t by Deft. and had no interest in favor of the party calling him, that he was a competent witness.

Ward vs. Haydon and another, 2 Esp. N. P. C. 553

Raven vs. Dunning 3 Esp. N. P. C. 25. Buller N. P. 98.

But the latest case I have seen, decided in the Com. Pleas in England in 1831, appears to me to lay down the correct rule.

This was the case of Worrall vs. Ja^s Jones, Wm Baker & Ed. Jones, 7 Bingh. 395—Debt on Bond, conditioned for the pay^t of rent by Edward Jones, as tenant to the Plff, pursuant to an ag^{rt} made in Jany 1806.

The two Jones's suffered Judg^t by default, and Baker pleaded that the tenancy under the ag^{rt} ceased on March 1816, up to which time all rent had been paid. And the issue to be tried was, whether the tenancy under the ag^{rt} had ceased—

At the trial before Bosanquet, Justice, the Plff called Ed. Jones, one of the Defts as a Witness to prove that his tenancy under the ag^{rt} continued to 1829.

His testimony was objected to, on the ground, that he was a party to the record, but the testimony was rec^d, subject to a motion to the Court as to its admissibility, and the Plff recovered a verdict.

A rule *nisi* for a new trial was obtained on the ground that the Witness had been improperly rec^d.

On the argument the cases were fully cited.

Tindal, Ch. Jus. delivered the opinion of the Court in which he says—"No case has been cited, nor can any be found, in which a Witness has been refused upon the objection in the abstract, that he was a party to the suit; on the contrary, many have been brought forward, in which parties to the suit, who have suffered judg^t by default, have been admitted as Wit. against their own interest: and the only inquiry seems to have been, in a majority of the cases, whether the party called was interested in the event of the suit or not; and the admission or rejection of the Witness has depended on the result of this inquiry.

The exclusion on the ground of *interest* is a known principle of the law of Evidence; and so much did Lord Chief Baron Gilbert consider this as the only solid objection against the evidence of a *party* to the *suit,* that after laying it down as a general rule, that no man interested in the matter in question can be a Witness for himself, he states, that several corollaries may be deduced from this rule; of which he gives, as the first "That the Plff or Deft cannot be a Witness in his own cause; for these are the persons who have a most immediate interest, and it is not to be presumed that a man who complains without cause, or defends without Justice, should have honesty enough to confess it." "That a party to the record["] continues Ch. J. Tindall ["]should not be *compelled against* his *consent* to become a Witness in a court of law, is [a rule] founded in good sense and sound policy; it forms the point of the decision in the case [of] the King vs. Woodburn 10

East 395, and the decision of that case leads to the necessary inference, that if the party consents to be examined, he is then an admissible Witness. ["]

He adds "We think, therefore, when the party to the Suit, who has suffered judg^t by default, waives the objection and consents to be examined, and is called against his own interest, there is no ground, either on principle or authority, for rejecting him."

The case at bar is precisely like the case in 7 Bingh. Here the principal in the contract was called, and consented to be examined as a Witness. If judg^t should be rendered against all the Defts he could not compel a contribution, as it was his own proper debt. And the only interest he could have would be in the failure of Plff to establish the point contract, and against that interest he was called to testify—and waiving his strict legal objection, and consenting to testify, I may say with the Court in the Case of Worrall vs. Jones and others, "there is no ground, either on principle or authority for rejecting him"—

(Qn? Judm't set aside?)
James M. Aynur
     vs.   The Same question
Wm W. Knowlton,
Wm Phelps and   Did the Wit. consent?
Olmstead Chamberlain

EDITOR'S NOTE: The above opinion, in the handwriting of Chief Justice Fletcher, was found in file No. 249, First Circuit—Law. The Journal, Fourth Circuit, contains the following entry: p. 19 (Jan. 21, 1842) reserved question filed; case submitted without argument. Volume I of the Journal, First Circuit, contains the following entry: p. 170 (March 31, 1842) answer certified to Supreme Court, Fourth Circuit that defendant Sparhawk is a competent witness on the part of the plaintiff. Also see Calendar, First Circuit—Law, case No. 249.

JAMES F. ROYCE *versus* THOMAS BRADBURN
March 31, 1842.

Supreme Court, First Circuit. Certiorari to two justices of the peace, Washtenaw County. Opinion by Whipple, J. Judgment reversed.

E. Mundy, attorney for plaintiff.

E. Lawrence & O. Hawkins, attorney for defendant.

EDITOR'S NOTE: The original MS. opinion in the above case has not been found. In printed form it appears in a footnote in 2 Douglass (Mich.) 377 (1849). It deals with forcible entry and detainer, privity of parties, etc. Volume I of the Journal, First Circuit, contains the following entry: p. 165 (March 31, 1842) judgment reversed. Also see Calendar, First Circuit—Law, Vol. I, case No. 242. File No. 242, First Circuit—Law, contains copies of orders made in the case.

Supreme Court Rules

EDITOR's NOTE: The following rules have been copied from journals of the Supreme Court. It is possible that other rules were recorded in the missing journal for the Second Circuit. In 1838 the Legislature directed the Supreme Court to formulate rules for practice in both the Supreme and Circuit Courts in all matters not expressly provided by law (Rev. St. 1838, Part III, Title I, Ch. I, Sec. 5, p. 358), and that within two years and at least once in every seven years thereafter, the Court should revise the rules to simplify and shorten proceedings, etc. (*ibid.*).

January 3, 1837.

ORDERED that the rules of practice of the Supreme Court of the late Territory of Michigan be adopted as the rules of practice of this Court until the further order of Court.

[*Journal, First Circuit,* Vol. I, p. 1]

January 13, 1837.

ORDERED that in all cases on writ of Error now pending in this Court for the first circuit where the pleadings are not completed, Errors shall be assigned in twenty days from the date of this order, and Joinder in Error shall be filed in twenty days after the time hereby limited for filing the assignment of Errors, where the Defendant in Error has appeared—and where there has been no appearance, the Defendant in Error shall join in Error in twenty days after a notice served on him that Errors have been assigned—and when the plaintiff shall be in default under this rule, Judgment of non pros may be entered against the plaintiff, or the Court may inspect the record and enter final Judgment at the option of the Defendant—and when the Defendant shall be in default the plaintiff may proceed Ex parte.

ORDERED that in all cases on writ of Error to be brought

into this Court sitting in the first Circuit where the writ shall
be returnable on the first Tuesday of June next the plaintiff
shall assign Errors on the day next succeeding the return day;
and the Defendant shall join in Error in two days after service of a notice that Errors have been assigned, where the Defendant shall reside within thirty miles of the place where the
Court shall be held—and where the Defendant resides more
than thirty miles from such place, joinder in Error shall be
filed within such additional time after the service of such
notice, as a computation of the distance of Defendants residence shall give, allowing one day for every twenty miles
over and above the first thirty miles, Excluding Sunday; and
in cases of default under this rule, the same proceeding, shall
be had as provided in the rule relative to causes in Error now
pending in this Court for the first Circuit.

ORDERED that the first Tuesday of June next Ensuing be
and said day is hereby fixed by this Court as a return day, to
which all writs lawfully issuing out of this Court until that
day may be made returnable.

[*Journal, First Circuit,* Vol. I, p. 21]

June 28, 1837

1. Ordered that in cases on certiorari to a justices court, it
   shall not be necessary to make a formal assignment of
   errors in law, but instead thereof a brief shall be made, in
   which shall be specified the points of error relied on together with the authorities to which reference shall be
   made in argument: and that it shall be the duty of consel
   for each party making a brief to furnish one copy to the
   opposite consel, and one for each member of the Court.
2. Ordered that in cases on writ of error, assignment of
   errors shall be filed on or before the first day of the term,
   to which the Writ is made returnable, and joinder in error

shall be filed thereto, at or before the opening of the Court on the second day of the term: and that in cases of Certiorari to a justices court where errors in fact are intended to be relied on, the assignment of such facts & the joinder in error shall be filed severally within the times respectively limited in this rule, for filing assignment of errors in joinder in cases on writ of error, unless the court in either of the above cases for special reasons shall allow or direct a longer or shorter time for filing such assignment or joinder.

3. Ordered that in cases of certiorari to a justices Court, the Plaintiff in error or his consel, at any time after service of the writ of certiorari, may serve a written notice, personally on the defendant in error, to appear on the first, or any other certain day of the term to which the writ shall be made returnable, and hear & answer the errors to be assigned in the cause which notice shall be served at least twelve days before the first day of the next term, and on proof of the service of such notice & no appearance being entered for the defendant, the Court will proceed to hear the cause *ex parte*.

4. Ordered that in cases in writ of error, the Plaintiff at his option may coerce the appearance of the defendant in error, by a writ of *Sceri facias audiendum errores*, or by a personal service of a notice to appear and join in error on the first or other specified day of the term to which the writ shall be made returnable—notice to be served on the defendants at least twelve days before the first day of the term on which the defendant was notified to appear.

5. Ordered that in cases, where by any rule of this Court, personal service of a notice or a copy of a rule is required to be made, a service thereof by copy left at the place of residence of the party, with some member of the family, in

which the party resides, of the age of fourteen years, or service upon the Attorney of the party shall be deemed as personal service.

[*Journal, Third Circuit*, pp. 2-3]

January 13, 1838.

ORDERED 1. On the return of a writ of Error or Certiorari, if the defendant in Error shall fail or neglect to cause his appearance to be entered during the term to which the writ of Error or Certiorari shall be made returnable, the plaintiff in Error may Enter a rule at any time thereafter in the Common rule Book requiring the Defendant in Error to cause his appearance to be Entered within sixty days after the service of notice of said rule, or that his default be Entered.

2. The service of such notice may be on the said Defendant *personally* or by putting the same into the Post Office directed to his residence, or by affixing the same in some conspicuous place in the Clerks office, and upon filing an affidavit of such service the plaintiff in Error may cause the Defendants default to be entered in the Book of Common rules.

[*Journal, First Circuit*, Vol. I, p. 41-42]

January 12, 1839.

Ordered by the Court that in all cases pending in the Chancery side of this Court, in which Subpoena has been returned served, and in which no pleadings have been filed by the defendant, that the defendant file his plea answer or demurrer to the Complainant's bill of Complaint within sixty days from this day; and that the Complainant file his replication or Exceptions to such answer within thirty days thereafter.

[*Journal, First Circuit*, Vol. I, p. 59]

February 27, 1839.

Ordered that the rules adopted by this Court for the Government of the practice of the different Circuit Courts of this State, so far as the same relate to the obtaining of commissions to take the depositions of witnesses shall apply to, and be the order of, this Court until further order.

[*Journal, First Circuit,* Vol. I, p. 72]

January 21, 1841.

It is ordered by the Court that in actions of Right made returnable to this Court at the present term. Declaration be filed in Sixty days from the first day of the term and Subsequent pleadings in twenty days thereafter Alternately.

[*Journal, Fourth Circuit,* p. 6]

January 4, 1842.

Ordered that Saturday the eight day of January instant be a general return day for process issuing from this Court.

[*Journal, First Circuit,* Vol. I, p. 126]

January 7, 1842.

Ordered that in Cases of Writs of Error issued out of & returnable to this Court. The Defendant in Error may take a rule upon the Plaintiff in Error to appear and bring in or file the Record in Two days from the return day of the Writ of Error—And after record is filed, the Defendant in Error may take a rule upon the Plaintiff in Error to assign Errors in two days and after Errors are assigned, the Plaintiff in Error may take a rule upon the Defendant in Error to plead or demur to such assignment or join therein in Two days. And in case of Default in either case under this rule on proof of a service of a copy of the rule upon the opposite party or his attorney—& if the default be on the part of the Plaintiff he shall be non-prossed, and if the default be on the part of the Defendant, the judgment shall be reversed—Provided however that the Court may, in its discretion, on special cause shewn, extend the time for either of the said rules and may set aside any default under this rule.

[*Journal, First Circuit,* Vol. I, p. 132]

Circuit Court Rules

EDITOR's NOTE: The following rules are reprinted from a pamphlet located in the Burton Historical Collections, Public Library, Detroit. The original record of these rules will be found in Volume I of the Journal of the Supreme Court, First Circuit, commencing at page 68.

[*]RULES   [*p. 1]

FOR THE

CIRCUIT COURTS

IN THE

STATE OF MICHIGAN;

ADOPTED BY THE SUPREME COURT, FEBRUARY, 1839.

DETROIT.

J. S. & S. A. BAGG, PRINTERS.

1839.

180

[*p. 3]

[*]CIRCUIT COURT RULES

Rule 1

Attorneys to have agents.

Who may be such.

How appointed.

Every attorney shall have an agent in each place where there is a circuit court held in this state, except in the city or town where such attorney keeps his office. No person shall be an agent unless he be an attorney of the court, clerk of the court, or deputy clerk. The appointment of agents shall be made in writing, signed by the attorney, and filed in the clerk's office; and the clerk shall keep a catalogue of the appointments filed in the office, with the attorneys' names alphabetically arranged.

Rule 2.

Service of papers. On whom made.

Where the attorney for the adverse party resides more than two miles from the place of holding court, service of papers contemplated by these rules may be made on an agent; but if he has no such agent, such service may be made by putting the notice or papers in the post office, directed to the attorney at his place of residence, to be ascertained according to the best information and belief of the person making such service.

Rule 3.

Notices to be in writing.

All notices shall be in writing, and shall be served on the attorney in the cause, or his agent; and where a party who is also an attorney of this court, shall prosecute in person, or, if a defendant, shall give notice that he is an attorney and will defend in person, all notices and other papers shall be served on him in like manner; and where the object is to bring the party into contempt for disobeying any rule or order of the court, the service shall be on such party personally, unless otherwise specially ordered by the court.

Rule 4.

Notices and papers may be served on an attorney or his agent, by leaving the same with him or his agent, or with his clerk in his office, or with a person having charge thereof; or when no person is to be found in the office, by leaving the same, between the hours of six in the [*]morning and nine in the evening, in some suitable and conspicuous place in such office; or if the office be not open so as to admit of service therein, then by leaving the same at the attorney's residence, with some person of suitable age and discretion.

How to be served.

[*p. 4]

Rule 5.

Where a party, other than an attorney of this court, prosecutes or defends in person, the service of papers may be on such party personally, or by putting the same into the post office, directed to him at his place of residence. And no service of notice or papers in the ordinary proceedings in a cause shall be necessary to be made on a defendant who has not appeared therein and given notice to the plaintiff's attorney of his intention to defend the suit, except where the defendant is returned imprisoned for want of bail, in which case a copy of the declaration shall be delivered to him, or to the sheriff or jailer in whose custody he shall be; and when an exception is entered to bail, and no notice of retainer of an attorney to defend is given, notice of such exception shall be delivered to the sheriff or one of his deputies.

When an attorney is a party.

When service not necessary.

Rule 6.

No private agreement or consent between the parties or their attorneys, in respect to the proceedings in a cause, shall be binding unless the same shall have been reduced to the form of a rule by consent, and entered

All agreements to be in writing.

accordingly in the book of common rules; or unless evidence thereof shall be in writing, subscribed by the party, or his attorney, against whom the same shall be alleged.

Rule 7.

Original writs may be issued in vacation, or in term time, and made returnable in any day in term.

Rule 8.

Every rule to which a party would, according to the practice of the court, be entitled of course, without showing special cause, shall be denominated a common rule; and every other rule shall be denominated a special rule. All common rules, and all rules by consent of parties, shall be entered with the clerk at his office, in a book to be provided by him for that purpose, to be called the "Common Rule Book," and may be entered at any time, as well in vacation as during term; and the day when the rule shall be entered shall be noted therein, and the party may enter such rule as he may conceive himself entitled to, of course, but at his peril.

[*]Rule 9.

The day on which any rule shall be entered, or order, notice, pleading or paper served, shall be excluded in the computation of the time for complying with the exigency of such rule, order or notice, pleading or paper, and the day on which a compliance therewith is required, shall be included, except where it shall fall on a Sunday, in which case the party shall have the next day to comply therewith. When by the terms of any order an act is directed to be performed instanter, it shall be done in twenty-four hours.

Rule 10.

In all suits originally commenced in the circuit court, declarations shall be filed with the clerk of the court within sixty days from the first day of the term to which the writ is made returnable, and the defendant shall plead thereto within thirty days from the expiration of the time to declare; and all subsequent pleadings shall respectively be filed within ten days each after the other, until issue of fact or law be joined.

Time for filing pleadings.

Declaration in sixty days.

Pleas in thirty.

Subsequent pleadings in ten days each.

Rule 11.

In suits commenced by the service of declaration, the defendant shall be entitled to the same time to plead subsequent to the next succeeding term after the service of declaration, as is provided by the preceding rule in cases commenced by original writs, and all subsequent pleadings shall be in accordance with said rule; and in cases against a number of defendants, where process shall not have been served on all of them, declaration may be filed against all the defendants, and a copy thereof served on the defendant or defendants not served with process, and such defendant or defendants shall plead thereto in thirty days after notice of the filing thereof and service of such copy, and in case such defendant or defendants shall not plead thereto in such time, the plaintiff, on affidavit filed of such service, may enter the appearance and default of such defendant or defendants; subsequent pleadings to be filed in ten days each consecutively, as under the preceding rules.

Suits by declaration.

Time to file plea to.

When all the defend'ts not served with process.

How to proceed against.

Rule 12.

When an attorney is retained to defend a cause, notice of retainer shall be served on the plaintiff's at-

Notice of retainer.

torney within fifty days from the first day of the term to which the writ is made returnable; and in cases commenced by declaration, within fifty days from the first day of the next succeeding after service thereof.

Rule 13.

When the defendant's attorney to be served with copy of declaration.

[*p. 6]

When the plaintiff's attorney receives notice of retainer, as is provided in the preceding rule, he shall, at or before the time limited for filing [*]declaration, serve a copy thereof on the defendant's attorney; and if such notice of retainer be not received until after the time above stated, then a copy of such declaration shall be served within ten days after receiving such notice.

Rule 14.

When copies of pleading to be served.

After the service of a copy of such declaration, the party filing any pleading, whether plaintiff or defendant, shall, on or before the day limited for filing any such, serve a copy of such pleading on the attorney of the opposite party.

Rule 15.

When no special bail filed.

Defendants cannot plead or take default.

Defendn't accepting service.

When a defendant has been taken upon a capias ad respondendum, and has given satisfactory appearance bail, the plaintiff may proceed to final judgment, which proceeding shall not release the appearance bail. Until the defendant has appeared and perfected special bail, he is not entitled to a copy of the declaration, nor can he plead thereto, nor take any default against the plaintiff; and where the defendant in any original writ accepts service, his appearance may be entered and he will be considered in court.

Rule 16.

If the plaintiff shall make default in declaring, then the defendant, or if either party shall make default in answering, then the opposite party, may have the default entered in the common rule book; but it shall not be competent to enter such default unless on receiving notice of retainer as aforesaid, copies of the pleadings in the cause have been served, as provided by these rules.

Default in pleading.

To be entered in common rule book.

Rule 17.

The defendant's default being duly entered, the plaintiff shall not be bound afterwards to accept a plea, unless the defendant, as soon as he shall know that the default has been entered, shall serve an affidavit of merits, plead issuably and pay or tender the costs of the default.

No plea to be afterwards accepted, except on service of affidavit of merits and pleading issuably.

Rule 18.

The party in whose favor default shall have been entered, may at any time after four days in term shall have intervened, have a rule entered in the common rule book to make such default absolute, and for such judgment as the party is entitled to by reason of the default. If such default be taken by plaintiff for want of plea, he shall, by said rule, in cases where it is competent, make reference to the clerk to assess the damages; and in cases where they must be assessed by a jury, said rule shall direct that such jury be called to make the assessment.

When default to be made absolute.

Plaintiff to obtain assessment of damages by clerk or jury.

[*]Rule 19.

The assessment being made as provided by the preceding rule, the court shall enter final judgment thereon.

[*p. 7]

Judgment to be entered on assessment.

Rule 20.

Pleas in abatement
—when to be filed.

Pleas in abatement, or to the jurisdiction, and all other dilatory pleas, may be filed without any rule for a special, or a general special, imparlance within the time limited by the tenth rule.

Rule 21.

Motion to set aside
proceedings for
misnomer.

The court will not entertain a motion to set aside the proceedings in a cause, on the ground of misnomer of the party arrested, but will leave him to his remedy by a plea in abatement.

Rule 22.

When plaintiff may
discontinue his suit.

The plaintiff may at any time, upon notice to the defendant or his attorney, and on the payment of all the costs taxed in the cause, discontinue his suit in the common rule book.

Rule 23.

Attorney to endorse
on pleadings his
taxed costs, and
number of folios.

Every attorney filing any pleading in a cause, shall endorse thereon the costs allowed him by law therefor, and the number of folios in the draft and copies thereof.

Rule 24.

Motion to set aside
default—when to
be made.
In cases of special
motion, affidavits
and papers to be
filed when made,
and to be served
on opposite
attorney.

All motions to set aside a default shall be made and filed within the four first days of the term next after the default shall have been entered; and in all cases of special motions (except a motion for a continuance) the affidavits and other papers on which the same may be founded, shall be filed at the time of making the motion, and copies thereof shall be served on the attorney of the opposite party on or before the day of making such motion.

Rule 25.

All motions shall be in writing, shall have endorsed thereon the names of the parties and their respective attorneys; and no motion which is resisted shall be argued on the day it is made, without the consent of parties, unless the court, on good cause being shown, otherwise direct.

Motions to be in writing—to be endorsed.

When resisted to lay over one day.

Unless for cause.

Rule 26.

When either party shall demur to any pleading, he shall briefly but plainly specify the objections, in matters of substance, as well as those of form, upon which he intends to rely on the argument; and if the [*]pleading shall be adjudged bad for any cause not so specified, the party pleading, when allowed to amend on terms, will be permitted to do so without costs.

Demurrers to be special.

*[*p. 8]*

If not, party may amend without costs.

Rule 27.

The plaintiff may at any time before the default for not replying shall be entered, if the plea shall be a special plea, or a plea in abatement, or within ten days after service of a copy of the plea, if it shall be the general issue, amend his declaration. After plea, either party may, before default for not answering shall be entered, amend the pleading to be answered; and where there shall be a demurrer to a declaration or other pleading, such pleading may be amended at any time before the default for not joining in demurrer shall be entered. The respective parties may amend under this rule, of course, and without costs, but shall not be entitled so to amend more than once. Under this rule new counts or pleas may be added.

When plaintiff may amend.

When either party may.

May amend, of course, without costs.

But once.
May add counts or pleas.

Rule 28.

No rule to amend shall be required, but a copy of the amended pleading, endorsed "amended narr.," "plea," &c., (as the case may be) shall be filed and served, with a notice that the same is a copy of the

pleading as amended. And the time to plead, or answer, if notice thereof has been given, shall be from the day of service of such copy of the amended pleading.

Rule 29.

In cases in which the defendant is entitled to demand a bill of particulars, the plaintiff shall furnish such on being served with a notice requiring the same by the defendant or his attorney, and if such bill be demanded before the expiration of the time for filing plea, the defendant shall have like time to plead after receiving the bill of particulars to which he was entitled at the time of serving such notice.

Rule 30.

If the plaintiff shall unreasonably neglect to furnish a bill of particulars, or if the bill of particulars delivered be insufficient, the court may in its discretion nonsuit the plaintiff, allow further time to furnish it, or require a more particular bill to be delivered.

Rule 31.

In cases where it is competent for the plaintiff to call upon the defendant for a bill of the particulars of his setoff, the defendant shall furnish such on the written request of the plaintiff or his attorney; and in case it be not furnished within thirty days after such

[*p. 9]

request, the [*]plaintiff may, by rule entered in the

common rule book, order the plea under which a setoff is claimed, if it requires a replication, to be struck out; and if it be the general issue, with a notice of setoff, the court may exclude all testimony touching it from going to the jury. Where the bill of particulars is demanded and furnished in cases where a replication is necessary, the plaintiff shall have the same time to reply that was unexpired of the rule at the time of demanding such bill.

When neglected to be furnished.

Time for pleading in such cases.

Rule 32.

Application may be made by petition to any circuit court, in term time, or to the presiding judge thereof, in vacation, to compel the production and discovery of books, papers, and documents relating to the merits of any suit pending in such court, or of any defence to such suit, in the following cases:

Mode of coercing the production and discovery of books, documents, &c, relating to a suit.

First. By the plaintiff, to compel the discovery of papers or documents in the possession or under the control of the defendant, which may be necessary to enable the plaintiff to declare or to answer any pleading of the defendant.

To enable plaintiff to declare.

Second. The plaintiff may be compelled to make the discovery of papers or documents, where the same shall be necessary to enable the defendant to answer any pleading of the petitioner.

Or defendant to plead.

Third. The plaintiff may be compelled, after declaring, and the defendant after pleading, to produce and discover all papers or documents on which the action, or defence, is founded.

The plaintiff after declaring, and defendant after pleading.

Fourth. After issue joined in any action, either party may be compelled to produce and discover all such books, papers, and documents as may be necessary to enable

After issue joined.

the party applying for such discovery to prepare for the trial of the cause.

Rule 33.

The petition for such discovery shall state the facts and circumstances on which the same is claimed, and shall be verified by affidavit, stating that the books, papers, and documents whereof discovery is sought, are not in the possession nor under the control of the party applying therefor, and that the party making such affidavit is advised by his counsel, and verily believes, that the discovery of the books, papers, or documents mentioned in such petition is necessary to enable him to declare, or answer, or to prepare for trial, as the case may be.

Rule 34.

The rule granting the discovery shall specify the mode in which the same is to be made, which may be either by requiring the party to [*]deliver sworn copies of matters to be discovered, or by requiring him to produce and deposite the same with the clerk of the court in which the trial is to be had. The order shall

also specify the time within which the discovery is to be made; and when the papers are required to be deposited, the order shall specify the time for which the deposite shall continue.

Rule 35.

The court, or presiding judge thereof, in granting such order, shall be governed by the principles and practice of the court of chancery in compelling discoveries, except that the costs of such proceedings shall always be awarded in the discretion of the court.

Rule 36.

Every such order may be vacated by the court, or the judge granting the same,

First. Upon satisfactory evidence that it ought not to have been granted.

Second. Upon the discovery sought being obtained.

Third. Upon the party required to make the discovery denying, on oath, the possession or control of the books, papers, or documents ordered so to be produced.

When order may be vacated.

Rule 37.

The order directing the discovery of books, papers, or documents shall operate as a stay of all other proceedings in the cause, until such order shall have been complied with, or vacated; and the party obtaining such order, after the same shall have been complied with, or vacated, shall have the like time to declare, plead, or answer, to which he was entitled at the time of the making the order.

Order to operate as a stay of proceedings until complied with.

Rule 38.

In case of the party refusing or neglecting to obey such order for a discovery within such time as the court shall deem reasonable, the court may nonsuit him, or may strike out any plea or notice he may have given, or may debar him from any particular defence in relation to which such discovery was sought; and the power of the court to compel such discovery shall be confined to the remedies herein provided, and shall not extend to authorize any other proceedings against the person or property of the party so refusing or neglecting.

In case order is disobeyed.

Rule 39.

When complied
with.

[*p. 11]

Its effect.

The books, papers, and documents, or sworn copies thereof, produced under any order made in pursuance of the preceding rules, shall [*]have the same effect, when used by the party requiring them, as if produced upon notice, according to the practice of the court.

Rule 40.

In action of
covenant motion of
special matter may
be given.

In actions of debt, or covenant, on any sealed instrument, a plea of non est factum shall be so far deemed a general issue as to entitle the defendant to accompany the same with a notice of special matter intended be given in evidence, as a defence to the action, provided if specially pleaded it would be a bar to such action.

Rule 41.

On argument
demurrers court to
be furnished with
a copy of special
causes of demurrer,
and pleading
demurred to.

The party filing a demurrer to a part of any pleading, shall, before proceeding to the argument, furnish the court with a copy of the part demurred to, and also of the special causes of demurrer, if any, filed; and if it be a general demurrer, a copy of the whole pleading demurred to shall be furnished, in default of which the demurrer shall be overruled.

Rule 42.

Application for
commission, to
whom to be made.

Application for a commission to take the deposition of any witness without this state, may be made to any circuit court, or to a judge thereof in vacation, in all cases provided for in the revised statutes.

Rule 43.

What to state.

Such application must be founded on an affidavit, stating that the cause is at issue, the names of the witnesses and their residence, and that they are without this state; and also that their testimony is material, without which the party cannot safely proceed to the trial of the cause, as he is advised by counsel and verily believes.

Rule 44.

Notice of such application shall be served on the adverse party, at least eight days before the time of making such application, if made to a judge in vacation.

Notice of.

Rule 45.

When an order for granting a commission shall be made by a judge in vacation, such order shall be filed in the office of the clerk of the court in which the cause is pending before issuing such commission, and shall be granted only in the like cases and upon the same terms that the court would award such commission, and shall be subject to the control of the court in all respects.

Order to be filed.

Rule 46.

The commissioners named by the party applying for a commission will, of course, be appointed, unless the opposite party object to any [*]commissioner, and show sufficient cause, by affidavit, when a substitution will be made.

When any of the commissioners objected to. [*p. 12]

Rule 47.

The interrogatories shall be settled by a judge of the circuit court, in vacation, and a copy thereof, and a notice of the time and place of settling the same, shall be served on the adverse party at least four days before the time designated in the notice.

Interrogations to be settled by a judge. On notice to opposite party.

Rule 48.

Deposition, &c., how to be returned.

The judge may in his discretion direct the commission, interrogatories, and depositions to be returned by an agent, or private person, or by mail, directed to the clerk of the court out of which the commission issued.

Rule 49.

Manner of executing commission.

The persons to whom such commission shall be directed, or any one of them, unless otherwise expressly directed therein, shall execute the same as follows:

To swear witnesses.

First. They, or any of them, shall publicly administer an oath to the witnesses named in the commission, that the answers given by such witnesses to the interrogatories proposed to them shall be the truth, the whole truth, and nothing but the truth.

Examination to be in writing and signed and certified.

Second. They shall cause the examination of each witness to be reduced to writing, and to be subscribed by him and certified by such of the commissioners as are present at the taking of the same.

If exhibits produced.

Third. If any exhibits are produced and proved before them, they shall be annexed to the depositions to which they relate, and shall, in like manner, be subscribed by the witness proving the same. (This section must be understood to refer to such papers as can be produced upon the examination. If the paper referred to be a record, not subject to the control of the party or the commissioners, it will be sufficient to annex a copy, and the original may be produced on the trial, separate from the commission.)

If papers cannot be produced.

Duty of commissioners.

Fourth. The commissioners, or commissioner, shall subscribe each sheet of the depositions, shall annex all the depositions and exhibits to the commission upon which the return shall be endorsed, and shall close them up under their, or his, seals, and shall address the same, when so closed, to the clerk of the court from which the commission issued, at his place of residence.

To whom deposition, &c., to be directed.

Fifth. If there is a direction on the commission to return the same by mail, they, or he, shall immediately deposite the packet, so directed, in the nearest post office.

If required to be returned by mail.

[*]*Sixth.* If there be a direction on the commission to return the same by an agent of the party who sued out the same, the packet, so directed, shall be delivered to such agent.

[*p. 13]

When by an agent.

Seventh. A copy of this rule must be annexed to every commission issued under these rules.

A copy of this rule to be annexed to all commissions.

Rule 50.

The clerk, upon receiving such commission and return, shall open the same, and immediately endorse thereon the time and manner of receiving them, and file such commission and return.

The clerk to open, endorse and file the same.

Rule 51.

Depositions of any witness taken within this state, in all cases provided for in the revised statutes, shall be received, opened, endorsed, and filed by the clerk, in the same manner as is provided for in the preceding rules for taking depositions of witnesses without this state under a commission.

Depositions taken within the state.

Rule 52.

All objections of form as to the taking of depositions to be read in evidence, shall be filed in writing at least one day before the cause is called for trial.

Exceptions to depositions to be filed before trial.

Rule 53.

When a deposition has been filed, if not read on the trial by the party taking it, it may be used by the other party if he sees fit.

Rule 54.

Whenever it shall be necessary in any affidavit to swear to the advice of counsel, the party shall, in addition to what has usually been inserted, swear that he has fully and fairly stated his case to his counsel, and shall give the name of such counsel.

Rule 55.

When a party applies for the continuance of a cause a second time, the affidavit must state, in addition to the usual requirements, the facts which the party expects to prove by the absent witness, and the diligence he has used to procure his attendance; but it shall be optional with the opposite party to proceed to trial if he admit the facts expected to be proved.

Rule 56.

Where a rule is granted upon payment of costs, a copy of the rule and of the taxed bill of costs must be served upon the opposite party, at the same time exhibiting to him a certified copy of the original rule;

[*p. 14]

[*]and if the costs be not paid on demand, and proof, by affidavit, shall be made of the personal demand of such sum of money, and of a refusal to pay it, the court may issue a precept to commit the person so disobeying to prison, until such sum, and the costs and expenses of the proceeding, be paid.

Rule 57.

It shall be the duty of the clerk of each of the circuit courts, previous to each term, to make out a docket of the causes at issue, arranging them according to the date of their issues, which docket shall be denominated "Issues of Fact;" also, a separate docket of causes which may not be at issue, or which may be for assessment of damages, either by the clerk, court, or jury, arranging them according to the time of commencing the suits, which docket shall be denominated "Imparlances;" also, another docket of all cases in which an issue at law is joined, arranging them according to the date of such issues, which shall be denominated "The Law Docket;" and also, a docket of all original appearances to the term.

Clerks to make out dockets.

1, "Issues of fact."

2, "Imparlances."

3, "Law docket."

4, "Appearance docket."

Rule 58.

The clerk of each circuit court shall make two copies of each of said dockets, one for the court and the other for the bar.

Clerks to make two copies of the dockets.

Rule 59.

All appeals shall be placed on the docket of issues of fact.

Appeals.

Rule 60.

Causes shall be heard according to their standing on the dockets, unless otherwise ordered by the court.

Order of trying causes.

Rule 61.

On the trial of causes, one counsel on each side only shall examine or cross-examine a witness, and two counsel only on each side shall sum up the cause to the jury, unless the court shall otherwise order.

One counsel only to examine witnesses and only two on each side to address jury.

Rule 62.

The party having the affirmative shall commence the evidence, and counsel may in all cases, previously to the opening of the evidence, make a statement of their case; the defendant making his statement immediately after the statement of the plaintiff, and before the evidence of the plaintiff be given, or after the evidence of the plaintiff shall have been given and before his own evidence is given, at his election.

[*]Rule 63.

Not more than two counsel on each side shall be heard on the argument of any motion, the mover being entitled to open the argument and to reply to the argument of the opposite attorney. Only one counsel can be heard on any reply.

Rule 64.

The clerk of every circuit court shall provide a book, to be denominated "The Special Motion Book," in which the attorneys shall, in term time, enter all special motions to be made to the court.

Rule 65.

The motions so made shall be heard by the court according to the order in which they stand in the special motion book, unless otherwise ordered on good cause shown.

Rule 66.

Motions for new trials shall be made and filed, with the reasons and grounds on which such motions are made, within two days after the rendition of the verdict.

Rule 67.

Motions in arrest of judgment, with the reasons and grounds on which they are founded, shall be made and filed within two days after the rendition of the verdict; or if a motion for a new trial has been interposed and overruled, then within two days after the overruling of such motion.

Motions in arrest of judgment, with the reasons, when to be filed.

Rule 68.

The time limited for moving to set aside defaults, or for making defaults absolute, or for filing motions and reasons for new trial, or in arrest of judgment, may be shortened or extended by the circuit courts respectively in their discretion.

Rules in certain cases may be shortened or enlarged by the court.

Rule 69.

On the argument of motions for new trial, or in arrest of judgment, the party making such motion will furnish the court with a copy of the reasons on which such motion is founded, and also a brief.

On argument of motion for new trial, counsel to furnish the reasons and a brief.

Rule 70.

Whenever a stay of proceedings may be necessary in order to make a special motion, the presiding judge may grant an order for that purpose; and service of such order, with copies of the affidavits on which it is grounded, and the notice of the motion, shall operate as a stay of [*]proceedings until the order of the court is had in the premises, unless the judge should in the mean time supersede or set aside such order. But the proceedings shall not be stayed for a longer time than to enable the party to make his motion, according

Presiding judge may grant a stay of proceedings.

[*p. 16]

How long to operate as a stay.

to the practice of the court, and if made, until the decision of the court thereon.

Rule 71.

The clerk shall endorse on every paper the day on which the same is filed. Parties must take notice of the filing of papers at their peril; and the clerk shall not suffer or permit any writ, pleading, affidavit, deposition, or other paper whatever, on file in his office, to be taken therefrom without the order of the court; but parties interested in any such, may inspect the same in his office, and take copies thereof.

Rule 72.

All cases not disposed of at any term shall stand continued to the next term, and shall be considered as continued from term to term until finally disposed of, without any special entry of a continuance.

Rule 73.

These rules shall take effect in the county of Wayne on the sixteenth day of February instant, and in each of the other counties in this state, excepting in the counties of Michilimackinac and Chippewa, on the fifteenth day of March next; and in the counties of Chippewa and Michilimackinac on the first day of May next; and shall govern the practice in the several circuit courts in this state until altered by the supreme court, or any two of the justices thereof; provided, however, that any of said

circuit courts may make such further and additional rules as may be deemed necessary, but which shall not be inconsistent, or conflict, with these rules or any of them;

and provided also, that either of said courts, or any judge thereof, may, upon good cause shown by affidavit or otherwise, in any case grant an extension of the time limited by any of these rules for filing pleadings, or for complying with the exigency of any rule, order, or notice.

Rule 74.

All rules and parts of rules made anterior to this day by said circuit courts, or any or either of them, or by any one or more of the judges of any or either of said courts, and all rules of practice which now obtain in any of said courts, are hereby rescinded, abolished, and repealed. This rule to take effect in the several counties in this state at the times respectively provided in the last rule above for the taking effect of the preceding rules in the counties respectively.

All former rules repealed.

[*]Rule 75.

[*p. 17]

It shall be the duty of the clerk of the supreme court for the first circuit, forthwith to cause these rules to be printed, and to transmit a copy thereof to the clerk of each of the circuit courts in this state; and it shall also be the duty of every such clerk to copy the said rules in their respective common rule books.

Clerk of supreme court of first circuit to send copies of these rules to the clerks of the circuit courts who are to copy them in rule books.

Adopted 16th February, 1839.

INDEX

WITH REFERENCE TO THE NUMBER OF THE RULES

W

Index Digest of Opinions

ARBITRATION

Delivery of an award of arbitrators (addressed to the court) to the clerk of the court in vacation is a delivery to the court, 129.

The rule that an award made without notice is void does not apply where the parties appeared before the arbitrators and agreed that they might, after viewing the land involved, make an award without notice and without hearing evidence, 129.

Where an award is silent with respect to notice of hearing, it is fair and reasonable to intend that notice was given, 129.

An agreement that arbitrators may, after viewing the land involved, make an award without notice and without hearing evidence, does not annul the original agreement for arbitration, 129.

ARREST

The fact that a nonresident is about to leave the county is not a sufficient basis for issuing a warrant for his arrest, 1.

ASSIGNMENT See 155.

ASSIGNMENT OF ERROR See Error.

ATTACHMENT See also 161.

Although it appears that a writ of attachment directed to the sheriff of another county was levied by summoning a person of that county who appeared and admitted that he had money and effects belonging to the defendants, the court is without jurisdiction to render judgment unless it appears that a writ of attachment was first directed to the sheriff of the county in which the attachment suit was commenced and levied on property in that county. A suit in attachment must be "pending" before a writ may be issued to another county, 156.

ATTORNEY

It is not error to permit an attorney to appear without express authority after he has appeared several times without objection, 9.

If, after dissolution of a law partnership, a client knows that his claim is being collected by the surviving partner, he cannot recover from the retiring partner money misappropriated by the surviving partner, 30.

AWARD See Arbitration.

BILLS AND NOTES See Negotiable instruments.

BOATS AND VESSELS See 161.

CAPIAS AD SATISFACIENDUM

A sheriff, being a ministerial officer, must obey the command of a writ of capias ad satisfaciendum with respect to the county in which the prisoner shall be confined, 95.

A writ of capias ad satisfaciendum issued from the circuit court of G. County directing the sheriff of O. County to imprison a judgment debtor in G. County is void insofar as it fixes the place of imprisonment, 95.

CERTIORARI

An erroneous instruction to jurors that they were bound to allow a certain credit to the defendant is not harmless error on certiorari brought by the defendant, 17.

Where there is "some evidence" to support the judgment of a justice of the peace, the Supreme Court on certiorari "will not stop to enquire whether it was so full or ample as to render the case entirely free from doubt, 23.

On certiorari to a justice of the peace the appellate court need not consider a point not raised below, 23.

Prior to 1838 a summary judgment by a justice of the peace against an officer for failure to return an execution, could be reviewed by certiorari even though the statute authorizing the summary judgment expressly prohibited an appeal, 85.

Under the statutes of 1838 a summary judgment by a justice of the peace against an officer for failure to return an execution, can be reviewed on appeal in the nature of certiorari, even though the statute authorizing the summary judgment expressly prohibits an appeal, 85.

CHANCELLOR
Statutes passed in 1836 authorizing the transfer of cases from territorial courts to state courts did not include cases in which the chancellor served as counsel, 4.

CHANCERY See Equity.

CITIES See Municipal ordinances.

COMMON COUNTS See Pleading.

COMPLAINT See 107, 150.

CONFLICT OF LAWS See 161.

CONSTITUTION See also 150.
The schedule of the Constitution of 1835, declaring that all writs, actions, etc., pending in the territorial courts shall continue, preserves these matters only until the legislature acts, 4.

CONTINUANCE See 107.

CORPORATIONS See 68.

COURTS See also 150.
Statutes passed in 1836 authorizing transfer of cases from territorial courts to state courts did not include cases in which the chancellor served as counsel, 4.

CRIMES See Larceny; Malicious killing of livestock; Perjury.

DAMAGES
In an action for libel (that plaintiff and three others had "robbed" a ballot box by taking out ballots for Crary and putting in ballots for Wells, leaving only 157 ballots for Crary), evidence that 200 persons had voted for Crary is inadmissible in mitigation of damages in the absence of evidence connecting the plaintiff with the "robbery", 65.

DEPUTY SHERIFF See Officers.

DIRECTED VERDICTS See Instructions to juries.

DOWER

The clearing of wild land not being waste, it is proper to endow a widow in wild land, 69.

ELECTIONS

In an action for libel (that plaintiff and three others had "robbed" a ballot box by taking out ballots for Crary and putting in ballots for Wells, leaving only 157 ballots for Crary), evidence that 200 persons had voted for Crary is inadmissible in mitigation of damages in the absence of evidence connecting the plaintiff with the "robbery," 65.

Proof that a person was clerk at the polls and had lawful custody of the ballots does not connect him with an alleged "robbery" of the ballot box, 65.

EQUITY *See also* 94.

A bill in equity which alleges that the plaintiff assigned a land contract to one of the defendants to secure him and another defendant against liability as indorsers on certain notes is not demurrable on the ground that it appears the assignment was made in fraud of creditors, although the bill also speaks of securing a retreat for the plaintiff and his family, refers to a nominal consideration, and alleges that the assignee was to hold the contract subject to the plaintiff's directions, 70.

A bill in equity which directly charges that a person to whom a land contract was assigned for a particular purpose violated his trust by disposing of the contract in a manner not warranted by the terms of the assignment alleges enough to show an equity between the plaintiff and the assignee, 70.

A bill in equity which alleges that the maker of a land contract procured from a trustee, to whom the contract had been assigned for a particular purpose, a wrongful assignment so as to destroy the plaintiff's interest in the land, and then conveyed the land to a third person, alleges enough to show an equity between the plaintiff and the maker of the contract, 70.

A bill in equity which alleges that the purchaser of certain land knew that it had been sold to the plaintiff under a land contract states an equitable claim against said purchaser, 70.

A bill in equity which claims a general right in which all the defendants are interested is not multifarious although each defendant has a separate and distinct interest, 70.

ERROR *See also* 155.

Where a case is submitted to a trial court on an agreed statement of facts which does not "contain all the facts necessary to turn the case into a question of law", the trial court's determination of the facts is conclusive if the statement contains evidence tending to prove the facts found, 30.

In the absence of statutory authority an agreed statement of facts is not a part of the court's record and, therefore, cannot be considered on writ of error, 30.

A writ of error sued out in the names of two of three persons against whom a joint judgment was rendered should be quashed unless an amendment is allowed, 161.

At common law a writ of error may not be amended by adding a party, 161.

Statute authorizing amendments in substance does not apply to proceedings in error, 161.

In the absence of statute, usage, or court rule changing the common law, proceedings in error may be amended only in form, 161.

ESCAPE
In an action for the escape of a person taken in execution, it is not necessary that the jury find specially that the officer consented or was negligent. A general verdict is sufficient, 9.
In an action against a sheriff for an escape, the sheriff's deputy who released the prisoner on an insufficient bond was interested in the event of the action, and, therefore, was properly rejected as a witness, 9.
In an action for an escape, it is error to reject as a witness the escaped prisoner when called by the defendant. If interested, his interest is against the party calling him, 9.

EVIDENCE *Also see* Witnesses.
In an action against an indorser of a promissory note, the certificate of a notary public that he presented the note for payment, that payment was refused, and that he mailed notice of protest, is not admissible to prove these facts, 27.
Whether the declaration of a defendant sued for trespass can be used against a codefendant sued as a joint tort feasor, quaere, 122.
Testimony by a witness that it was his uniform practice to give indorsers of promissory notes notice of nonpayment, is "no evidence" that notice was given in the particular case, 151.

EXECUTION
In a summary proceeding against an officer for failing to levy or return a writ of execution, a justice of the peace does not exceed his jurisdiction by rendering a judgment for more than $100, 13.
A renewal of an execution at the instance of the officer without the request or consent of the plaintiff will not defeat a claim against the officer for failing to levy or return the writ in time, 13.
Prior to 1838 a summary judgment by a justice of the peace against an officer for failure to return an execution, could be reviewed by certiorari, 85.
Under the statutes of 1838 a summary judgment by a justice of the peace against an officer for failure to return an execution, can be reviewed on appeal in the nature of certiorari, 85.

FORCIBLE ENTRY AND DETAINER *See* 50, 107, 155, 171.

FRAUD *Also see* Statute of frauds.
In an action of replevin the plaintiff may prove that a sale by the original owner to the defendant was in fraud of creditors, 146.

GENERAL APPEARANCE *See* Process.

GENERAL ISSUE *See* Pleading.

GENERAL VERDICT *See* Verdict.

GRAND JURY *See* Indictments.

HARMLESS ERROR
An erroneous instruction to jurors that they were bound to allow a certain

credit to defendant is not harmless error on certiorari brought by the defendant, 17.

INDICTMENTS *See* also 150.

Although, in an indictment for perjury, it is not necessary to allege that issue was joined in the action in which the perjury is alleged to have been committed, such an allegation is descriptive and must be proved strictly, 97.

An indictment which charges that defendants killed certain hogs of one D. and did "thereby" destroy the personal property of said D., does not embrace two distinct offenses, viz., (1) the killing of another's livestock, and (2) the destruction of another's personal property, 104.

INDORSERS *See* Negotiable instruments.

INSTRUCTIONS TO JURIES

In an action for work and labor in a justice's court, it is error for the justice to instruct the jury that inasmuch as the defendant has proved that the plaintiff received one-half of certain crops, the jurors are bound by their oaths to allow the defendant credit for the same, 17.

Where in an action for trespass there is any legal testimony, however slight, against one of the defendants, the court may not direct a verdict for that defendant in order that he may testify in behalf of a codefendant, 122.

ISSUE *See* Pleading.

JOINDER OF ISSUE *See* Pleading.

JOINT PARTIES *See* Parties.

JOINT TENANCY

Payment of rent to one of three joint owners is a discharge of the joint claim, 21.

JUDGMENTS *Also see* Summary proceedings.

Where rent is sued for in a justice's court in the names of three joint owners and one of them informs the justice that the rent has been paid, it is error for the justice to render judgment against the defendant in his absence at the instance of the other joint owners, 21.

JURISDICTION

In a summary proceeding against an officer for failing to levy or return a writ of execution, a justice of the peace does not exceed his jurisdiction by rendering a judgment for more than $100, 13.

JURY *See* also 155.

In justices' courts jurors are judges of the law as well as of the facts, 17.

JUSTICES OF THE PEACE *See* also 107.

A person sued in a justice's court must be sued in the county of his residence, except, etc., 1.

In a summary proceeding against an officer for failure to levy or return a writ of execution, a justice of the peace does not exceed his jurisdiction by rendering a judgment for more than $100, 13.

In justices' courts jurors are judges of the law as well as of the facts, 17.

Prior to 1838 a summary judgment by a justice of the peace against an officer for failure to return an execution could be reviewed by certiorari, 85.

Under the statutes of 1838 a summary judgment by a justice of the peace against an officer for failure to return an execution can be reviewed on appeal in the nature of certiorari, 85.

LARCENY
Repeal of a statute under which a larceny was committed does not exempt the defendant from the punishment prescribed by the statute, the repealing statute having expressly provided against such exemption except to the extent that any punishment was mitigated by the repealing statute, 142.

Where a statute reducing the punishment for a larceny previously committed is repealed, the defendant may be punished under the statute in force when the larceny was committed, 142.

LEGISLATIVE POWER
Once an action has abated the legislature has no power to revive it, 4.

LEVY See Attachment; Execution.

LIBEL
In an action for libel (that plaintiff and three others had "robbed" a ballot box by taking out ballots for Crary and putting in ballots for Wells, leaving only 157 ballots for Crary), evidence that 200 persons had voted for Crary is inadmissible in mitigation of damages in the absence of evidence connecting the plaintiff with the "robbery", 65.

LIENS See 161.

MALICIOUS KILLING OF LIVESTOCK
An indictment which charges that defendants killed certain hogs of one D. and did "thereby" destroy the personal property of said D., does not embrace two distinct offenses, viz. (1) the killing of another's livestock, and (2) the destruction of another's personal property, 104.

MAYOR'S COURT See Courts.

MITIGATION OF DAMAGES See Damages.

MULTIFARIOUSNESS See Pleading.

MUNICIPAL ORDINANCES See also 150.
A city ordinance providing that "no person shall sell meat except in stalls rented from the corporation" is invalid, being unreasonable and in restraint of trade (opinion of one judge), 36.

NEGOTIABLE INSTRUMENTS
In an action against an indorser of a promissory note, the certificate of a notary public that he presented the note for payment, that payment was refused, and that he mailed notice of protest, is not admissible to prove these facts, 27.

In the absence of evidence a court cannot presume that a memorandum at the foot of a promissory note ("At 12 per cent int. D.P.") was made when the note was made or that "D.P." means David Paddock, one of the makers of the note, 62.

The fact that an indorser of a promissory note received security from the maker to indemnify him against liability as an indorser does not make him absolutely liable without demand on the maker and notice to the indorser of nonpayment, 108.

In an action by the indorsee of a promissory note against the indorser, a declaration which alleges that the defendant received from the maker certain property to indemnify him as indorser and that the defendant has not "sustained any damages by reason of his not having received notice of the nonpayment of the note" is demurrable, 108.

Testimony by a witness that it was his uniform practice to give indorsers of promissory notes notice of nonpayment, is "no evidence" that notice was given in the particular case, 151.

NONSUIT

The fact that a witness called by the plaintiff on rebuttal testified that one of the defendants had declared during the trial "that he had no hand in taking the property" did not justify a conclusion by the court that the plaintiff had abandoned his action against that defendant, 122.

NOTARIES PUBLIC

In an action against an indorser of a promissory note, the certificate of a notary public that he presented the note for payment, that payment was refused, and that he mailed notice of protest, is not admissible to prove this fact, 27.

NOTICE TO QUIT See 155.

NUNCUPATIVE WILLS See Wills.

OFFICERS

In an action against a sheriff for an escape, the sheriff's deputy, who released the prisoner on an insufficient bond, was interested in the event of the action, and, therefore, properly rejected as a witness, 9.

In a summary proceeding against an officer for failing to levy or return a writ of execution, a justice of the peace does not exceed his jurisdiction by rendering a judgment for more than $100, 13.

A renewal of an execution at the instance of the officer without the request or consent of the plaintiff will not defeat a claim against the officer for failing to levy or return the writ in time, 13.

Prior to 1838 a summary judgment by a justice of the peace against an officer for failure to return an execution could be reviewed on certiorari, 85.

Under the statutes of 1838 a summary judgment by a justice of the peace against an officer for failure to return an execution can be reviewed on appeal in the nature of certiorari, 85.

A sheriff, being a ministerial officer, must obey the command of a writ of capias ad satisfaciendum with respect to the county in which the prisoner shall be confined, 95.

ORDINANCES See Muncipal ordinances.

PARTIES See also 155.

Where rent is sued for in a justice's court in the names of three joint owners and one of them informs the justice that the rent has been paid, it is error for the justice to render judgment against the defendant in his absence at the instance of the other joint owners, 21.

A writ of error sued out in the names of two of three persons against whom a joint judgment was rendered should be quashed, 161.

PARTNERSHIPS

Testimony by a person claiming to be agent that he was "authorized by the *defendants* to . . . employ workmen for them" is sufficient basis for inferring that the defendants, sued as "traders under the style of the Detroit Iron Co." constituted such company, 23.

If, after dissolution of a law partnership, a client knows that his claim is being collected by the surviving partner, he cannot recover from the retiring partner money misappropriated by the surviving partner, 23.

PAYMENT

Payment of rent to one of three joint owners is a discharge of the joint claim, 21.

PERJURY

Although, in an indictment for perjury, it is not necessary to allege that issue was joined in the action in which the perjury is alleged to have been committed, such an allegation is descriptive and must be proved strictly, 97.

PLEADING *See* also 50, 68, 94, 107.

Where the defendant has pleaded the general issue and a special plea, and the return of the justice states that issue was joined, the appellate court will presume that the plaintiff added a similiter to the general issue and traversed the special plea, 9.

The omission of a similiter is a mere matter of form which is aided by verdict, 9.

Where labor is performed under a subsisting special agreement, recovery may not be had under the common counts. But if the agreement has been fully performed by the plaintiff or rescinded by mutual consent, common counts may be used, 17.

Where it does not appear that a memorandum at the foot of a promissory note is a substantial part of the note, proof of the note and memorandum is not a material variance from a pleading which describes the note without mentioning the memorandum, 62.

A bill in equity which claims a general right in which all of the defendants are interested is not multifarious although each defendant has a separate and distinct interest, 70.

Proof (1) that a plaintiff, in an action on a jail-limits bond before a justice of the peace, filed the bond as his declaration; (2) that the defendants filed no plea; (3) that, on appeal to the circuit court, the transcript of the justice stated "The plaintiff declares on a limit bond on file", which bond was attached to the transcript; (4) that defendants in the circuit court filed a plea of nil debit; and (5) that no similiter was added, or other pleadings filed—is not proof that issue was joined in the circuit court, 97.

PRESENTMENT *See* Indictment; Negotiable instruments.

PRIVITY *See* 171.

PROCESS *Also see* Attachment; Capias; Execution.

All objections to process are waived by a general appearance, 23.

PROMISSORY NOTES *See* Negotiable instruments.

PROTEST *See* Negotiable instruments.

RENEWAL OF EXECUTION *See* Execution.

REPEAL *See* Statutes.

REPLEVIN
Property held on a writ of replevin may be replevied by a third person, 146.
In an action of replevin the plaintiff may prove that a sale by the original owner to the defendant was in fraud of creditors, 146.

RESTRAINT OF TRADE
A city ordinance providing that "no person shall sell meat except in stalls rented from the corporation" is invalid, being unreasonable and in restraint of trade (opinion of one judge), 36.

RETURN OF EXECUTION *See* Execution.

REVIVAL OF ACTIONS *See* Abatement.

SHERIFF *See* Officers.

SIMILITER *See* Pleading.

SPECIAL VERDICT *See* Verdict.

SPECIFIC PERFORMANCE *See* 94.

STATUTE OF FRAUDS *See* 94.

STATUTES
Repeal of a statute under which a crime was committed does not exempt the defendant from the punishment prescribed by the statute, the repealing statute having provided expressly against such exemption except to the extent that any punishment was mitigated by the repealing statute, 142.
Where a statute reducing punishment for a crime previously committed is repealed, the defendant may be punished under the statute in force when the crime was committed, 142.

SUMMARY PROCEEDINGS *See* also 150.
In a summary proceeding against an officer for failing to levy or return a writ of execution, a justice of the peace does not exceed his jurisdiction by rendering a judgment for more than $100, 13.
Prior to 1838 a summary judgment by a justice of the peace against an officer for failure to return an execution, could be reviewed by certiorari even though the statute authorizing the summary judgment expressly prohibited an appeal, 85.
Under the statutes of 1838 a summary judgment by a justice of the peace against an officer for failure to return an execution, can be reviewed on appeal in the nature of the certiorari even though the statute authorizing the summary judgment expressly prohibits an appeal, 85.

SURVIVAL OF ACTIONS *See* Abatement.

TRUSTS *See* Equity.

VARIANCE *See* Indictments; Pleading.

VENUE
A person sued in a justice's court must be sued in the county of his residence, except, etc., 1.

VERDICT *Also see* Instructions to juries.
In an action for the escape of a person taken in execution it is not necessary that the jury find especially that the officer consented or was negligent. A general verdict is sufficient, 9.

WARRANT OF ATTORNEY *See* Attorney.

WASTE
The clearing of wild land not being waste, it is proper to endow a widow in wild land, 69.

WILD LANDS
The clearing of wild land not being waste, it is proper to endow a widow in wild land, 69.

WILLS
A declaration by a person in his last sickness, which was read over to him, approved by him, and declared by him to be his will in the presence of five persons who signed as witnesses at his request, is a nuncupative will, and not a written will which is defective because not signed by the testator, 50.
A valid nuncupative will which purports to dispose of both real and personal property may be allowed to stand as to the personalty, 50.
For the proper execution of a will it is necessary that all the witnesses see the act of signing, or the testator must acknowledge that he signed it, or declare that it is his will, 136.

WITNESSES
In an action against a sheriff for an escape the sheriff's deputy who released the prisoner on an insufficient bond was interested in the event of the action, and, therefore, properly rejected as a witness, 9.
In an action for an escape it is error to reject as a witness the escaped prisoner when called by the defendant. If interested, his interest is against the party calling him, 9.
Where in an action for trespass there is any testimony, however slight, against one of the defendants, the court may not direct a verdict for that defendant in order that he may testify in behalf of a codefendant ,122.
A person sued as principal, who has defaulted and consents to testify, is a competent witness for the plaintiff against a codefendant sued as secondarily liable on the same contract, 166.

WRITS *See* Attachment; Capias ad satisfaciendum; Certiorari; Execution; Error; Replevin.